The Best
About
Backpacking

A Sierra Club Totebook®

The Best
About
Backpacking

Edited by Denise Van Lear

Sierra Club • San Francisco

My special thanks go to the numerous publishers, literary agents and authors who granted permission to let us use segments of their books; Bob Wood of *Pleasure Packing* fame for his continued enthusiasm; Bill Kelmsley, publisher of *Backpacker Magazine*; Bill Niemi of Eddie Bauer for the grand tour; to the editorial staff of Sierra Club Books for making it flow.

Most of all I wish to thank my friends and well wishers from the mountaineering community—Leon Greenman, who got me started, Guy and Laura, Ira, Herb, and Art, especially and always.

—Denise Van Lear

Contents

Introduction 9
1. Getting Ready/*Robert S. Wood* 13
   Trip Planning 14
   Preparation 20
   Conditioning 26
   Packing Up 32
2. Footwear and Walking/*Colin Fletcher* 36
   Boots 36
   Socks 55
   Camp Footwear 58
   Aids and Attachments 60
   Care of Feet 72
   Walking: The Foundations in Action 79
3. The Outfit/*Albert Saijo* 90
   Underwear 92
   Shirts 92
   Pants 93
   Outer Uppers 94
   Shell Parka 96
   Poncho 97
   Odds and Ends 98
4. Picking Packs/*Harvey Manning* 101
   Rucksacks 103
   Packframe and Bag: Details of Construction . . . 110
   Stuff Bag 120

Choosing a Packframe and Bag.............. 121

5. Bed is a Bag/*Harvey Manning* 130
   Construction 132
   Selecting a Sleeping Bag 150
   Care of the Bag 161
   Sleeping Pad, Air Mattress, Ground Sheet 166

6. Home is a Tent/*Richard Langer* 172
   The Tarp Tent 175
   Security is a Real Tent 178
   Forest Tents 182
   Alpine Tents 192
   Checking Out a Tent 196
   Making Your Own 197
   Mending a Tent 198
   Stakes 199

7. Good Eats/*Robert S. Wood* 202
   Calories 205
   Packaging 207
   A Balanced Diet 208
   Food Planning 212
   Recipes 232

8. The Wilderness Kitchen/*Robert S. Wood* 236
   Types of Fuels 238
   Types of Stoves 243
   Grills 248
   Lighting the Fire 250
   Cook Kit 252
   Clean Up 259

9. Camp/*Albert Saijo* 261
   Setting Up 261
   Sanitation 265
   Sleep 266
   Breaking Camp 266

10. The Littlest Camper/*Richard Langer* 269

The Wilderness Nursery 272
Through a Small Child's Eyes 275
11. Backpacking in Winter/*Raymond Bridge* 277
Walking in Snow...................... 279
Snowshoes and Skis...................... 281
Snow Conditions 287
Camping 290
Cooking and Water 294
Other Winter Camping Notes 295
12. The Backcountry Navigator/*Bjorn Kjellstrom* 296
Map...................... 296
Compass...................... 308
The Real Thing...................... 315
13. The Weather Eye/*Robert L. Mooers, Jr.* 316
Some Old (Semi-) Reliable Weather Signs 317
What Makes Weather 318
Air Masses and Weather Fronts 319
Cloud Identification 321
Approach of a Cold Front 327
Approach of a Warm Front 328
Lightening Strikes 329
14. Dealing With Heat and Cold/*Alan E. Nourse,M.D.* 331
Dealing with the Heat 331
Dealing with the Cold 342
15. Out/*Albert Saijo* 360
Appendices
The Authors 365
Some Organizations of Interest to Backpackers 369
Wilderness Areas 376
Chapters and Offices of the Sierra Club 381

Introduction

Harvey Manning called it "the first genuinely modern book on hiking . . . the first with humor, and the first with an ecological conscience." He was referring to *Going Light with Backpack or Burro*, a concise little volume first published by the Sierra Club in 1951 at a time when the sky-land trails were still lonely and the pack frames were fashioned from wood. Through the years, *Going Light* endured frequent revision mandated by the changing philosophies of backcountry travel. Yet one philosophy prevailed. David Brower, editor of the original volume, put it like this in his preface: "We hope that somehow these pages will stimulate and encourage those who feel they should like to be up there—up where the trails are. And we're anxious not only that they be encouraged to seek, but also that they be persuaded to protect to the utmost the wild places they have sought—and lived with and loved."

Today more than ever there is a need for the seekers to protect the wild places they have loved. For one thing, their numbers have multiplied dramatically since 1951—to the extent, some say, that backpackers now threaten to subdue the earth with their Vibram soles.

Worse, not all of those who seek wear backpacks. There is another breed (more often than not astride an off-road vehicle) which comes to the woods to assess the land's potential for other uses, such as mining and logging and road-building and the construction of sundry other public works destined for obsolescence. And that is why the wilderness still needs friends who know how to go light and walk softly, and who are willing to oppose the spoilers and preserve the places that have served them so well.

Going light implies more than the size or the weight of your pack. It implies a state of mind, a new kind of conscience. Conspicuous consumption was no great problem in the early 1950s, but it is today. And all round us are seekers whose sole quest seems to be the acquisition of gadgets and garments itemized on someone's "comprehensive equipment list," and whose approach to the literature of backpacking is no better than that of the sartorial popinjay shopping through some fashion catalogue. We are not advocating here that you disregard the consumer suggestions offered by our contributors. We are simply recommending restraint. If you are a beginner in the backcountry, you might consider starting off with nothing more than a good pair of boots. Get out and walk. And if the activity still appeals to you, then advance to the next step. Put an apple in a hankie, tie the hankie to a stick, swing the stick over your shoulder and hit the trail once more. The rest will come soon enough.

Possibly one of the best reasons to hit the trail is to develop a sense of proportion. In most cases, that means a sense of humility. The mountains and forests were here long before we were. They don't need *us*. And we can't improve them. We have been instructed to believe that "parks are for people," but that is only half of the truth. Yellowstone, for example, is also for bears. The North Rim of the Grand Canyon is also for Kaibab squirrels. The Everglades are also for alligators. Disneyland is for people. But you won't need a backpack to get there; no, nor a hankie-on-a-stick.

Having brought forth the "first" of its kind in backpacking literature, the Sierra Club in the 1950s and 1960s turned to the more immediate challenge of protecting the wild places from encroachment. Meanwhile, backpacking blossomed as one of the most popular forms of outdoor recreation in the United States, and a host of other publishers proceeded to define and refine the activity between the covers of new books. Some of what got published was not so good. It fostered a *user* attitude, as if wilderness were something to be stalked and slain and mounted above the mantlepiece. But much of what did arrive on the bookshelves was excellent. And so the Sierra Club decided to acquire for this new volume the right to reprint some of the best about backpacking that had been published by others over the past decade.

To tackle the difficult job of selecting the best, we turned to Denise Van Lear, an experienced backpacker and mountaineer in her own right. Ms. Van Lear had just completed for *Backpacker* magazine, where she is a contributing editor, a comprehensive analysis of the current literature. And from that springboard, she proceeded to assemble the material for this book. Thus, you will meet in the pages that follow such authorities as Colin Fletcher, Harvey Manning, Robert Wood, Richard Langer and Albert Saijo, among others. And we think that as you read what each has to say here, you will be moved to acquaint yourself with the original volumes from which their contributions were extracted.

A final word about backcountry practices: No one writer, nor all of them together, has all the answers —yet. There is still much we do not know about the environmental impact of human waste in the wild, about whether the use of camp fires is ecologically responsible under any circumstance short of an emergency, about what to do with food scraps. For this reason, we are obligated to state that the views of the authors of this book do not always reflect the opinion of the publisher.

Now, on with the book. And go lightly.

—*The editors*
Sierra Club Books

Getting Ready

From *Pleasure Packing*.
By Robert S. Wood

Nothing dooms a trip like slipshod preparation. It only takes one or two little mistakes. Many a veteran backpacker has seen a trip ruined for lack of a map, knife, salt or match. Still more common is the beginner who, determined to camp in comfort, can barely stagger up the trail under a gargantuan load. The line between comfort and misery is far too thin for any backpacker to take getting ready lightly.

But preparing to go backpacking need not be drudgery. There is keen pleasure in working out a route for a fine summer trip on a dark and drizzly January night. And there is satisfaction in planning a trip into wild and distant country that delicately balances the weight of food and gear against the necessity of traveling light. The more that is accomplished beforehand at home—getting in shape, experimenting with foods, memorizing maps, breaking in boots—the smoother and more carefree the trip will be.

By systematizing the job to reduce the work, one can make getting ready a pleasant prologue to the trip. The subject divides itself conveniently into four distinct phases: (1) Trip Planning: where, when and how to go, (2) **Preparation**: deciding exactly what to take, then getting it together, (3) Physical Conditioning: getting in shape before the trip, and (4) Packing Up: getting to the trailhead and making up packs.

Trip Planning

As backpacking becomes more popular, it becomes easier and easier for the beginner to get started. Probably the best sources of help are the big organizations like the Sierra Club, Mazamas and Mountaineers based in the West, and the Adirondack, Appalachian and Green Mountain clubs based in the East. Not only are they unexcelled sources of information about their respective territories, they offer organized outings of all types on which the beginner can safely become acquainted with the country and acquire experience with equipment and technique. In addition to the big clubs with their wide-ranging programs, there are innumerable local hiking clubs. These can usually be located by contacting the Federation of Western Outdoor Clubs, Route 3, P.O. Box 172, Carmel, Calif. 93921, or the Appalachian Trail Conference, 1718 N St., N.W., Washington, D.C. 20036. [*See Appendix for further information.*]

If I were suddenly transplanted to some unfamiliar part of the country, the first thing I would do is join both the local and regional hiking, mountaineering or conservation organizations. From these sources I would collect all the published data on nearby wild areas. Then, based on my reading, I would purchase, in the largest scale available, the appropriate topographic maps and study the country. From the administering government agencies, I would obtain regulations and the necessary permits and licenses. From club members, lectures, slide shows and sporting goods stores, I would discover what sort of clothing, equipment and techniques were required. Depending on the nature of the country, I might make a few excursions with the mountaineering club before going off on my own.

Trip planning, like wilderness travel, requires the ability to read and use maps. Probably no other skill is more important to all aspects of backpacking. No one should enter wild country unsupervised without appropriate maps and the ability to use them. Of course a map is useless if directions are unknown, so a compass becomes a necessity. There is a tendency among amateurs and strangers to the outdoors to regard the compass as a toy for Boy Scouts. But in strange country where landmarks are unfamiliar, a compass is no less than indispensable. Many times I have worked out my true location or avoided a wrong turn by referring to a plastic compass that weighs a fraction of an ounce and costs less than a dollar.

Since there is no substitute for proficiency with map and compass, the inexperienced backpacker is well advised to invest his spare time in mastering both. [*See chapter on "The Backcountry Navigator."*]

The Itinerary

There are various ways to travel the country. Newcomers to the outdoors may want to car camp at the trailhead for a day or two and make exploratory day trips into the wilds until they become acclimated and

find an appealing campsite that seems within their
reach. Families and other groups with limited range
often set up a base camp within an easy walk of the car
and then make daily side trips into surrounding country.

Groups with greater mobility or the urge to move
may decide to shift their base camp one or more times;
others make a practice of packing up and moving every
other day. Inexperienced or cautious backpackers
often take the shortest route to their goal, then retrace
their steps going home. More practiced and imaginative
hikers go to some pains to plot a route that makes some
kind of circle or loop in order to see more country and
avoid treading the same ground twice.

Another popular plan is the shuttle trip. Two cars
drive the party to the exit trailhead, where one car is
left. Sandwiched into the second car, the party then
drives to the entrance of the trailhead to begin a backpacking traverse between the two. There is also the rare
and exotic "double shuttle" in which two traversing
parties start at opposite ends of the same route and
trade car keys when they pass on the trail.

Some backpackers find a greater sense of adventure
in deliberately planning no itinerary, going where and
when the spirit moves them. Others, similarly moti-
vated, spurn trails altogether in favor of cross-country
travel, finding pleasure in avoiding people and the
beaten path. Since true wilderness does not begin until
the trail has been left behind, it should probably be the
goal of most backpackers to travel cross-country, even
if only for an hour's day hike from base camp.

I like to start thinking about future trips while I am

still in the mountains. I find myself wondering, for instance, whether the rocky, trailless canyon I am passing could be ascended, under pack, to the lake that lies above. As I move along, I try to estimate the difficulty of reaching passes, following ridges and crossing slopes, with an eye toward future trips. I study the topographical map to learn what lies on the other side of the mountain and to compare the bunching of contour lines with those on slopes I can see or have already climbed. And I often take pictures of country that interests me for reference in planning future trips.

This type of on-the-spot research becomes invaluable for plotting feasible cross-country routes in trailless country. A glance up a canyon on this year's trip may warn me against including it in next year's itinerary because the gentle slope suggested by the "topo" map turns out to be a series of ledges and cliffs. Or I confidently plan a route down a forbiddingly steep slope because I know it to be an easy sand and scree slide.

Timing

The question inevitably asked by strangers to the wilderness is how fast will I travel? Or, how far should I plan to go in a day? There are no specific answers, only generalities. On relatively level trails at moderate elevations, a lightly burdened, long-legged well-conditioned man may manage four miles per hour. At elevations over 6,000 feet in rolling country, a well-acclimated backpacker is moving extremely well if he can cover three miles per hour. The average back-

packer, fresh from the city, with a full pack, heading
up into the mountains will be lucky to average two
miles per hour. These speeds are for hikers who keep
moving and should probably be cut in half for those
who want to poke along, smell the flowers, take pictures and enjoy the view.

People who are overburdened or climbing steeply or
moving cross country may average only one mile per
hour. Children, the elderly and hikers strongly affected
by the altitude may manage as little as half a mile an
hour. A friend of mine has devised a useful formula for
predicting his speed. He plans every hour to cover two
miles if the trail is flat or mildly descending. For each
1,000 feet of rise he adds another hour. For steeply
descending trail he adds half an hour per 1,000 feet,
increasing that to a full hour for extremely steep downhill. By plotting a rough profile of the trail from the
topo map and applying his formula, he can estimate
quite accurately the time needed to walk it with a
moderate—under 30 pound—load.

How far one should attempt to go in a given day is
equally hard to answer. The first day out is always the
hardest, especially if the hiker has gained a mile or two
of altitude between home and the trailhead, carries a
healthy pack and is in less than top physical condition.
In these circumstances, five miles may be a full day's
work. Well-conditioned backpackers who know their
capabilities may cover ten or more miles the first day
and not suffer unduly, but most people will be happier if
they schedule considerably less. On succeeding days it
becomes possible to cover more ground with less discomfort. I have covered 15 or 20 miles on the third or

fourth day with greater comfort than I felt after eight miles the first day.

There is no particular virtue in covering great distances. I have received more pleasure, solitude and a sense of wilderness from backpacking less than two miles cross country into a neglected corner than I have from following 60 miles of well-traveled trail and camping in battered, over-used campsites. I customarily spend the summer on the edge of California's Desolation Wilderness, a place of extremely heavy use, but I know any number of charming, well-watered off-trail spots within an hour or two of the trailheads where I can camp in peace on virgin ground. As backcountry use continues to increase, backpackers determined to find solitude and unspoiled country will have to invest more time dreaming over their maps to find the less obvious routes that lie between the trails.

When to go is often determined by school and business vacation schedules. In California's High Sierra, spring, summer and fall are compressed into three or four months and consequently it makes a great deal of difference whether a trip is scheduled for June or August. Often it will snow every day for a week in early June, yet the country is dusty and parched by August. The beginner should gather all the information he can about likely conditions in his area for various seasons. If there is one season to avoid, it is probably spring. Even if the weather is miraculously fair, the ground is almost certain to be wet. Spring is a good time to car camp in comfort and settle for day hikes into the wilderness. Fishing reports, snowmelt reports and weather forecasts are all good sources of current information on conditions.

Climate and weather, more than anything else, determine what needs to be carried for warmth and shelter. Every year I meet people shivering in thin clothing in the snow in early season and sweating in down parkas in the middle of summer, simply because they had not sufficiently researched likely conditions. Where it is possible to schedule a trip on the basis of weather, one can simply check daily with the Weather Bureau until conditions are right and the long-range forecast is clear. I never plan even a casual overnight jaunt without learning all I can about expected weather. Comfortable backpacking is hard enough without deliberately setting out into the path of an approaching storm. [*See chapter on "The Weather Eye."*]

Preparation

Once the route has been determined, the length of the trip decided and the starting date set, it becomes possible to determine what must be taken along. Actually, I like to begin my preparations before the end of the previous trip. In camp on the last leg of a trip, or perhaps at the trailhead—after exchanging my pack for an ice cold drink—I sit down with my notebook while memories are fresh, and make pertinent notes about the trip. I criticize the food, recording both the noteworthy successes and the dishes that need never be carried again. I might write down, for instance, that breakfasts were a little skimpy so the cereal allotment should be increased from three ounces per meal to four.

Triumphs and failures of clothing and equipment are duly noted. Unused food, clothing and gear are listed for future scrutiny. I write down items that were forgotten and others that would have added comfort if I had had the foresight to bring them. Breakdowns are noted; so are needed repairs and ideas for equipment modification. Everything relevant to making the next trip more comfortable goes into the notebook—while the lessons of the present trip are still vivid in my mind.

Later, in the process of dismantling my pack, my notebook is kept handy for jotting down other things: the need to replenish bandaids and aspirin, a reminder to move a knot on my pack frame that rubbed my back, the need to carry a heavier grade of plastic bag for carrying garbage. When I put away my gear—after cleaning it and making repairs—I file my notebook for future reference.

By making notes before the memory fades, I accomplish three things: (1) I give myself the best possible chance to increase my enjoyment of future trips, (2) I avoid repeating mistakes for failure to remember them, and (3) by putting it all in writing, I avoid the mental drudgery of having to start planning each trip from scratch. Fifteen minutes spent making notes at the end of a trip will save two hours of preparation a month later; I cannot recommend this procedure too highly.

When I put away my gear at the end of a trip, I sort it into a series of cardboard cartons, one for containers, another for food, a third for cooking gear, and so on. These cartons are stored together, along with my notebooks, menus and checklists from previous trips, under two of the bunks in my cabin. Checklists, I believe, are as vital to comfortable backpacking as comfortable boots or a comfortable bed.

The checklist takes the place of a perfect memory, and the longer it runs the more security it provides. Every time I buy a new piece of gear, I add it to my checklist, but I rarely can bring myself to cross anything off, even the items I have not dreamed of carrying in years. Like other backpackers interested in comfort, I enjoy reading other people's lists. The abridged checklist that follows may serve as a starter for newcomers to backpacking—but only as a starter. A checklist is a highly personal thing and the beginner must eventually construct his own, updating it after each trip to make sure it contains every scrap of gear he owns.

Equipment Weight List
*items kept in use

Packs	lbs.-oz.		lbs.-oz.
Frame and packbag	3-12	*Moleskin shirt	13
Daypack	9	*Hiking shorts	10
Fanny pack	5½	*Bathing suit (shorts)	4½
Belt pack	2	Turtle-neck sweater	11
		Down sweater	17
Clothing		Down parka	1-8
*Parka shell	7½	Storm suit	1-5
*Felt hat	3	*Rag socks	4
*Tropical cap	2	*Inner socks	1
Tennis hat	2	*Wick Dry socks	3½
*String shirt	7	*Thermal socks	2½

	lbs.-oz.
*Lightweight boots	3-4
*Medium-weight boots	4-2
*Moccasins	13
*Trousers	16
*Bandanna	¾
*Denim shirt	8
Watch cap	2
Dark glasses	1½
Gaiters-7''	4
*Foam-lined leather gloves	3
*Wool mittens	3
*Boxer shorts	3
*Mountain parka	1-4
Balaclava	3

Shelter

	lbs.-oz.
10' × 10' tarp tent	2-11
Space rescue blanket	2
Poncho	1-0
Forest tent	4-8
Tent fly	1-4

Beds

	lbs.-oz.
Superlight sleeping bag (stuffed)	3-5
Foam pad (54'')	1-12
Foam pad (48'')	1-9
Foam pad (36'')	1-0
Bivouac cover	17
5' × 8' ground sheet: 3 mil	12
5' × 8' ground cloth: 4 mil	15
⅜'' Ensolite, 19'' × 42''	14

Cook gear

	lbs.-oz.
Pocketknife	1½
Fork-spoon	1½
Bluet with cartridge	1-13
Extra cartridge	10
1 qt. bottle	5
1 pt. bottle	2½
Pot tongs	1½
Sigg pot, lid	9
Scouring pad	½
Emerycloth-backed sponge	½
Salt mix shaker (filled)	2
Matches (wooden)	1
Toilet paper	2
Plastic cup	1½
Teflon frying pan	1-0
Steel frying pan	12
Primus 71L Stove	10
Primus stove box	10
1½ pt. gas can (empty)	5½
1 liter wine skin	4
Aluminum measuring cup	¾
1 qt. plastic canteen	5
Plastic bucket-basin	3½

	lbs.-oz.		lbs.-oz.
Soup ladle	1½	Insect repellant	
Tea kettle	3	(Cutters)	1
1 gal. jug	4	Large stuff sack	4
Grill	6	*Guidebook	9
Camp Trails grill	4	Personal kit	3
		*Camera & film	13
Miscellaneous		*Fly rod, reel, line	7½
Thermometer	¾	*Paperback book	7
Compass	½	*Notebook, pencil	2
Map(s)	?	*Loaded creel	9
50′ cord (550 lb. test)	3	Flashlight	3
Snakebite kit		First aid kit (large)	9
(Cutters)	1	First aid kit (small)	6

Once a new trip has been planned, I can turn to the preparation stage with much of the work already done. Having determined where, when and for how long I am going, I get myself a pair of empty cartons, assemble my notebooks and spread out my checklist. I read my notes from the previous trip, then I make my way down the list, considering each entry in terms of my needs for the trip in question. Items with asterisks are skipped over on the first reading because they are not stored in the cartons. (My camera, fly rod, boots and socks and most of my clothing, for instance, are usually kept in other places or are in use.) Each item selected is fished out of its storage box and put in the appropriate trip box. One box is for community gear (food, cooking paraphernalia, first aid kit, etc.), the other is for my personal gear (sleeping bag, clothing, etc.).

If I feel any uncertainty about an item, I include it. When I cannot make up my mind between a wool sweater and a down jacket, I put in both. Since I never actually make up my pack until I have reached the trailhead, I will have plenty of time to make a choice. When I have worked my way through the contents of the equipment boxes, I go to work on the asterisked items. Sometimes a few of these are unavailable (socks may need washing, film for the camera may have to be bought), so I put a list of missing items in the appropriate box. Having considered every item on my list at least twice, I put away the equipment boxes and start to inspect my selections.

Utensils and containers may need washing and airing, the pack will need to have its pockets cleaned out and its rigging checked, sleeping bags, mattresses and ground sheets need to be spread out in the sun and inspected for holes, grime, pitch and the like. First aid kits and flashlight batteries need to be checked; so do emergency supplies and personal kits. Every piece of equipment should have at least a cursory inspection to make certain that it will function as expected.

With the equipment all assembled (or at least planned and noted) I consult old menus and the comments made at the end of previous trips. After figuring the required number of breakfasts, lunches and dinners, I consider the appetites and preferences of party members, the likelihood of our catching trout and the possibility of our staying out a little longer than planned. Then I compose a tentative menu which will be discussed and probably changed before the actual shopping begins.

Once the menu is set and the food acquired, most of it needs to be repackaged. Some people go so far as to separately package every meal so they need only dig out the appropriately labeled bag. In my view, this sort of packaging is excessive for short or casual trips where measurements need not be precise and where an extra ounce of cereal for breakfast for several days will not result in starvation the last day out.

My repackaging consists of stripping away all cardboard, paper, cellophane and light plastic and replacing it with large, heavy-duty polyethylene bags. I like to tie the long neck of the bag into an overhand knot rather than struggle with rubber bands, twistys, paper clips or heat sealing. Bags that will repeatedly be opened (gorp, cereal) and thus subject to more wear are usually doubled. I buy the heaviest bags I can find, rather than risk the puncture and spilling inevitable with flimsy bags that are cheap or free. After repackaging appropriately, I put fresh food (butter, meat, cheese) in the refrigerator. Everything else goes into the food box—including a boldly written reminder to collect the refrigerated food before leaving.

On the evening before departure, I assemble the clothes I expect to put on in the morning and set them beside my bed. I also gather the clothes and food and drink that I will look forward to finding in the car at the end of the trip. As a final step, I run quickly down my checklist one last time. Everything should now be ready.

Conditioning

Many a trip has been ruined—and I speak from experience—by the failure to get in halfway reasonable shape beforehand. I can remember trips which seemed to be one long nightmare of aching legs, bursting lungs and a desperate effort to keep up with the party. It is simply impossible to turn from sedentary city life to high-altitude wilderness backpacking without a certain amount of physical strain. It is, however, possible to leave a lot of the discomfort at home.

At home, the conditioning can be as gradual as the hiker cares to make it, thus spreading and actually reducing the discomfort. It can be performed within easy reach of a hot shower, soft bed and the assurance that today's blisters can be babied tomorrow. On the trip itself, there is more than enough discomfort from hiking under load at high altitude, sleeping on the ground, wind, sweaty clothes—without unnecessarily adding a lack of physical preparation.

There is no better investment of time during the several weeks prior to a demanding trip than a program of conditioning that will bridge part of the gap between city living and wilderness travel. It is far better to discover blisters while walking near home than it is at 10,000 feet in a cold, windy camp, with ten miles to cover the following day.

It is perfectly possible for a sedentary city worker in his spare time to significantly improve the capability of his legs, lungs, shoulders, feet and skin, depending on his condition, in anywhere from a week to a month. The program actually required will depend on many factors: age, experience, physical condition, time available, determination, rigorousness of the trip contemplated, etc.

The following program is suggested for a badly out-of-shape, no-longer-young backpacker planning an ambitious two-week trip which will begin on a weekend. About three weeks ahead of time our man should, with the aid of a city map, mark out rather precise one- two- and three-mile courses that begin and end with his home. Traffic lights, crowded sidewalks, even stop signs should be avoided so there is no necessity to stop.

After work, instead of opening a beer, our man should go walking. Early risers may prefer to get up and walk at dawn; it is a marvelous time to be about. Since our man is in really rotten shape, he may have trouble the first time just getting around a one-mile course. Nevertheless, he should time his walk in order to chart his improvement. If he is too sore after that first walk, he can take the next day off. Weight lifters and long-distance runners often work out on rest days. On the third day, our man should try two miles and try not to stop. A brisk pace is actually more comfortable and less tiring than starting and stopping or an aimless saunter.

At the end of the first week, our man should be able to cover the mile courses in 20 to 30 minutes and the two miles in less than an hour. By the end of the second week he should be able to do three miles in an hour; the weekend before he leaves he ought to walk the three miles twice in a period of two hours. Walking regularly (at least every other day) and briskly (charting the times and always trying to improve) will strengthen the legs and provide endurance.

To develop the lungs and toughen the knees there is nothing like running. Once the body is used to walking, it is safe to go running. I find shorter distances (50 to 200 yards) of hard running to be more effective than a mile of slow jogging. The high school track is a good place to run. To increase my wind I run until I am gasping, then I run another 20 yards before slowing to a walk. When our man runs out of breath, he should walk very slowly until his breathing returns to normal and then start running again. By the end of two weeks, he will find his wind greatly improved and he should be able to navigate the one-mile course, alternately running and walking. As his lung capacity grows and begins to catch up to his leg development, he will begin to feel fatigue in his knees. The ideally conditioned backpacker on a difficult stretch should feel approximately equal discomfort in his knees and lungs.

To condition the shoulders to the pull of his pack, it is only necessary for our man—probably the second or third week—to start wearing it on his walks. Books make good ballast and ten or 15 pounds should be enough for the first tour of his routes under load. This can be increased to 25 shortly before the actual trip. Since backpacks are not made for running, our man will want to alternate unladen run-walk tours of his routes with pack-carrying tours. So far, all of his work has probably been on flat, paved sidewalk. But backpacking usually means traversing rough, steep country, so our man should hunt out the steepest, roughest terrain in the area and work out a course or two for the final week of conditioning.

Only on steep trails are the conditions in mountain wilderness closely approximated. The knees need the unique strains produced by going up and down hill and the ankles need rough and rocky terrain to develop toughness and resistance to sprain. No amount of walking or running on city sidewalks can accomplish the same thing. I find the bulldozed fire trails in the steep Berkeley hills behind my home to be perfect. When I was working at a desk job and wanted to get ready for a weekend trip, I would drive to the fire trails on the preceding Sunday, Tuesday and Thursday evenings and spend an hour or two running uphill until either my legs or lungs forced me to stop. Then I would slow to a walk until I was sufficiently recovered to run again. A great amount of conditioning can be compressed into a week in this manner—providing the body is in reasonably good shape beforehand.

In addition to run-walk tours in the hills, our man should carry a loaded pack on perhaps a total of ten miles worth of walking trips through the hills. The weight of the pack will condition the shoulders, knees, ankles and feet to the strain and jarring that rough country provides. Hiking in the hills with a pack and run-walk tours without one—this is the real conditioning. Walking and running on city sidewalks is only "pre-conditioning" for people unaccustomed to vigorous exercise.

From the beginning of this program, the feet need to receive special consideration. On all his excursions, our man should be wearing the boots and socks he will take on this trip. This will break in the boots and mate them to the feet before the trip begins, and it will toughen the feet sufficiently to prevent chafing and blistering in the wilds. Undoubtedly, the most overlooked and easiest part of foot conditioning is cutting the toenails.

Long toenails will make boots seem too short and can be painfully crippling on downhill stretches. Cutting long toenails the night before a trip will result in pain and inflamation on the trail. Great discomfort (and worn sock toes) can be prevented by awareness of the problem. I try to keep my toenails reasonably short with frequent cutting, but I also remind myself, sometimes in writing, to cut my toenails four or five days before a trip.

I think the best way to toughen up feet is to make a practice of going barefoot. Before a trip I go barefoot around the house and I like to go for short barefoot walks. Concrete sidewalks are great tougheners and callous builders. I have the idea that sunlight and fresh air are healthy for feet, certainly a lot healthier than damp, constricting shoes. I spend enough time barefoot to sport a pretty tan on the tops of my feet by the end of the summer. Tanning can be extremely important to the comfort and pleasure of a trip. People who take lily-white skin to high altitudes become horribly burned unless they keep themselves carefully and continuously covered.

A tan acquired in the city or at the beach will never fully protect the hiker against fierce high-altitude sunlight but it will enable him to travel with only normal discretion without risk of serious burning. Nothing is worse than having to hike in the heat completely shrouded from the sun—unless it is suffering with sunburned shoulders that will have to carry a pack the next day. Trying to safely tan white skin by short periods of exposure to fierce high-altitude sun is a bothersome, inconvenient process on a backpacking trip.

Our man will be well advised to start cultivating a tan
by getting out in the sun (in a bathing suit if he expects to
hike in shorts) on weekends from the beginning of his
conditioning period—taking care to use discretion and
sunburn preventatives. If there is anything more vulnerable to mountain sunshine than city skin it is sunburned city skin that has freshly peeled. Special care
should be taken to avoid burning the nose to prevent
starting a cycle of peeling, burning and repeeling.

Not many backpackers will need to take the full
conditioning course outlined above, but most people
will enjoy a more comfortable trip to the extent that
they complete their conditioning at home.

Packing Up

With trip planning, preparation and conditioning out of
the way, all that remains is to pack up and go. For most
people, that means taking a car to the trailhead; and
sometimes that journey is the hardest trip their car ever
makes. On more than a few trips, the biggest adventure,
the greatest challenge and the hardest work is getting
the car to the trailhead and back. I have slipped off the
road, gotten stuck in the mud and hung up on rocks. I
have run out of water and gas, blown out tires, smashed
into rocks and killed the motor fording creeks.
Trailheads have a habit of lying deserted at the ends of
unmaintained rocky roads, so it behooves the backpacker to take more than a casual interest in the condition of his car.

Backpackers are often so intent on getting their gear
into the car and getting away that they forget to carry

the extra food, drink, clothing and money that is so welcome at the end of a trip. For purposes of acclimation and an early start, I like to drive from home to the trailhead on the eve of the trip in order to sleep at the highest elevation possible. To simplify matters, I usually take a car-camping sleeping bag and mattress to insure a good rest. If I have to cook I take along a separate stove, food and utensils rather than rummage in my backpacking gear. When possible, it is usually most convenient to eat in a restaurant.

While driving to the trailhead, I try to get a final weather forecast on the car radio. Sometimes at the last available pay phone, I call the nearest Weather Bureau or airport or Highway Patrol office to get an extended forecast. On the basis of this information, together with weather conditions at the trailhead, I make my final selection of protective gear: tents, rain suits, ponchos, ground sheets, tarps, parkas, mittens, caps and sweaters. My usual procedure, after deciding what to carry, is to spread out an old tarp, brought along for that purpose, and empty on to it all the food and community gear.

Then, if there are two of us, one of us divides the pile on the basis of both weight and bulk into two equal stacks; the other man gets first choice. It is probably a good idea to employ a scale to be precise, but we generally just heft comparable items at arms' length and hope that compensating errors will cancel out major differences. Sometimes one man, because of his pack, will be short on space and may request less bulky items, but both hikers still split the weight evenly, unless there is a marked difference in their size. Carrying ability is usually proportional to body weight.

After combining my share of the community gear with my personal equipment, I start to make up my pack, laying it flat on the ground on the shoulder straps. First I set aside clothing that may be needed in a hurry, trail food, notebook, pencil, compass, first aid kit, camera, lip salve, sunburn cream, bandanna, mosquito dope and anything else I expect to need on the trail. Then, starting at the top of the pack, I make a layer of the heaviest, densest items in such a way that the weight will lie as high and as close to my back as possible. From the remaining gear I take those items least likely to be needed and, working my way to the top, fill the remainder of the pack snugly. If I am hiking in shorts, my long trousers are packed on top for easy access, or in the lower compartment of a divided bag.

The gear set aside to be used on the trail is then systematically divided between the pack's outside pockets. To find things fast, it helps to use the same arrangement for every trip. For instance, I make a habit of sprinkling wooden kitchen matches in every pocket, but the main supply always rides in the upper right-hand pocket. With the last of the small items stowed, I stuff my rolled foam mattress into (or onto) the top of the pack bag and cinch down the flap over it. My sleeping bag is then strapped or snapped beneath the three-quarter packbag. Last to be attached is my two-piece fly rod, broken down, but with the reel still attached.

With the pack made up and hoisted onto the hood of the car for easy mounting, I go through my pockets, reload the car, hide my wallet after extracting two or three dimes for pay phone use, and lock the car. Normally I hide the keys nearby, rather than take the chance of losing them. After making sure I know what direction I want to go, I slip into my pack and adjust the buckles so the weight is borne equally by my shoulders and hips. With nothing further to detain me, I pop a lemondrop in my mouth and set forth up the trail.

Footwear and Walking

The chapter "Foundations" from
The Complete Walker.
By Colin Fletcher

The foundations of the house on your back are your feet
and their footgear, and the cornerstone is a good pair of

Boots.*

Although some "serious" hikers own two or more pairs
of boots, to meet different conditions, one pair should
be enough to fill most people's walking needs. But
they must be carefully chosen.

First, they must be stout enough to protect and support your feet with the heaviest load you expect to
carry. Your feet are used to supporting your full body-
weight, and provided you do not add much to it they
will, once hardened by practice, carry you comfortably
over long distances even on thin soles and uppers. Soles
for this unladen kind of walking, though they must be
stouter than those of city shoes, need be no more than
five-sixteenths of an inch thick. The uppers can be thin
leather, suede, or even canvas. For my money, the
uppers should protect and support the ankles, but there

---

*There is no omission here. On this page as well as page 67 Mr.
Fletcher has ended the sentence with a subhead. The eds./Sierra
Club Books.*

are some walkers who go in for oxfords. A fair number, including a few backpackers, manage to cover long distances in basketball or even tennis shoes. They're welcome.

As soon as you carry a pack and so add appreciably to the burden on your feet, they need extra protection and support. Remember that you may be increasing their normal load by a third. For cushioning effect as well as for durability and traction, by far the most popular soles today are heavily lugged rubber-and-synthetic compound types such as the Vibram and Galibier. The one-half-inch thickness is probably best for general use. (This measurement is of the sole itself, with lugs; it does not include the softer mid-sole embodied in most good hiking boots, which helps the cushioning effect.) If you expect to do any rock climbing or to operate a great deal in snow, thicker soles might be an advantage—for rigidity in rock climbing, insulation on snow.

Vibram soles come in two types and four qualities. The Roccia is a relatively thin, soft sole, fine for lightweight walking boots. The Montagna is thicker, harder and less flexible, and will take rougher wear. These names are always stamped on the sole's Vibram label. Italian Vibrams may have yellow or black labels: Yellow means a high-carbon sole of the finest quality; black indicates a lower carbon content, but still a very good sole. Vibrams are now made under license in Switzerland and the U.S. Both carry black labels or imprints. The Swiss soles are at least as good as the Italian originals, but the U.S. version is said to be of poorer quality. Every article imported into the U.S. must bear

an imprint stating country of origin, and you will find
it somewhere on the sole, though not necessarily on
the Vibram label. U.S.-made Vibrams sold here may
show no country of origin. The British Commando,
once fairly popular, no longer seems to be generally
available in the U.S. The French Galibier is comparable to the best Vibram.

Some lightweight, less expensive boots now have
molded soles, bonded direct to leather uppers. Because
there are no stitches around the welt—the line along
which sole and uppers meet, the line along which water
is most liable to infiltrate a boot—this system has
theoretical advantages. But aside from residual doubts
about the effectiveness of the bonding, there is the
difficulty that worn soles are at present not replaceable.
Worse still, neither are heels, which form a single unit
with the soles. So it seems doubtful whether bonded
soles will ever become worthwhile on high-quality
boots, which should outlast several soles and heels.

The standard (or Goodyear) welt has exposed stitching. It lies along a narrow ledge that encircles the boot
where sole joins uppers—a ledge that might have been
designed to collect moisture and dirt. That is one reason
the welt is a danger point: unless proper precautions are
taken—and sometimes even then—water seeps into
socks and feet; and dirt and other abrasives can play
havoc with the stitching. At least one bootmaker, Vasque, sells a special device for applying Epoxy to exposed welt-stitching. Some good boots designed for wet
conditions have a strip of leather known as a storm welt
sewn in along the junction line. Look, and ye shall find.
There is another kind of welt that some people consider

better. Count me in—I've used it for ten years now, on Pivetta boots, with zero travail. In this welt, the uppers are turned inward and then sewn to the sole. Stitches are therefore protected from abrasion. And the boot has no ledge to collect water and dirt. Lacking a ledge, the sole ends almost flush with the uppers, is less flexible at the edges, and therefore gives you better purchase for rock climbing—and for the kind of scrambling you're sure to do from time to time in cross-country walking. Unfortunately, this in-turned kind of welt cannot be made by a fully mechanized process and is therefore found only on certain rather more expensive boots, including, for example, some made by Fabiano and Vasque.

Uppers must be stout enough to support foot muscles that are being strained by an abnormal load, and to afford adequate protection. But they must be pliant enough to allow feet to bulge outward slightly when under a heavy load. They must also, when properly treated, be very close to waterproof.

There is still no substitute for good leather uppers —smooth-finish, rough-out or suede. Smooth-finish boots come with the smooth, outside-of-the-animal surface facing outward. Rough-outs have the leather reversed. Suede is generally the inside half of a split hide; it therefore has two rough sides—and it has been further roughened by an abrading machine.

The first edition of this book stated: "Virtually all really high-quality boots have smooth-side-out uppers." Even in 1968 that may have been a questionable statement. Today it is nonsense: the majority of hiking boots now seem to come with rough-out uppers. Untreated, they are said to be more waterproof than smooth-finish boots. Treated, smooth-finish uppers may seal a shade better; but they leave the thin "skin" of the hide—which forms the leather's most effective water-barrier—highly susceptible to rupture from normal wear and tear. The surface of rough-outs is less tough, but scuff marks or even shallow cuts matter very little because the vital "skin" remains protected, way inside. Rough-outs, assert some pundits, are therefore better. Other pundits counter-assert, fiercely. In the end, what seems to count is the quality of the leather. Above all, it should be "full grain" (i.e. unsplit, whole, intact). Because most of today's high-quality boots are lined, checking for full grain is difficult. Like it or not, you mostly have to rely on the integrity of maker and retailer.

Suede boots are relatively inexpensive, light, and cool to wear. But the porosity that makes them cool also makes them difficult to waterproof. They are useful for dry, not-too-rugged use—and for certain kinds of rock climbing.

The fewer seams in the uppers, the more rugged the boot (because it is at the seams that most boots first show wear). A single-seamed boot is the strongest kind—and also, because it demands the very best leather, in large pieces, the most expensive. A many-seamed boot will probably stand up well enough if you keep to trails. If you do much cross-country work, especially on talus, it probably won't.

A thin leather lining increases a boot's warmth and may possibly reduce friction. A thin padding such as foam rubber between uppers and lining makes the boot very easy to break in and comfortable and warm to wear. It also gives your feet extra protection. But there is some danger that in deserts and other fiery places it may make them uncomfortably hot. A Los Angeles firm, Bare/Foot/Gear, makes foam-padded boots with sweat-resistant leather linings and recommends—but does not insist—that you wear them without socks.

In extreme cases, terrain can affect your choice. Jagged volcanic rock or steep talus will soon knock hell out of thin or poor-quality material, both soles and uppers. And tough going like that can also bruise poorly protected feet. So if you expect to cross a lot of really rough country it may be as well to increase stoutness and/or quality a notch all around.

But extra stoutness means extra weight, and that can be critical. It is all too easy to pare away at the ounces that go into your pack and to overlook the boots. Yet the successful 1953 Mount Everest Expedition came to the conclusion that in terms of physical effort one pound on the feet is equivalent to five pounds on the back. As usual, then, you have to compromise. But remember that although it is obviously stupid to wear unnecessarily heavy boots, choosing too light a pair is asking for trouble.

Many people consider that ankle boots—six or seven inches high—are too low. But it seems to me that, except in heavy brush country, taller boots do not add enough protection to warrant the extra weight. They are also hotter—though that means "warmer" in cold weather. Even more seriously, they tend to restrict your calf muscles.

A few boots incorporate gaiter-like structures built

onto the tops to seal the gap between boot and sock against snow, pebbles, or even water. These scree collars or snow protectors (they also go by other names) are clearly worth considering if the boots will be used exclusively or even largely under conditions that cry out for such protection.

The requirements I have outlined do not really restrict you very much. Today's equipment catalogues list and illustrate such an array of boots that studying them can cause severe mental indigestion.

The simplest way out—once you've grasped, roughly, the range of boots available—is to find a store with a salesman you feel you can trust (easier said than done, of course) and tell him what you expect to use the boots for, and also (if that's the way you operate) how much you're prepared to spend. If you plan to walk unladen, and only on civilized surfaces, you can probably skip the store and wear whatever has always been most comfortable for you, from tennis shoes on up. If you'll be carrying only mild loads and sticking to well-manicured trails, look at what the catalogues call "light" or "medium hiking boots," or perhaps "trail boots." For heavy loads, very rough or soggy trails, or cross-country work, consider only those listed as "heavy hiking boots" or something similar. Be careful of "climbing boots." They may or may not be suitable for prolonged walking.

Among boots generally acknowledged as first class are the German Lowa and Bass, the Italian Fabiano and Vasque (formerly Voyageur), and the French Galibier. I'm afraid I can report first-hand on none of them: it is a long time since I wore anything but

Italian Pivetta boots. For a decade I have used the heaviest Pivetta, the "Eiger," described as a "mountaineering boot." The black, smooth-finish uppers are seven inches high and protect my ankles very adequately. The latest models have a soft, padded cuff designed to reduce the sad, supra-ankle soreness endemic to most boots that are new or have not been worn for some time. The uppers have only one seam—on the inner side of each boot. Nowhere does any stitching go all the way through the boot. The heel—where seams are particularly liable to split—is, except for a small incision for the pull-loop, solid leather. The boot has a hard toe and strong heel counter. A steel shank built into the center sole imparts necessary stiffness. Lacing is through eyelets. The calfskin lining is padded around the ankle section with thin foam rubber. Sole: Vibram Montagna, cemented on; the bond reinforced at heel and toe with brass screws. Welt: turned-in type, and sole trimmed flush with uppers. My size 10 Eigers weighed five pounds, twelve ounces when new. Present cost: $45.

Now I don't want to suggest that these boots are necessarily "the best" on the market, whatever that might mean. Like most people, I have actually tried very few different kinds. And I came to these by the orthodox route: a combination of chance and whim and experience and personal prejudice, mitigated by a saleman's advice. But I've used successive Eigers in daytime shade temperatures ranging from 20°F to over 100°F on snow and sand, in places as different as Grand Canyon and Kilimanjaro. And I'm satisfied. I have yet to come across a pair of boots that looked as though they would prove better for all-around use.

My only possible complaint is that the foam padding perhaps makes them rather hot for desert use; but I do not really have a yardstick by which to measure this factor. The padding certainly makes for greater comfort and for warmth in snow and reduces both the time and trauma involved in breaking in a new pair.

When I described my Eigers in the first edition of this book I did not realize that the only place in the world they are sold is The Ski Hut. The Pivetta line of boots has been developed over the past twenty years by Trail-wise (Ski Hut) in conjunction with the Italian maker, working from a modified U.S. marching last, and is not sold in Italy or anywhere else except the U.S. Most Pivetta models are now increasingly available at retail stores across the U.S., but so few Eigers are made that they are never wholesaled.* Still, I shall let my description stand—because Eigers are the only boots I know cuff to sole; because the important things, anyway, are the factors governing choice; and because boots very similar to Pivettas are now beginning to appear on the U.S. market.

Naturally, special conditions may call for special boots.

Two summers of slogging through trailless tracts of western Vancouver Island convinced me that for cross-country travel in rain forests, where your route often lies over or along slippery fallen tree trunks, and where undergrowth is always snatching at your legs, the only satisfactory footwear is a pair of caulked knee

*News just in that a few will in future be wholesaled. But that will push their price up to around $60.

boots. By no means everyone agrees; but then, who would expect them to?

Another summer in the muskeg-and-lake country of Canada's Northwest Territories taught me that in such places you need a stout and roomy pair of leather-topped rubber boots (worn with thick insoles and two pairs of socks). The Maine Hunting Shoe made by L. L. Bean of Freeport, Maine, is the standard, though there are others. A generic name for the breed is "Shoepac." Ten-inch boots are probably the most popular, but they come in all heights from six to sixteen inches. I understand that boots of this type are admirable for much eastern wilderness—the sort of flat, soggy terrain in which old tote roads skirt or even run through spruce and cedar swamps. They're especially good when hiking is largely a means to camping or hunting or fishing, and a day's backpacking may amount to no more than five miles and is unlikely to exceed twelve. In recent years, leather-topped rubber boots have been challenged by rubber boots heavily insulated with fiber glass or some similar material. Opinion seems to be divided. Some people find them unbearably hot.

In certain parts of the country—because of local conditions or innate human conservatism or both—a specific style of boot may remain as traditional as the dialect. You can always ask a reputable dealer about parochial preferences. Of course, there's no law that says you have to take his advice.

In really cold weather—especially at high altitudes—it may be necessary to wear extra-thick boots (a size or two larger than usual, to accommodate more sock). You may even need overboots. Recently,

Ocaté and other firms have come up with foam boots for ultra-cold conditions. But here we are coming close to the fringe of "just plain walking."

Insoles

Many boots—and especially those with hand-stitched soles (because the stitching may protrude and chafe your feet)—need insoles. In emergencies I have used cardboard cutouts from cereal boxes (they last about six hours), regular foam-rubber insoles of the kind you can pick up at a drug store (intolerably hot), and makeshift devices fashioned from asbestos gasket sheeting bought at a wayside garage (effective, though they tend to curl). The best material I've tried so far is plain leather, but Dale Vent/O/Soles ("woven saran—ventilates at each step"; $2.25 a pair from *Walking News,* P.O. Box 352, New York, N.Y. 10013) look as if they just may have possibilities.

It is probably an advantage to glue the insoles in. If they are left loose, though, you can transfer an old pair, already well molded to the contours of your soles, into a new pair of boots and so cut down appreciably the grief of breaking them in.

Laces and Lacing

Braided nylon laces are extremely strong. I have never had one break on me. They do not rot, absorb water, dry out stiff, or become brittle in extreme cold. Unlike leather laces, they are never eaten by mice or their allies. And the newer, flattened kind have largely overcome the annoying tendency of the old, round version to slip out of the top eyelets when your boots are unlaced.

I used to follow tradition and carry a spare pair of laces, but long ago decided to rely on a length of my ubiquitous ⅛-inch nylon cord.

There are four distinct systems for lacing boots: grommeted eyelets; swivel eyelets (small D-rings attached by the straight side to clips fixed to the outside of the uppers); open hooks (similarly attached); and "speed lacing" (closed, tunnel-like hooks through which the laces pass easily and can be tightened, bottom to top, with a single sharp pull). Some boots have speed lacing or eyelets—grommeted or swivel—partway up, then hooks to the top. And there are other combinations. Boots with speed lacing, hooks or swivel eyelets are easier to take off or put on than those with grommeted eyelets, and also lace quicker and more simply. Indeed, if you are wearing big gloves in severe cold, open hooks may be the only practical solution. But under normal conditions I prefer the old-fashioned and almost indestructible grommeted eyelets. Even if a grommet wears through or works loose, the hole is still usable. Hooks and swivel eyelets, on the other hand, can and do break off and pull loose—leaving you miles from Godknowswhere with a boot that is not only imperfectly laced but may also let water in. What's more, hooks can snag on undergrowth and other boot laces; somehow I can rarely get this danger, which is no doubt very slight, clean out of my mind. Still, grommeted eyelets are now perhaps the least common lace system on

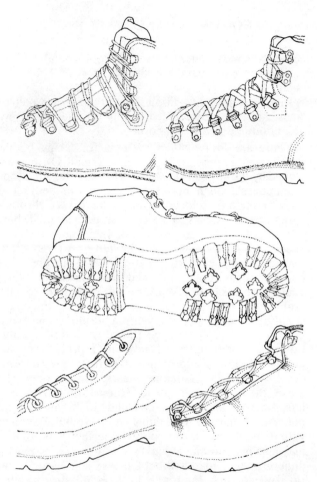

Top: Open hook and D-ring. Bottom: Grommeted eyelets and speed lacing. The heavily-lugged Vibram sole is one of the most popular today.

hiking boots—a fact that may be not unconnected with their being the most troublesome for manufacturers to install.

Laces should not be drawn too tight in the lower eyelets or hooks: the pressure can block the necessary wriggle-freedom of your toes and may even constrict circulation. But on the vertical part of the boot the laces must be tight enough to prevent your foot from sliding forward under the kind of pressure you generate when walking downhill.

Tall boots should be normally laced up to the ankle; but if the calf section, especially when of soft leather, can be left rather looser, then you get better ventilation and less muscle constriction. A reader suggests using separate laces, top and bottom. Or you can block the transfer of tension from tightly to loosely laced sectors by crisscrossing the laces three or four times at the ankle.

Fitting New Boots

Think of yourself as trying to put a glove on your foot. But do not picture a skintight glove. What you need is a boot that fits snugly at the broadest part of the foot (the trick is deciding exactly what "snugly" means, and in the end you have to make your own decision, based on experience) but which leaves one finger's width of free room in front of the toes. You check this toe space by unlacing the boot, standing up without a pack, and pressing forward until your toes meet the end of the boot. If you can just slide a forefinger down into the gap left at the heel, that part of the fit is about right. With the

boot laced, you should be able to wriggle your toes
fairly freely (the shape of the toe cap is important; for
most feet, the broader and squarer the better). But it is
vital that, with the boot laced tightly up the vertical
part, there is as little movement as possible at the heel,
upward or sideways. The difficulty is that new boots
are relatively stiff, and that with wear all boots mold
themselves to the shape of your feet. You simply have
to guess how much change will take place—how much
the sides will "give," and how well that stiff-feeling
heel will conform to the contours of your particular
foot. Cheaper boots tend to alter more than good-
quality ones, especially if they are unlined; buy them a
little on the tight side. I find that with my Pivettas
—presumably because of their lining and foam padding
and high-quality leather—a good fit in the store seems
to mean a good fit on the mountain.

Do not, by the way, pay too much attention to sizes.
Base your decision on the feel of the boot. If the size is
not the same as last time, it doesn't matter a damn.
Different boots marked as the same size may vary appreciably.

If you feel confident that the salesman knows what he
is talking about, lean heavily on his advice. Even if you
hike like crazy, all year round, you buy new boots only
once every few years, and you tend to forget the rules.
But the salesman is at it all day and every day. Frankly,
I found when I came to write this section that I really
couldn't quite remember what I looked for. So I talked
to a backpacker-salesman I trusted and—after checking with other sources—have gratefully incorporated
most of his testament. All I can say about the way I've

managed to apply the rules in the past is that I've
only once been dissatisfied with any hiking boots I've
bought—and that was probably due to a manufacturing
defect. Mind you, it may take me an hour to select
the pair I want.

If you live far from any dealer that carries the kind of
boot you want, you may have to mail order. I hear that
the best firms are very good at matching outline
sketches of feet. Follow their instructions meticu-
lously, that's all—particularly in making the foot
sketches. And deal only with reputable people who
offer what seems to be an honest guarantee.

Breaking In New Boots

All new boots need slow and careful breaking in. Until
some of the stiffness has gone and insoles and uppers
have begun to conform to the contours of your feet,
they are almost sure to be uncomfortable. And they'll
be great at generating blisters. I have heard people
advise: "Just put your new boots on and soak them in
water for a while and then go out and walk. You'll never
have any trouble." It sounds pretty drastic treatment to
me, and I have never tried it. (But one experienced
mountaineer I know, who had always felt as I do about
the soaking theory, once tried it out as a crash program
and found that it worked. Perhaps it's relevant, though,
that he says he hasn't repeated it.) All I do is take short,
easy walks, with little or no load at first, and gradually
increase load and distance. At the very beginning, even
wearing the boots around the house helps (advantage:
most good stores will change a poorly fitting pair that

has not been worn outdoors). Naturally, boots should be well waxed as soon as you buy them.

For a major backpacking expedition—the kind that threatens to wear out a pair of boots—you obviously have to start with new ones. After all, you wouldn't set out on a transcontinental road rally with worn tires. For such expeditions, breaking in the new boots can become a problem. The theory is simple: the boots will take care of themselves during those practice hikes you plan to take for several weeks beforehand in slowly increasing doses that will painlessly harden your feet and muscles. But I have found that in practice the press of administrative arrangements just before the start rises to such a frantic peak that there is no time for any practice hikes worthy of the name. So you start with flabby muscles, soft feet—and stiff boots. And this is no laughing matter. It is not simply that sore feet soon take the joy out of walking. They can make walking impossible. Just before my Grand Canyon trip, while putting out a food cache and at the same time trying rather belatedly to harden my feet and soften a new pair of boots, I attempted too much in a single day, generated a blister, developed an infected heel, and had to postpone the start for a week. Fortunately, I had planned an easy first week's shakedown cruise. But even with an old pair of insoles in the boots, my feet barely carried me through the second critical and much harder week of the trip. I offer no solution to this kind of problem (which can also crop up on shorter journeys), but I suggest that you at least make every effort to allow time for a gentle shakedown cruise at the beginning.

Care of Boots

Leather uppers must be conditioned with wax or oil. But which conditioners should be used and which avoided on what kinds of leather is something that dissolves the experts into raucous disagreement. As far as I can make out, the tentative current gospel reads: on "dry-tanned" leather (which forms the uppers on most hiking boots), use wax and/or silicone, *but never use oil or grease*; on oil-tanned leather (which is normally softer and more flexible, as on the upperworks of many calf-length boots), use oil or grease. Moral: when you buy new boots, make sure you know what treatment they demand.

For summer use, the ideal is to apply the conditioner lightly so that your feet can "breathe" through leather that will be reasonably water-repellent. In snow or wet, condition heavily. The leather will become waterproof; but it cannot then "breathe." That's the theory, anyway. Frankly, I find that in hot weather I need plenty of conditioner to keep the bloody boots soft.

For many years I used Kiwi neutral wax on my Pivettas but found that they tended to dry out too fast on long journeys, even though I applied an average of one 2½ ounce can a week. Then I switched to Sno-Seal, a wax and silicone mixture, and found that it kept the leather supple for very much longer. Recently I have begun using Leath-R-Seal, a wax and shellac combination with several apparent advantages: it is reputed to penetrate the leather more deeply than Sno-Seal; it is apparently an effective seam-sealer; it does not weaken the cement that bonds the various layers of the soles (as the solvent in certain silicone mixtures can do); and it can be applied cold. It is the cold application that really attracts me. You are supposed to apply Sno-Seal "over direct heat," and I find it a damned nuisance. Even at home, let alone in the field, the chore tends to get put off. There is also some danger of "cooking" your boots (though one reader suggests heating the Sno-Seal instead of the boots, spooning or brushing it on, then standing the boots in direct sunlight for two or three hours).*

Whenever your boots show the slightest sign of drying out—and also when you get home after a trip of any magnitude—clean and dry them and rub the chosen dressing well into the leather with fingers or a rag, particularly at seams and welts. With silicone and oil, avoid the sole. Sample dressings—Sno-Seal; 85 cents per 8-ounce can, 55 cents per 4-ounce can; Leather-R-Seal: $1.40 per 5½-fluid-ounce bottle (heavy and breakable, unfortunately, and with a fragile plastic cap); Herbert's Leather Dressing (neats-foot oil): 40 cents per 8-ounce can.

If your boots get thoroughly wet, dry them slowly. Packing loosely with newspaper or toilet paper helps absorb internal moisture. Never put wet boots close to a fire: the soles may curl up and the leather lose some of its life. Somebody once gave me a pair of cunning devices for preventing wet soles from curling. Called "stretchers," they're made of light alloy and plastic-

---

*Now, the newest Sno-Seal has been "improved with silicones," and you no longer need heat your boots, only "keep warm" until the Snow-Seal is fully absorbed.

covered cord, and are designed to apply tension that counteracts the tendency of drying soles to curl toward their uppers. Unfortunately, you cannot use them on boots that, like my Pivettas, have turned-in welts and therefore no ledge.

The interiors of boots left standing for any length of time may sprout a green mold. I have yet to try, as a reader suggests, prophylactic spraying with a fungicide powder (B.F.I., Quinsana, Desenex), but it sounds like a far from sterile idea.

Socks

The best sock thickness depends on whether you tend to suffer from hot feet, cold feet, tender feet, or none of these afflictions. In theory it would seem obvious to put on a thicker pair of socks in cold weather. But if your boots fit perfectly with the socks you normally wear they will pinch with a thicker pair. You are left with two alternatives: buying a second pair of boots, or getting by with the usual socks. (If conditions are severe enough to justify overboots, you probably need two pairs of thick socks and big boots anyway.) I normally wear only one pair of socks at a time, but many people, perhaps even a majority of backpackers, find that two pairs—the thinner ones inside—help reduce friction between feet and boots.

On almost every count—resilience, sweat absorption, insulation and general comfort—wool is the material. But nylon reinforcement—a small percentage throughout, with a boost at heels and toes—increases durability without detracting appreciably from the other qualities. At least, this is what I believed for many years. And I wore medium-weight wool socks (4 ounces) that met these requirements and were also shrink resistant. Then these socks ceased to be available. As a stop-gap, and also to give a trial to a new product, I turned with some skepticism to Wick-Dry (4½ ounces; $2.60). These socks have two layers. The inner layer of moisture-repellent orlon and nylon is designed to "wick" perspiration to the outer layer of moisture-absorbing yarn (the socks are 10 percent cotton), where it evaporates. The first trials turned out to be less than stringent, but the new socks seemed about as efficient as the old ones. So I went on using them. They've not yet had a really tough test under fierce desert conditions or in temperatures below about 20°F, and I retain a sort of residual skepticism; but on the whole I still don't seem to find any marked difference from wool. I guess I ought to have something firmer to report on such a fundamental matter. At this point, though, I'm afraid I don't.*

Whatever socks I'm wearing, I want them long enough to turn down over ankle boots when I'm wearing shorts—which is almost always. An ordinary rubber band keeps stones and dirt from falling down between socks and ankle.

I carry three pairs of socks at a time. The two spare

---

*I've now gone back to wool—to the gray "Norwegian boot socks" that are almost standard western hikers' wear (4½ ounces and $3.50 a pair). Funny thing, though: I'm damned if I can produce any stunningly convincing reasons for my reconversion. I needed a new pair of boots and had to decide what thickness sock I'd fit them with, that's all. Sorry.

pairs travel in the flap pocket of the pack—or if it lacks such a pocket, in some other easily accessible place. In very hot weather I often change socks every hour and tie the sweat-drenched pair on top of the pack to dry. A three-foot length of nylon cord knotted to the upper crossbar of the packframe secures the tops of these socks with a clove hitch; and tucking the socks under the pack's closure strings prevents them from slipping off to one side (well, usually prevents). When not in use, the cord tucks down behind the nylon mesh back support. In cooler country I may wear the same socks all day, or almost all day, but any dirty pairs hang purifying on top of the pack. If a dirty pair have to go inside the pack for any reason (such as rain or snatching tree branches or recently washed socks that monopolize the outside drier) I segregate them hygienically in a plastic bag.

A pair of socks no doubt lasts longer for some people than for others. In the six months and thousand-plus map-miles of my California trip (many more on the ground) I wore out nine pairs.

Care of Socks

Woolen socks must be washed carefully. Some backpackers carry packages of Woolite, specially made for washing wool in cold water. But you eliminate one item and do almost as good a job if you use soap, which may be in your toilet gear anyway. Avoid detergent; it removes vital oils from the wool. Trak is safe for wool, and a most convenient maid-of-all-work. But whatever you use, rinse the socks thoroughly. An advantage of Wick-Dry socks is that you need exercise less care.

If no washing agent is available, plain rinsing out of dirty socks, even in cold water, does a surprising lot of good.

Strictly speaking, socks should be dried away from the sun and lying flat rather than hanging, but even with wool I have often broken both rules without apparent penalty. I find, in any case, that drying out socks on top of the pack as I walk is often the only way I get to dry them out at all. (Warning: wet socks are heavy, and when spread out to dry on a rock will stay put in moderate winds; but as they dry out, so the tendency to flight increases. Solution: always hobble them with rocks, full canteens, or what have you.)

Try to wash your socks fairly often. In hot weather that may mean once a day. Dirty socks insulate poorly, absorb little sweat, and because they are no longer soft and resilient can quickly cause abrasions.

The only time I wore a hole in a sock while out and away, I patched it with a small foam-rubber disk cut from a sheet of "moleskin." The repair turned out to be astonishingly effective.

Camp Footwear

Wearing boots around camp is usually a nuisance, can often be uncomfortable, and may even amount to a serious inefficiency. (Toward the end of my first week's real traveling in Grand Canyon my feet became so sore that I rested a day and a half beside a spring. Because I had moccasins, which slip off and on very easily, I was able to expose my feet almost continually to the air and never to the painful pressures of boots. If I had had to wear the boots for the many small chores that always need doing around camp, I am sure my feet would not have recovered as quickly as they did.)

Unless you feel confident that conditions will allow you to go barefoot in camp—and they almost never will—the only answer is to carry lightweight campwear.

I have found nothing to equal moccasins with an external composition sole about a quarter of an inch thick—not the hard and slippery kind but a softer, lighter, off-crepe type that grips almost any surface, wet or dry. Such soles add little weight but keep out thorns and blunt the cutting—and bruising—edge of almost any stone. They wear well too. My last pair died only after a long career culminating in months of hard use in Africa, day after day, driving and around camp. I'm finding it difficult to buy a replacement pair light and non-slip enough but I'll keep trying. Those old moccasins were ideal. Among other things, I could, by adjusting the laces, vary their fit: loose for slipping on and off sore feet in camp; firm and safe if the feet were in good fettle and took me exploring up a nearby rockface.*

If the weight problem becomes acute, consider light unsoled moccasins (average, nine ounces; $7). But in stony country don't expect too much from the unprotected underleather. The pair I carried in Grand Canyon just about lasted out the two months.

When your feet are really sore, even camp moccasins can feel uncomfortable, particularly if they're new. One solution: pad toes and heels with toilet paper.

*Later: Just found a pair—Minnetonka Buffalo Moccasins (17 ounces, $10).

Aids and Attachments

Walking Staff

Although the vast majority of walkers never even think of using a walking staff, I unhesitatingly include it among the foundations of the house that travels on my back. I take my staff along almost as automatically as I take my pack. For many years now it has been a third leg to me—and much more besides.

On smooth surfaces the staff helps maintain an easy rhythm to my walking and gives me something to lean on when I stop to stand and stare. Over rough going of any kind, from tussocky grass to pockety rock, and also in a high wind, it converts me when I am heavily laden from an insecure biped into a confident triped. It does the same only more so when I have to scramble across a chasm or a big boulder or a mildly obstructive stretch of rock and keep reaching out sideways for a balancing aid or backwards for that little extra push up and over. And it does the same thing, even more critically and consistently, when I cross a steep, loose slope of talus or gravel or dirt, or wade a fast-flowing creek, or cross it on a log. In marshland or on precarious rock or snow, and in failing light or darkness anywhere, it tests doubtful footing ahead. It reconnoiters bushes or crevices that I suspect might harbor a rattlesnake. It often acts as the indispensable upright needed to rig a shelter from rain or sun with fly sheet or ground sheet or poncho. Occasionally, held down by a couple of heavy stones, it serves as ground anchor for the windward side of such a shelter. It has performed successfully as a fishing rod. It has acted as a marked measuring stick to be checked later, when a rule is available, for the exact length of fish, rattlesnakes, and other dead animals. It forms a rough but very ready monopod for steadying binoculars if my hands are shaking from exertion, or for a camera if I need to shoot with a shutter speed slower than 1/60 second. And day in and day out, at almost every halt, it props up my pack and gives me a soft and stable backrest. (As I am lazy enough to believe that being able to relax against a soft backrest for even a ten-minute halt is no minor matter, I am almost inclined to regard this function of my staff as one of its most vital.) Although I had never really considered the matter until this minute, I think the staff also gives me a false but subconsciously comforting feeling that I am not after all completely defenseless against attack by such enemies as snakes, bears, and men.

The staff still surprises and pleases me from time to time by accomplishing new and unexpected chores. I can pluck at least three from recent memories. Once, I decided halfway up a short rockface that it was unclimbable with the heavy pack on my back. I slipped the pack off and held it with knee pressure in a sloping crevice and took a short length of nylon cord from an outside pocket and tied it to the head of the staff and then to the pack frame. Then I jammed the foot of the staff on a convenient ledge and angled its head up against the bottom of the pack so that it held there without my knee and thereby freed the knee and the rest of me for the short and relatively simple climb (unencumbered) to the top of the rockface—where I had a safe stance from which to reach down without difficulty and pull up the pack and attached staff. One cool and windy afternoon, when I was booted and fully clothed, the staff rescued, with about an inch to spare, an empty plastic water canteen that the wind had blown into a river no less wet than any other river and a good deal bigger and stronger than most. And one night when I was camped in a cave I tied the staff onto the nylon cord from which my candle lantern was suspended—and thereby furnished myself with a convenient handle by which I could, without moving my lazy butt an inch, adjust the candle lantern into the various specific positions I wanted it for cooking, writing notes, or contemplating cave or universe.

The staff I used until recently was nothing much to look at: ordinary stout bamboo with an average diameter of 1⅜ inches—just right for a firm but comfortable grip.* After years of use, small cracks developed up and down its whole length, some of them decidedly threatening. Mostly, they stopped when they came to a knot mark, and the general structure remained sound. But each end-section had split so severely that, left to itself, it would flap like an empty banana skin, and over

---

*I don't know what kind of bamboo it is, but the man who gave it to me—near the start of my California walk, beside the Colorado River—said he had cut it on his own property near Los Angeles.

When I told him that I wanted the bamboo to replace a yucca staff I had broken in killing a rattlesnake he said, "Well, I hope you get a rattler with it. One of them killed my brother." But one of the few things the staff has never done is to kill a rattlesnake—at first because I did not want to risk breaking it or getting venom on it; and quite soon because, growing up, I came to realize that there is no reason except fear for killing rattlesnakes that live in places where they are unlikely to meet people.

the years I bandaged the wounds with several rings of rip-stop tape. Yet I have to confess that when I looked at the bamboo's weatherbeaten surface, and especially at the brown patina that had formed around the second knot, where my hand usually gripped, I felt sad at the thought that it would not last for ever. In other words, I had come to regard the staff with a warm affection. I suppose some people would call it a soggy sentimentality.

But a dozen years of grinding toil wore away the foot of the staff, inch by inch, until at last it measured only 3 feet, 10 inches. Reluctantly, I retired it. Its replacement, also bamboo, is 5 feet long—the original length of the old one—and weighs 15½ ounces. But it has already split rather severely, and although a couple of years' use have now pounded the beginnings of character into its shiny newness it has not really begun to command the affection I felt for the old one.

A possible but vanishing source of unimproved bamboo is your friendly neighborhood rug store, where they may still use bamboo poles instead of cardboard rolls as the inner cores of rolled carpeting.

I gather that my staff fixation has generated a bemused merriment among many readers of the first edition. But by no means among all of them. Two were even kind enough to send me staffs. One was the replacement bamboo. The other is an elegant aluminum job, complete with rubber foot and removable knurled top that screws onto a fitting the same size as the screw fitting of a camera tripod, thereby making the staff an instant monopod. Although I can all too easily imagine the metal becoming too hot and also too cold for comfort, the staff has proved entirely efficient. Yet I find I do not use it often: it is too mechanical looking, somehow, for the back country. (Yes, packframes are also aluminum and shiny. I know, I know. But still . . . .)

Several readers have sent stavic suggestions. A New Yorker writes that he bought from Honda Associates (485 Fifth Avenue—"Your Judo-Karate Service Center") an *Aikido bo,* or wooden defense stick (48 inches, 18 ounces, $6; 60 inches, 27 ounces, $7). The kind of wood seems uncertain, but the 5-foot model, well treated with linseed oil, has given good service. It apparently pays, though, to check very carefully that a new *bo* is not warped.*

---

*A letter I received from Vermont deserves special mention for more than its data on how to make an ultra-strong staff. The staff is interesting enough: a 6-foot bamboo, about 1¼-inch diameter, wrapped spirally with a single layer of 3-inch glass cloth tape in a 50% overlap and bonded with epoxy or polyester resin (from a boating supplies store); the top capped with a large rubber chair leg tip; the foot fitted with a large natural rubber crutch tip (Safe-T-Flex by Guardian of Los Angeles) that "lasts for many years and is a very good gripper on wet rocks, ice, etc."

This tip, says the writer, "stops the clatter of the stick on rocks; prevents the foot from wearing and splitting; provides mass near the ground that gives the stick a good 'pendulum' action—I find it easy to 'throw' forward and, while light (1.4 pounds), to have good dynamics." But the letter's meat lies in the asides that keep popping up at you: "I have to use a staff for propulsion because I go on one common and one wooden leg . . . . The only failures have been to have them stolen, and one that went over a waterfall (before me) . . . . I have used it for (among other things) poling canoes down rapids. The rubber cap keeps me from getting bruised in case I fall on it when pole vaulting down steep slopes . . . ." The letter ends: "Try this design" and I am sure the modest man was talking only about his staff.

Several outdoor suppliers now list staffs in their catalogues. Adventure Horizons of San Diego makes aluminum ones (5 feet and 4 feet, $8 post free). L. L. Bean offers a ¾-inch aircraft alloy tubing model that folds into three equal sections, has an internal heavy duty elastic cable that "positively locks extended sections and cannot accidentally come apart," tungsten carbide tip, molded polyvinyl grip and adjustable leather strap. (Color: black. 56 inches, 13¼ ounces; 58 inches, 13¾ ounces; 60 inches, 14¼ ounces. Any length: $10.) Bean, Moor & Mountain, The Ski Hut, and maybe other catalogues offer a wooden model, hand fashioned from kiln dried ash and finished in weatherproof walnut color, that has a leather wrist thong and is bound at the foot with a tapered brass ferrule fitted with an abrasion- and slip-resistant urethane tip (46, 50, 54 and 58 inches; average weight, 13 ounces; all lengths: $7).

There are many other kinds of staff. One reader was kind enough to send me a Wanderstock, or German walking stick. He says its metal tip "makes it almost prehensile on boulder fields and as a wading staff," and adds that the hooked end means you can "let it hang from the wrist for taking a picture or a leak." The Ski Hut, and perhaps other suppliers, catalogue these sticks. Then there's the Wauk-o-Long Survival Staff (42-, 48- and 54-inch lengths; $7.49, $7.98, and $8.49, respectively, from Springhart Corporation, Dayton, Ohio). Made of anodized aluminum, it "contains a set of plastic canisters for storing your own selection of survival gear or food (tare weight: 2½ pounds). It also has a rubber crutch tip at each end, a nylon wrist strap and dayglo grip pads.'' My Technological God!

One small but constantly recurring matter: you cannot conveniently lift a pack onto your back while holding a staff. Where possible, lean the staff against something before you lift the pack, so that once you're loaded up you can easily take hold of it. But even in open places there is no need to waste the not inconsiderable energy expended in bending down with a heavy load on your back: just hook one foot under the staff, lift it with your instep, and take hold of it when the top angles up within reach of your hand. With practice, you'll probably find yourself flipping the head of the staff up with your foot and catching it as its apogee. You'll soon get used to laying the staff ready for this maneuver on a low bush or stone or across a depression in the ground before you hoist up the pack, so that afterward you can slide a toe under it. If you forget the precaution and can't get a toe under, simply roll the staff up onto your instep with the heel of the other foot. It sounds gynmastic but is really very simple.

There are, I admit, times when a long staff becomes a nuisance.

If you have to swim across a fast river, for example, it can tangle dangerously with your legs. In calm water it's easy enough to pull the staff safely along behind on a length of nylon cord. But when a fast-water situation was plainly going to arise on a 1966 trip beside the Colorado River, I left my regular staff behind and on the first day cut a four-foot section from the stem of a dead agave, or century plant. With the thicker end carefully rounded it made a very serviceable third leg. During river crossings it tucked conveniently out of the way in the bindings of my packframe, protruding only very slightly at the top. The odd thing was that by the end of two weeks I was feeling for this little staff the same kind of affection that I lavished on my regular one—so much so that when it broke on the next-to-last day and I had to cut a fresh length of agave, I stuffed the scarred, foot-long stub into my pack and carried it all the way home. I guess "soggy sentimentality" is about right.

A staff is also a nuisance, even a hazard, if you have to do any climbing that demands the use of two unencumbered hands. Occasionally, on short and unexpected pitches, I've pulled the staff up after me on a nylon cord, or lowered it ahead. If you know you're likely to face some rock climbing, it may be worth leaving your regular staff behind and cutting a temporary one that can be discarded and replaced (climbing was a contributory reason for my doing so on that 1966 Colorado trip). If you expect to do very much climbing, there are two solutions. Either do without a staff of any kind; or take along an

Ice ax.

Even if you use the ax little if at all for ice work, it will serve as a reasonably efficient staff, even in its pack-prop role. And while you are climbing you can tie it out of the way on your pack. An ice ax (1¼-2 pounds; $24-35) is, incidentally, a splendid instrument for extracting stubborn tent pegs from packed snow—and in its old age, I'm told, for gardening.

When walking, hold the ax by the head, with the

pointed part of the head forward so that in case of a fall the danger to you is reduced. A rubber protector for the base tip can be used on hard surfaces, and definitely should be used when the ax is in the car or at home (1 ounce; 50¢). You can also get rubber covers for the ax head (1½ ounces, $1.75).

The technical use of an ice ax does not fall within the scope of a walking book.

Two other walking aids that lie close to the fringes of walking deserve brief mention:

Crampons

Although crampons are essentially ironmongery for climbers, they are sometimes worth carrying if you expect to cross ice or hard snow. And not only steep snow. A flat snowfield that has weathered hard may develop basins and ridges and even savage pinnacles that in naked boots create considerable and potentially dangerous obstacles. And not long ago I discovered by accident, when I climbed out onto the lip of an ice-covered gully on Mount Shasta, that when you are carrying a heavy load crampons can transform a sloping slab of very soft rock from a nasty barrier into a cakewalk.

For beginners, ten-point crampons are said to be best (22 ounces; $21). Twelve-pointers, with a pair of spikes protruding forward, can easily trip unwary users. Novices should exercise great care with *any* crampons; indeed, some experts suggest that a tyro may be better off with an ice ax alone.

When you buy crampons or rent them (at, say, $2 a weekend or $8 for two weeks), take pains to ensure that they fit your boots exactly, for both width and length. A loose pair can be extremely dangerous. Make sure too that you learn how to strap them on properly. I will not try to describe the correct method here: it is a complicated thing to verbalize but very simple to learn from a salesman.

Weighted down with stones, crampons make excellent tent pegs on hard surfaces that more orthodox pegs refuse to penetrate.

Snowshoes

My experience is meager, but I have learned that snowshoes permit you to move over the very surface of snow into which your booted legs plunge knee deep—and that immediately after a storm they will allow you to travel (sweating hard, but sinking in less than a foot at each step) across snow into which you would otherwise go on sinking forever if God had not arranged that human legs eventually converge. I have also learned that if you have an old hamstring injury, snowshoeing may let you in for some nagging discomfort. Also that, short of a shovel, there is nothing like a snowshoe for digging out your tent during and after a storm.

When I first inquired about the technique of snowshoeing, several people said, "Oh, you just put them on and go." And that seems to be about right. The vitally important thing is not to splay your feet out. At the very start, keep looking down to see how close together you can slide your feet without entrapping one snowshoe under the other; or, after a little practice, how far forward you must step in order to get away with lifting the edge of one shoe *just* over the edge of the other at the bulging widest part. Soon you find yourself moving along without thinking about how to put your feet down. Naturally, the closer the movement comes to normal walking, the less tiring it is.

Without a pack, the thing soon becomes simple. But if you are backpacking the chances are that the pack—what with a stout tent and warm clothing and big sleeping bag—will be hippopotamic; and although snowshoes make movement possible under conditions that would otherwise bog you down, you should be prepared for the discovery that snowshoeing can be a pretty laborious, not to say boring, business. But it has its moments. In really deep, soft, new snow you may get the disturbing notion that if you lose your balance and fall with that huge load on your back you will "drown."

At one end of the snowshoe spectrum lie little tear-shaped "bearpaws" (average 13 inches by 30 inches, weight 6 pounds), too awkwardly wide for normal cross-country use but apparently valuable around cabins or in thick brush where maneuverability is vital. At the other end come prodigious structures 5 feet long and more that look as if they would support an elephant on detergent foam. Terrain dictates the type. On the West Coast, long-tailed models are most popular; in New England, smaller, tailless, "modified bearpaws." Check locally. The only kind I have used are "trail shoes" measuring 10 inches by 56 inches and weighing 6 pounds. On them I was able to move comfortably over deep snow with a crust too weak to support my boots, and to move rather laboriously through a storm that had already dropped more than four feet of powder-soft snow. This was when I found out about the drowning threat. It was pretty hard work with a heavy pack anyway, and my solution was to break trail unladen, backtrack, and then pack forward over an easy, trampled trail. I can imagine experienced snowshoers extracting considerable amusement from this admission. But at least I emerged undunked.

When not in use, snowshoes can in reasonably open terrain be tied horizontally on your pack. Laying them across the top of the open pack and just pulling tight on the flap is often the simplest way. Where trees or brush are likely to snag the protruding ends, strap vertically.

Standard ash-and-rawhide-thong snowshoes need occasional revarnishing. (Spray varnishes are now available.) An alternative to buying your own (around $45) and having to maintain them is to rent a pair (say, $5 a weekend, $18 for two weeks) and let the store look after the varnishing.

Some wooden snowshoes now come with nylon or neoprene thongs, and they are said to be good. So are aluminum-framed models, provided they are kept well varnished. There are also all-plastic versions, and they are still said to be, roughly speaking, terrible: they break. But they're improving. One cognoscente suggests that they've already gone from terrible to bad, and that given time and research they may well carry the day.

The way to move across snow country is to ski. But on skis you are no longer walking. At least, that clearly used to be so. With Nordic skiing, which I have yet to try, the distinction seems less definite.

Care of Feet

Some people seem to have naturally tough feet. But if you are like me you know that it pays to take stringent precautions before and during any walk much longer than you are currently used to, or with a load much heavier than you have very recently carried. If you do not yet understand the value of such precautions, then you've never generated a big, joy-killing blister with many miles still to go.

Getting Your Feet Ready

This vital task is best achieved by practice—by taking time out beforehand to work up slowly from a few gentle miles, unladen (if you are in really bad shape), to a long day's slog with a load as big as you mean to carry. But somehow you rarely seem to have the time to take out, and even more rarely the determination to take it. The only substitute I know, and it's a poor one, is to toughen up the skin (soles, toes, and heels particularly) by regular applications of rubbing alcohol for a week or so beforehand. If you put the alcohol bottle beside your toothbrush, it is not too difficult to remember this simple half-minute chore, morning and night. It helps too, if you cannot get out for any serious walking, to wear your boots—especially new ones—as much as you can for a week or so beforehand, even if only around the house.

Some people who habitually get blisters in certain places on their feet say they ward them off by covering the sites in advance with tape or moleskin. And one reader writes: "If you go barefoot whenever you can, you'll most likely develop lovely leathery feet." I think he's got something too.

On the March

The important thing is to begin easily. Men—and whole families—who backpack into the bush for once-a-year vacations all too often find the whole week or fortnight ruined at the very beginning by too much ambition and too little discretion. Their feet never recover from the pounding of the first day or two. A gentle shakedown cruise—a day or a week, depending on the total length of the trip—can make all the difference. On my thousand-mile California walk, although I began with stiff new boots and soft city feet, I suffered only one blister—a minor affair generated by an ill-advised insole experiment. But I took great care in the first week and averaged barely seven miles a day, over very easy going. In Grand Canyon my feet fared less well. But I began with a barely cured infected heel, and because of it had worn nothing but moccasins for almost two weeks. If it had not been for two days of easy ambling at the start and a further four days of taking it fairly easy, I should probably have been crippled before I got fully started.

It's essential that you continue to take precautions until your feet are comfortably lasting out the longest day and the heaviest load—even with steady downhill work, which gives feet a much more brutal hammering than they get on the level or uphill. I rarely seem to reach this point for at least a week or two. Until then I go on applying rubbing alcohol. For years I carried about 5 ounces of it in a flat plastic bottle, but have now switched to one of those little plastic squeeze-bottles that drug stores sell for use with all kinds of liquids, from hand lotion to insect repellent. These bottles (¾ ounce; 40¢) have long, thin, internal tubes attached to their caps, and when squeezed they eject liquid contents in a fine spray. They are therefore much more economical than open-mouthed bottles, which tend to slosh too much alcohol onto your feet. For a normal week's walking I find the 2-ounce-size bottle adequate. But there are larger sizes. Before you pass a bottle for "combat" duty, try it in every position, including upside down, to check that the spray cap never leaks alcohol. I'm told that a useful source for good bottles (for this and other uses) is the nasal spray canister. The inner tops come out, they are the right size, and you can always pour the junk down the drain. My alcohol bottle travels, immediately accessible, in an outside pocket of the pack. Normally I rub my feet with a little alcohol morning and night, and in hot weather or when my feet are really sore I may do so several times a day. I also carry a 3-ounce or 1-ounce can of foot powder, in the same pocket of the pack. I always sprinkle the insides of my socks with it in the morning, and may do so again several times during the day.

Many experienced hikers deplore all this messing around. "Unless something is seriously wrong," I once heard an expert advise a beginner, "keep your boots on until you stop for the day. You'll have far less trouble with your feet that way." And no doubt such advice is sound enough for some people. I go to the other extreme. In hot weather I often take my boots off at each halt and let the air get at the perspiring feet. When my feet are really sore I anoint them with alcohol and powder at almost every hourly halt and also change socks, repowdering the pair that has been drying out on top of the pack. I sometimes used, if water was available, to wash my feet at almost every halt—a practice that a lot of people regard as skin-softening idiocy. I am now inclined to regard it—with considerable conviction, on the flimsiest of evidence—as skin-softening idiocy.

Taking your boots off and airing your feet whenever your can certainly makes good theoretical sense. Heat is the cause of all blisters. Locally, the heat comes from the friction of a rucked sock or an ill-fitting boot. But it seems reasonable to suppose that the overall temperature of your feet makes a big difference. I certainly find deserts the hardest places on feet. And it is not really surprising: few people realize how hot the ground underfoot can be. In Grand Canyon I repeatedly checked air and ground temperatures. With air temperature about 85°F I would get a ground reading on unshaded rock (and that meant just about any rock) of around 115° or 120°. On unshaded sand the mercury would go well past the last gradation of 120°. When air temperature climbed over 90° I had to be careful where I left the thermometer, for fear the mercury would blow off the top.*

---

*An article by A. Court in the *Geographical Review* (1949, No. 2, pages 214-20) gives these figures for extreme conditions in American deserts: air at five feet, 125°F.; at one foot, 150°; at one inch, 165°; at ground, 180°. [*Footnote continues on the next page.*]

Remedial Treatment

If, in spite of all your care, your feet need doctoring, start it early. The moment you feel what may be the beginnings of a blister, do something about it.

First remove any obvious and rectifiable local irritant, such as a fragment of stone or a rucked sock. Then cover the tender place. Cover it even if you can see nothing more than a faint redness. Cover it, in fact, if you can see nothing at all. Being a "hero" is being a bloody fool. The covering may only be needed for a few hours; if you take it off at night and let the air get at the skin you may not even need to replace it next morning. But if you do nothing at the first warning you may find yourself inside the hour with a blister that will last a week.

For covering, a piece of surgical tape or a Band-aid will do, provided its adhesive surface is efficient enough to prevent rucking—a requirement not always met when the trouble is on your toes.

By far the best patches I know are those cut from the oddly miraculous devices known as "moleskins." They're sold in most drug stores. Now it used to be that a moleskin was a moleskin was a moleskin. No more. These days you must choose between five variants. The original Moleskins, still sold under that name, are sheets of thin white felt, adhesive on one side. Kurotex

---

This kind of heat layering is by no means confined to deserts. Interesting temperatures recorded during World War II at a naval research center in Imperial Valley, California, on a day when the official air temperature touched 120°F., include 145° in the gasoline in a 50-gallon drum left in the sun, 155° in the vapor above the gasoline, and 190° on the seat of a jeep.

("A Superior Moleskin") seems to be the same only flesh-colored (well, flesh-colored for pinkish Caucasians, anyway). Kiro Felt is flesh-colored and double thickness. In Adhesive Foam ("Softer than Moleskin!"), latex foam replaces felt. In Molefoam, you get felt over foam. I've unfortunately failed to extract from the makers any coherent information about the advantages and disadvantages of each variant, so for the moment I'll stick to Moleskin and Kurotex. I mistrust the foam: it must surely hold the heat. But I see that Eastern Mountain Sports calls Molefoam the "greatest thing for blisters ever invented." (Moleskins and Kurotex come in convenient flat 1-ounce packages of four 3-by-4-inch strips, 45 cents; and in rolls in cans—7 by 10 inches, 50 cents; 7 by 30 inches, $1.15. Kiro Felt: two strips, $4^{5}/_{16}$ by $2\frac{7}{8}$ inches, 45 cents; roll in can, 7 by 10 inches, $1.10. Molefoam: $4\frac{3}{4}$-by-5-inch sheet, 43 cents. Adhesive Foam: 6-by-6-inch sheet, 33 cents.)

Moleskins—and, I assume, the variants—stick to skin like glue even after your feet get wet. In fact, it is sometimes quite a business peeling the thin protective layer of plastic off new patches. (The makers leave a helpful projecting band of this layer and advise you to remove the plastic before cutting patches to the required shape. But in order to preserve the adhesive qualities—which can be rather easily damaged by handling—I shape the patch first with a pair of scissors, carefully beveling all edges, then lever up one corner of the plastic with the scissors' point, and peel it off.) But mere adhesion does not begin to explain the extraordinary efficiency of moleskins. I suppose their secret has something to do with the resilience and sideways-sliding quality of the felt. Anyway, I know for a fact and with gratitude that they can stop embryonic friction trouble dead; can stifle the pain from any surface blister and often keep it from getting worse; and can even, apparently from mere cushioning, deaden the worst pain from those deep, dismal, often invisible blisters that occasionally form under heel or ball of foot.

My moleskins travel in my "office," and conveniently protect both scissors and signaling mirror.

If you generate a blister in spite of all your care—or because you were not careful enough—and if it is either very deep or is not yet very bulbous, the best treatment is probably just to cover it. But if the blister is close to the surface and has already inflated you will need to burst it before you can walk with comfort. Pierce it with a needle, from the side, down near the base of the balloon, so that all the liquid can drain away. (I carry several needles, primarily for repair work, in my water-proof matchsafe.) Sterilize the needle first, in a steriliz-ing agent if you carry one (rubbing alcohol won't do), but failing that in a flame—far better than nothing, in spite of the carbon deposits. If you have got to keep walking and if the loose skin of the balloon does not ruck up when deflated, it is probably best to leave the skin in place and cover it, and to cut it away only when the skin beneath has had time to harden. But if you can rest long enough for the skin to harden—which it does more quickly if exposed to the air—or if the deflated outer skin puckers so badly that it seems likely to cause further damage as you walk, remove it by scissoring carefully around the edges of the blister. Take care to keep the exposed area clean. And leave no dead skin likely to cause new chafing. If you must keep walking, and apply a moleskin or other adhesive cover, use a thin fragment of gauze to prevent the cover from sticking directly to the exposed and tender skin. A sprinkling of foot powder helps reduce friction further, and so does an antiseptic of a kind that will lubricate as well as reduce the danger of infection.

But never forget that a blister is a sign of failure. The efficient way to deal with foot trouble is to avoid it. Pre-harden. On the march, and especially in the early days of a trip, attend assiduously to preventive measures. And nip tribulations in the bud.

The Foundations in Action

A book on walking should no doubt have something to say about the simple, basic, physical act of walking.

On the most fundamental level, advice is probably useless. Anyone old enough to read has almost certainly grown too set in the way he puts one foot in front of the other to alter it materially without devoting a great deal of time and determination to the task. Unless, of course, there is something correctably wrong with his feet.

On the other hand, it is very easy to improve by a little conscious thought what I regard as the most important single element in the physical act of walking: rhythm. An easy, unbroken rhythm can carry you along hour after hour almost without your being aware that you are putting one foot in front of the other. At the end of a really long day you will be aware of the act all right, but as long as you maintain a steady rhythm very little of your mind need be concerned with it. And your muscles will complain far less than if you have walked all day in a series of jerky and semi-coordinated movements, sometimes pushing close to your limit, sometimes meandering.

With experience you automatically fall into your own rhythmic pace. (At least, mostly you do. There will still be days when you have to fight for it, and not always with total success.) But when you first take up real walking you may have to think deliberately about establishing a stride and a speed that feel comfortable. And both stride and speed may be rather different with and without a load.

You will almost certainly have to concentrate at first on the important matter of not disrupting the rhythm unless absolutely necessary. This means stepping short for a stride when you come to some minor obstacle such as a narrow ditch, or even marking time with one foot. I cannot emphasize this unbroken rhythm business too strongly.

Of course, rhythm is not always a simple matter of constant stride and speed. In fact it remains so only as long as you walk on a smooth and level surface. The moment you meet rough going underfoot or start up or down a gradient you have to modify stride or speed or both.

Climbing a gentle slope means nothing more than a mild shortening of stride, though leaning forward slightly may help too. But long before a mountainside gets so steep that you start reaching out for handholds, stride becomes a meaningless word. Now, you put your feet down almost side by side at one step, a foot or more apart at the next, depending on the immediate local gradients and footholds. Even the rate at which you move one leg past the other—slowly and deliberately and almost laboriously, though not quite—may vary in response to changes in the general gradient. But the old rhythm persists. I am not sure where the relationships lie. It is not—though I have sometimes thought so —that you continue to expend the same amount of energy. Steep climbing takes more out of you, always. But the fact remains that although you must change gear in an almost literal sense at the bottom and top of a steep hill you can maintain the deeper continuity of the old rhythm. The pulse is still there, somewhere, if you know where to feel for it.

Downhill walking, though less sweaty than climbing, is less easy than it ought to be. In theory you merely relinquish the potential energy you gained with such labor as you climbed; but in practice you do no such thing. At every step you expend a great deal of effort in holding yourself back—and this effort too demands a deliberate change of gear. If the gradient is at all severe you reduce both stride and speed as much as you think necessary to prevent yourself from hammering hell out of knees and ankles and feet (especially feet). Again, though, you find with practice that it is possible to maintain the essence of the old rhythm.

You may also have to apply a conscious effort to maintaining your rhythmic pace when you come to certain kinds of rough going—soft sand or gravel that drags at your feet like molasses; talus that slides away from under your feet like a treadmill; rough rock or tussocky grassland that soon disrupts an even stride; or prolonged sidehill work that puts an abnormal strain on foot and leg muscles and may also present something of a problem in balance.

Walking after dark, especially on pitch-black, moonless nights, can also destroy your customary rhythm. If you have been walking in daylight and simply keep going, little trouble seems to arise. But if you get up in the middle of the night and hike out into darkness you may have a surprise in store. I wrote in *The Thousand-Mile Summer* about the only time I traveled at night on my California walk. It was in Death Valley. The first night inside the Valley I had no sleeping bag, and I failed, dismally, to stay asleep. At three thirty I got up from the gully in which I had camped and headed north into the darkness. There was no moon. From the start I found myself walking in a curious and disturbing state of detachment. The paleness that was the dirt road refused to stay in positive contact with my feet, and I struggled along with laborious, unrhythmic steps. All around hovered hints of immense open spaces and distant, unconvincing slopes. Time had lost real meaning back in the gully; now it lacked even boundaries. When dawn gave the landscape a tenuous reality at last, I was still two hours away from my next cache. In those endless two hours I completely failed to reestablish my usual rhythmic pace.

Next night I was on the move by nine thirty. This time, bright moonlight made the physical world something real and conquerable. I could plant my feet firmly and confidently on the solid white road. But soon after eleven o'clock, the moon set. The world narrowed to hints of colossal open space, to a blur that achieved reality only through jabbing at my feet. Distance degenerated into marks on the map. Time was the creeping progress of watch hands. All through the long and cold and dismal night that followed I had to struggle to hold some semblance of my usual daytime rhythm. I succeeded only marginally. But I succeeded far better than on the previous night.

A delicate sense of balance is vital to good walking. And it's not just a matter of being able to cross steep slopes without tightening up. Your body should always be poised and relaxed so that you put down your feet, whatever their size and whatever your load, with something close to daintiness. Before I walked through Grand Canyon I met the one man who seemed to know much about hiking away from trails in its remote corners. Trying to get some idea of whether I would be able to cope with the rough, steep country that he crossed with such apparent ease, I asked him to tell me, honestly, if he were a good climber. "No," he said, "definitely not. I'd say I was a very mediocre climber indeed. But in the Canyon it's mostly walking, you know, even though it can be pretty tricky walking at times." He smiled. "I guess you could say, come to think of it, that maybe I don't dislodge quite as many stones as the next guy." And I knew then that he was a good walker.

One of the surest ways to tell an experienced walker from a beginner is the speed at which he starts walking. The beginner tends to tear away in the morning as if he meant to break every record in sight. By contrast, your experienced man seems to amble. But before long, and certainly by evening, their positions have reversed. The beginner is dragging. The expert, still swinging along at the same easy pace, is now the one who looks as though he has records in mind. One friend of mine, a real expert, says, "If you can't carry on a conversation, you're going too fast."

The trap to avoid at all costs, if you want to enjoy yourself, is spurious heroism—the delusion that your prowess as a walker rests on how dauntlessly you "pick 'em up and lay 'em down." It's a sadly common syndrome.

The actual speed at which you walk is a personal and idiosyncratic matter. Settle for whatever seems to suit you best. It is really a question of finding out what you can keep up hour after hour in various kinds of terrain carrying various loads. Until you know your own limits, aim for a slow, rhythmic, almost effortless pace. You'll be surprised, I think, at the ground you cover. The miles will come to meet you. In time, you'll learn that, generally speaking, the way to hurry is not to hurry but to keep going. To this end I have two walking speeds: slow and slower.

The halts you choose to take are a matter of personal preference, but frequent and irregular halts are a sure sign of an inexperienced hiker. Unladen, it may be a good thing to keep going hour after hour without disturbing your rhythm. But if you're carrying a sizable pack you will almost certainly find that, no matter how fit you are, you need to get the weight off your back for a short spell about once an hour. I halt every hour with fairly mechanical regularity, modifying slightly to suit terrain. I like to get to the top of a hill before I stop, for example; and I often halt a few minutes early or late to take advantage of convenient shade or water or a pleasing view. In theory, I rest for ten minutes. When I have a map, I sometimes mark the halting place and pencil in the exact time I stopped. I am no longer sure why I began doing this; but I do so now because I know only too well that it is horribly easy to let a halt drift on for fifteen, twenty, or even thirty minutes, and the penciled figures on the map act as a reminder and a spur. They also help me to judge how I am progressing across a given kind of country, and make it much easier to estimate how far I should be able to travel in the next hour or afternoon or day or week.

At each halt I take off the pack and prop it against a rock or a tree or my staff and lean against it with my back resting comfortably between the protruding outside pockets. I try to relax completely. Sometimes, warding off the attractions of scenery, animals, and the map, I succeed. I may even doze off for a few minutes. Getting started again may demand considerable will power, especially toward the end of a long day; but within a few paces I slip back into the old regular rhythm. With luck I will hold it, unbroken, for another fifty minutes.

Walking at High Altitudes

Even if you acclimate properly you must, once you get up high, walk differently. "How high" is not really answerable with a figure: your body, on any given day, will respond more accurately. But as a guideline it is probably safe to say that most people will have to adjust over 10,000 feet, and that many will have to do so a lot lower.

First, you must learn to modulate your rhythm—to dead slow. Even at sea level, there's nothing so becomes a walker as modest slowness and languidity;

But when the mountain air blows in your ears,
Then imitate the action of a tortoise;
Slacken the sinews, throttle down the blood,
Deflect ambition with delib'rate pace,
And lend the legs a loitering aspect;
Let them creep through the hours of the day
Like a brass clock; let the body dawdle
As languidly as doth a smoker
Drag slow-foot through the grass, like a tippler
O'erfilled with mild but tasteful potion.
Now ope the teeth, and stretch the nostril wide;
Draw slow the breath, and suck down every intake
To his full depth!—On, on, you noble Walker,

whose blood is thin from scaling this full height, and remember that not only during the first three days of your body's readjustment but on, on into the fourth and fifth, Henry, and beyond that for as long as you stay up high, you must strive to keep moving in this consciously imposed, almost ludicrous slow motion. If you do it properly you will not get breathless unless you go very high indeed. And your heart will not pound. (I maintain that if your muscles feel the strain of walking when you are up high then you are asking too much of your heart.) If you forget to hold your legs in check, and revert to something like your normal pace, you will begin to gasp and to feel your heart triphammering. You will therefore rest—and lose time and momentum. But if you tortoise along you can often keep going for the full regulation hour with no more distress than at sea level.

Remember too about those deep, slow breaths—preferably taken in rhythm with your steps: by dragging each breath down into the full depths of your lungs you will at least in part make up for the reduced oxygen-absorbing efficiency of your blood. If you find your brain is not functioning very well—and up high there will assuredly be times when it does not—stop and drag down several extra-deep breaths that expel every lurking unoxygenated residue from your lung cellars. You may begin to think better at once. And this treatment will as often as not remove or at least moderate the headaches that are apt to afflict you for a spell. I keep at headaches with such deep breathing and find I very rarely need resort to aspirins, which I regard as something to be avoided—even in bed, certainly on the move.

Once you have mastered these simple lessons you will be ready to sample the simple joys of walking around on top of the world.

There remains the matter of what you do with your mind while your body walks. Mostly, I find that everything takes care of itself. My mind soars or grubs along or meanders halfway in between, according to the sun or cloud, the wind or rain, the state of my metabolism, the demands of the hour, or other elements beyond my control. But there are times when, in the interests of efficient walking, you need to discipline your thoughts. If the way ahead looks long and tiresome and, above all, if it slopes steeply and inexorably upward, on and on, then you are liable to find that the prospect presses heavy on your mind and that the depression acts as a brake on your body and that its lethargy further depresses your mind—and so on. The syndrome is pandemic of mountains, and especially to those high enough for the thin air to brake directly on mind and body. In early November 1971 I went up Mount Whitney. I wandered up, acclimating slowly, savoring the emptiness and silence of the country (I had chosen November for horde-avoidance); but I was carrying a considerable load—my plan, soon scuttled by weather, was to camp on the summit—and on the long, final pull, each step became a wearisome, mind-demanding effort. Ahead, the trail curved on and up, on and up. As I climbed, the air grew thinner, even less sustaining. My mind sagged under the burden of step-by-step effort. And then I remembered something. My paperback for the trip was *Zen and the Art of Archery,* and while reading it in my tent the night before I had decided to try applying one of its lessons. I immediately began to do so. "I am the summit;" I told myself. "I am the summit. I am the summit." I focused my mind on the statement, close. And very soon, very easily, I believed it: my insignificant self and the apex of that huge blade of rock *were* the same thing—or at least they occupied the same point in space and time. Yet the space was in another sense still above me. The time, I think, was a nudge ahead in the future. Or perhaps it was the present. Anyway, I held the concept tight and firm, so that there was no room for anything else. (Ex-

cluding other ideas was not too difficult: at 14,000 feet
you can rarely cope with more than one at a time.)

It seemed to work. The effort of climbing—of pulling
self and load on and up, on and up, step by laborious
step—faded away. To say that I floated upward would,
I guess, be hyperbole; but when I reached the summit in
a physical sense I was, I think, less tired than I have
ever been at such a high and crowning moment.

The Outfit

From *The Backpacker*.
By Albert Saijo

Equipment should be judged on qualities such as durability, weight and performance. How well does it do the things it's supposed to do? A clumsy, shoddily made piece of equipment is a burden in wilderness where breakdown and malfunction can be a real problem. Equipment must feel right, which is a part of its design, the aesthetic of the matter, if you will. Why not say that equipment should be both right and beautiful, the most elegant solution of a need? Let it be neither more nor less than it has to be to do its job.

In this chapter we are concerned primarily with an outfit for temperate zone, spring to autumn trips into wilderness. Essentially, we want a basic outfit to which other items can be added according to personal needs and the needs of any particular trip. We also want an outfit that will be adequate in the widest range of conditions. Fortunately, mountain, forest and desert wilderness require much the same basic outfit.

We will be covering equipment in some detail, on the premise that if your equipment is squared away before you go into wilderness, you won't have to fuss over it once you're there.

First, let's try to work out the ideal set of clothes.

Though you should choose each item for its own qualities, you should also think about how it will combine with the other items of your set. You want to carry the minimum set of clothes that will serve over the widest range of conditions.

What do we ask of clothes? In the ideal climate we would be happiest lightly clothed or naked. Being warm-blooded creatures, however, we must maintain an internal temperature of approximately 98.6°F. Heat circulates through the body by way of the blood stream. When it gets hot, from weather or exertion, there is vaso-dilation, and the blood circulates excess heat away from the vital organs to surface tissue and the extremities. When it gets cold, vaso-constriction reduces the blood supply to surface tissue and extremities in order to conserve the heat of the vital organs. Thus the ideal set of clothes will allow us to ventilate heat away in warm weather and conserve body heat in the cold.

Bulky, heavy clothes were once thought the best protection against cold. Now we know that several light loose layers of the right material will do as well or better than a single layer of the same weight. The modern approach is to emphasize the conservation of body heat for warmth.

Clothes are such a personal item, however, that there can be no final word on them. Individual heat and cold tolerance varies too much to set down any general rules for clothes. Only by getting out into wilderness and experimenting will you find the set of clothes that best suits you. What follows are suggestions and possibilities, starting from the inside and working out.

Underwear

You may either get a set of special underwear or improvise some other combination. If you are going into country you know to be cold, not only mornings and evenings but through the day, it would be wise to consider a set of long underwear.

The most efficient underwear is the open-mesh or fishnet type. The principle here is to trap warm air next to the body in the mesh pockets, and at the same time allow body moisture to evaporate out. This is vital because your body perspires constantly. Even without exertion, it gives off a pint of water every eight hours in breath and fine perspiration.

Fishnet and underwear comes in cotton or wool-and-cotton combination. It has the disadvantage of not working unless it's under something, and by itself it won't keep insects off.

Then there are the traditional wool or cotton long johns. These unfortunately don't ventilate well, and so with the slightest exertion you begin to sweat in them. The sweat isn't evaporated but wicked right into the fabric and wet underwear doesn't have much insulating power. Don't take the whole set if you can get along with either the top or the bottom separately.

Instead of underwear, a cotton T-shirt may serve your needs, or a long-sleeved cotton turtle-neck or crew-neck shirt. These, or course, may serve as outer shirts, too.

Shirts

Possibilities here include a cotton or light-wool (about

10-ounce-weight fabric) shirt with long sleeves, long tail, buttoned-flap breast pockets, and buttons all the way down front; or the aforementioned cotton turtle- or crew-neck shirt, rib knit or jersey. Long sleeves keep off insects and a buttoned front makes the shirt adjustable. Think of the type of shirt that gives you the most comfort while working. Think of the kind of weather you're likely to meet.

Pants

For extended walking in rugged country, loose-fitting pants are best. In hiking, your legs are the most active part of your body and need cooling. Tight-legged pants tend to bind in the crotch and legs, especially if you have sweat into them, or have been caught by rain. On the other hand, some people feel their snug fit to be a comfort. Be sure pockets are strong. At least one back pocket should button down. Watch pockets are handy. Cuffs are useless. A light but tough twill fabric (like whipcord), either cotton or wool backed with synthetics, is the standard material for a good pair of outdoor pants.

Many backpackers swear by walking shorts. These too should be of a generous cut. If you don't want to take both pants and shorts, a pair of pants can be fixed so they will convert to shorts. Find a pair of wide-legged pants. Then draw the pant legs up inside themselves and hold with snaps or buttons. Don't forget a belt to keep your pants where you want them and to hang things from. But don't overload your belt. Or how about suspenders?

Outer Uppers

Through the day you're likely to be in shirt and pants,
your first layer of insulation. In the cold of morning and
night you'll want a garment that is heavier or has more
insulating power. This is your second layer of insulation.

Sweater: A light, fuzzy, open-weave, wool sweater
or a heavier, bulky-knit, Icelandic one could fill the bill.
But the light sweater may be too light against sustained
cold, while the Icelandic, though warm, may be too
heavy or too bulky for packing. Clothes are a compromise at best. A pullover is not very adjustable. If it
gets too hot, all you can do is take it off. If it gets cold
you can put a shell parka over it to increase its efficiency somewhat. Perhaps the most you can say for a
well-made sweater is that it has aesthetic appeal.

Heavy wool shirt: More efficient as second-layer
insulation would be a medium-to-heavy wool shirt (14-
to 20-ounce-weight fabric. It's more efficient than a
sweater because it's more adjustable to changing conditions. If it gets too warm, you can unbutton the front,
roll up the sleeves, or pull out the tail, depending on the
degree of ventilation you want. If it gets cold, you can
button up, tuck in the tail, and pull up the collar. A
heavy shirt can also be combined with a shell parka for
more warmth. A well-made shirt of about 20-ounce-
weight, 100 percent pure virgin wool fabric with its
thick soft nap is a beautiful garment to wear. Twill or
diagonal weave makes a strong fabric. Wool nap has
great insulating and water-shedding qualities, and unlike any other fabric, doesn't feel clammy when wet. In

fact, even when wet it continues to give warmth. A heavy wool shirt does, however, have the disadvantage of weight and bulk.

Light down jacket: Strictly from the point of view of efficiency—warmth per weight and bulk—nothing beats a waterfowl down garment. A light down jacket weighs from 16 to 20 ounces, as compared to 26 ounces for a heavy wool shirt. It has the advantage of compressibility: it will stuff into a sack about three by eight inches. Above all, it will provide all the warmth you'll need on a backpacking trip.

The ideal down jacket will have a nylon zipper down the front covered by a snap-down flap which allows closure with zipper open; elastic cuffs with snaps for better ventilation control at the waist; a drawstring around the bottom for vertical air-flow control; a down-filled collar that snaps under the chin to cut off air movement about the neck; and a couple of down-filled pockets for warming hands. All the better if it is cut longer by three inches or so in back; this will keep you covered even when you bend over.

The insulation of down jackets depends on loft—the volume to which the down can expand. The ideal down jacket will be filled with about nine ounces of down and have a thickness, or loft, of at least one and one half inches. A jacket of this type breathes well, allowing moisture to escape, while retaining body heat as insulation.

As in all down articles the outer fabric must be light and soft enough to allow the down to expand to its full loft, and at the same time be resistant to wear. Nylon is the preferred fabric for its strength and lightness. A fabric of about two-ounce weight is generally used.

The disadvantages of a down jacket are the difficulty of drying it out if it gets wet through, and the weakness of nylon against fire damage—even a small coal popping out of a fire can burn right through nylon fabric.

Down vest: If you took the light down jacket and cut off its sleeves, you would be left with the down vest. The idea of the vest is to keep your torso warm. If the torso with its vital organs is kept warm, heat will not be called in from the extremities and you'll feel warm all over.

Shell Parka

The shell parka is the windproof, water-repellent layer of our set of clothes. To work properly, insulating clothes must be able to breathe out body moisture. But clothes that breathe are subject to wind and rain penetration. The shell parka is designed to give some protection against wind and rain, but in order to do its job right it must itself breathe, or body moisture would be captured and condense on its inside surface. In other words, a parka can't be perfectly windproof, it can only be more windproof—of more tightly woven fabric —than the clothes it covers. For the same reason, it can't be waterproof. It will repel water for a short time and then soak through. It is mainly protection against dry, windy cold.

Shell parkas come in light and heavier weights. For summer backpacking the light shell parka, a garment weighing about a pound, will do. Ideally it should be fingertip length and have a hood. The fabric (about two-and-one-half-ounce nylon) should be double layered through the upper sleeves, upper body and hood. For good adjustability it should have a two-way nylon zipper down front that opens from top and bottom with a snap-fastened overlap. The zipper should close high to chin level. The hood should have a drawstring around the front to adjust the face opening. A draw-cord inside the waist and a closure system for the cuffs (snaps, buttons or Velcro tabs) give added ventilation control. It should have at least two zippered pockets (on the generous side), and perhaps a zippered compartment across the back. With all its uses, a shell parka is a handy garment to own.

Poncho

This is the wonderful, versatile and essential piece of equipment that waterproofs your outfit. A poncho is made of either sheet plastic or nylon fabric coated with rubber or plastic. Basically, it's a rectangle of waterproof material with a hole in the center for the head to go through, and a hood fixed around the hole to cover the head. It simply drapes over you like a tent. Snap closures are set along the side.

The poncho covers both you and your pack should you be caught by rain on the trail. With it on, you can keep walking, or stop and crouch under it till the weather clears. It can be pitched as an emergency shelter. At night it can be used as a ground cloth under your sleeping bag. If your shell parka proves inadequate in a biting cold wind, the poncho will give the needed extra protection. Its very loose closure system allows good ventilation control.

Someday you will want to have a good poncho. The sheet-plastic ponchos, though inexpensive, just don't stand up to hard use. They tend to stiffen, crack and tear as they weather. The ideal poncho would be made of light but strong nylon fabric (about two-and-one-half-ounce weight) coated with a tough plastic resin—a fabric that will remain pliant even in cold. Ponchos are now made in two sizes, standard (84 by 70 inches) and packframe (100 by 70 inches). The packframe size is designed to cover both you and your pack and still fall low enough to give some protection to the back of your legs—something that a standard poncho does inadequately. The packframe size seems indicated. It has snaps down each side, grommets set in the corners and a hood with a drawstring. For better ventilation control and ease in putting it on, a zipper at the neck may be included.

Odds and Ends

Hat: The head is the only extremity where blood supply is never reduced. Since it has no vaso-constriction mechanism, it receives a constant supply of blood regardless of changes in heat and cold. Because of this, it radiates more heat than any other part of the body. Thus, covering your head when it's cold will help heat the rest of the body. When it's hot, uncovering the head will help cool the body.

There are varieties of headgear. For cold, a wool-knit watch cap would be adequate. A balaclava, a knit hood which covers the entire head, might be considered for the protection it gives the neck. In hot weather, what-

The balaclava can be worn with the hood up or down.
The snug-fitting watch-cap is practical for winter hiking.
Summer hats should have a wide brim and high crown.

ever you put on your head to keep off the sun should have good air circulation.

Bandanna: This is always a handy item especially for improvising headgear. Large size is best.

Mittens: Consider wool mittens for early- and late-season trips to the mountains.

Picking Packs

From *Backpacking: One Step at a Time*.
By Harvey Manning

Candy bar and apple in pockets, cup on belt, sweater around waist, camera over shoulder—off and away the happy hiker strides.

Good enough for an afternoon stroll. For a long trail day, though, or a short one if much lunch or children's clothing is to be hauled or mushrooms are to be gathered, stuffing pockets and draping the body interferes with free-action walking. The answer? A pack, of course.

At any distance from the road the hiker must carry the Ten Essentials (extra clothing, sunglasses, first aid kit, extra food, flashlight and extra cells, map, compass, matches, fire starters and knife). The articles weigh little but won't fit conveniently in pockets. Again the answer is a pack—to avoid the dangerous temptation to leave the essentials behind and risk discomfort or disaster.

Borderline hikers seem to distrust and fear packs, perhaps because of their once-deserved evil reputation as back-manglers, or perhaps out of humility—who can say? Walk any popular trail near a tourist center and see people who are hikers at heart (or they wouldn't have left the parking lot) lugging picnic hampers or sacks of sandwiches by hand, loads of sweaters under arms, and

cameras and canteens and binoculars strung from
shoulders, bouncing and banging. And see the more
sophisticated others wearing spiffy "mountain pants"
and hardly able to lift their legs because of jamful
"cargo carriers."

The borderline hiker is wise not to rush prematurely
into purchase of a pack. He may never wish to take
walks longer than a couple hours on easy, safe trails. Or
despite a first flurry of enthusiasm may get bitten by one
fly too many and take up sailing. However, once he
crosses the border and decides to go walking for good
and real and far, it is pack time.

Agreed. But *what* pack? No other item of equipment,
not even boots, presents so many complicated options.
The bewildering assortment available reflects the importance of the pack—which ranks with boots and
sleeping bag as one of the Big Three Decisions facing a
backpacker. It also reflects the continuing creative experimentation by manufacturers, each questing the Ultimate.

Or rather, the Ultimates, since no one pack is ideal
for every realm or every activity of the wilderness
world, and since there is widespread disagreement
among manufacturers as to what constitutes the ideal.
The hiker can quickly rule out many (but not all) packs
designed specifically for skiing and climbing, but there
still remain numerous choices.

The starting point is: What will the pack be used for?
Afternoon strolls, full-day rambles; occasional over-
nights, every-weekend, year-after-year, long-distance
backpacks; ten-day, heavy-loaded, semi-expeditions
—the requirements differ.

And then, how fares the bank account? The affluent hiker can buy several packs for various purposes and in each case pick the highest-price model available. But poverty-stricken youths and parents impoverished by numerous offspring must spend carefully, seeking multi-purpose packs and the best possible combination of comfort, convenience, durability, and economy.

More will be said later about choosing a pack, or packs, but first the subject must be broken into digestible chunks. To sort things out, one major distinction is between the rucksack, mainly for day hikes but in the upper ranges of the category usable for short backpacking expeditions, and the packframe and bag, which can do day duty quite well but is chiefly intended for overnight and longer trips.

Rucksacks

Belt and Waist Bags

Pouches that fasten to the belt with loops and belt bags (also called waist packs, fanny packs) that strap around the waist supplement pockets for short walks, carrying from a few ounces to several pounds. Photographers often use them for gadgetry to which quick access is desired.

Frameless Rucksack (Knapsacks)

A frameless rucksack serves for day-hike loads of five to 20 pounds. The weight hangs directly from the shoulders but with a moderate amount of gear causes no discomfort or strain. Stowing must be done carefully to avoid sharp edges stabbing the back; clothing or a small piece of Ensolite (plastic foam) can be placed as padding.

Many rucksacks are designed for the rigors and complexities of climbing and ski-mountaineering and have extremely stout construction, hauling loops, and devices for carrying ice axes, crampons, and skis. These features are of no interest to the hiker, whose needs are simple; he can narrow his choice by avoiding the "tough" and heavy models.

Some backpackers carry a light rucksack for day hikes in the course of an extended trip; to avoid an extra piece of gear they may use the sack as a stuff bag for the sleeping bag (or buy a stuff bag with carrying straps).

For average hiking a very acceptable rucksack is one made of cotton or waterproof nylon, some 15 inches wide, 16 inches high, and five inches deep, with two outside zippered pockets for quick-access items, weighing one pound and selling for around $10.

The beginner might do well to buy such a rucksack and not read the following paragraphs. However, for individual needs and tastes there are numerous other choices with various combinations of the features discussed below.

Features of frameless rucksacks: Nylon rucksacks perhaps offer the best combination of strength, lightness, and water repellency. Those of cotton or cotton canvas are usually somewhat heavier and less waterproof than well-coated nylon but generally don't cost as much, are more abrasion-resistant and more durable pound for pound, breathe freely so the back does not get sweaty, and hold shape better than comparatively limp nylon and thus don't form an "egg" on the back quite so readily. Leather rucksacks are expensive, heavy, rugged, and stylish; they go well with lederhosen.

To protect the area that takes the most wear, heavy-duty rucksacks have a bottom of leather, vinyl, or heavy-coated reinforced nylon.

Rucksacks vary widely in size, ranging from little sacks for little kids to big ones for big-time climbers. For light trail use the size mentioned above (15 inches by 16 inches by 5 inches) suffices. However, better to buy a large sack and never fill it completely than one too small, which when stuffed to capacity rides on the back like a hard-boiled egg, bouncing-banging on the spine at each step. Many hikers therefore prefer a bag with dimensions of about 14 inches by 18 inches by 7 inches.

The weight of a rucksack is a consideration when it is to be taken on a long backpack for side-trip use, but of minor consequence for day trips. The range in models suitable for the average hiker is from one-half pound for children's sacks to about two pounds.

Outside pockets, often omitted from climbers' rucksacks because they snag on rocks, are convenient for the hiker. Some models have one pocket, others two. Zipper closures are most common; straps and buckles are more foolproof but more trouble. Some pockets are detachable.

Rucksacks for climbers and skiers usually have a waist strap to hold the bag close to the body. The feature has utility for a hiker mainly if he likes to run downhill.

The shoulder straps may be of leather for durability, or canvas, or nylon. Sacks intended for heavy loads may have padded straps. Extra slide-on pads can be purchased for soft shoulders.

The top flap may tie with a single strap and buckle or with two; in either case an extra sweater, or parka can be carried conveniently under the flap. Some flaps contain a zippered pocket, which may be inside for maps or outside for storage.

Among other special features, rucksacks may have rustproof metal parts, fittings (that is, the patches on the bag to which straps and buckles are attached) of leather or woven nylon, inner pockets accessible from the outside via a zipper, a waterproof inner shell, a compartmented interior with two sections separated by a flap.

A toggle, a light, spring-loaded clamp, is very useful for locking the drawstrings.

Depending on the material and the size and special features, frameless rucksacks (omitting those for climbing) range in price from less than $5 to around $20.

Frame Rucksacks

Intermediate (so to speak) between the frameless rucksack and the packframe-and-bag combination is the rucksack with a light frame of aluminum tubing, steel staves, slats, or tubes, fiberglass rods, or other materials. Some frames are flexible, others rigid. The intent of the frame is to allow for more comfortable carrying of heavier loads than with a frameless sack—perhaps as much as 40 pounds in some designs—and thus the di-

Knapsack

Frame Rucksack (front)   *Frame Rucksack (back)*

mensions tend to be larger. However, the two categories overlap almost completely: some light-duty rucksacks have frames and some frameless rucksacks are very big and designed for quite heavy loads. In general, very general, the frame gives more comfort for equivalent loads and offers the back some protection against sharp objects in the bag so less care is required in stowing gear.

Day hikers who transport more than the average amount of gear—and in this group fall parents with small children, fussy photographers, and collectors of botanical or geological specimens—often prefer a frame rucksack. In some models the frame can be easily removed so the sack can be stowed in a larger pack, such as for sidetrips during a long backpack. (Similarly, for overnight trips some hikers remove the bag from the packframe, stow gear in the rucksack and lash it to the packframe, and thus have the rucksack available for side-trips.)

Many frame (and some frameless) rucksacks are spacious enough for overnight hauls or even up to three or four days; the sleeping bag can be carried under the top flap. However, even with a waist strap to hold the bag to the body, the weight is suspended entirely from the shoulders and forces a forward lean to get the center of gravity over the feet, putting a strain on back muscles that can be wearisome when the way is long. By very careful distribution of gear quite heavy loads can be carried with rucksacks, but the average hiker finds that at 25 pounds or so it is time to proceed to a packframe.

Though the best combination for the beginner probably is a frameless rucksack for day trips and a pack-frame for overnight, as time goes on, a hiker may want a frame rucksack for intermediate purposes.

Many veterans never use a rucksack of any kind. For day walks and sidetrips on long hikes they simply carry their packframe and bag, which gives less freedom of movement than a rucksack but eliminates the expense of an extra piece of equipment; also by this method they never discover, in time of need, that the Ten Essentials are in the other pack.

But to look at it from the other direction, some ruck-sacks spacious enough for overnight use cost consider-ably less than packframes and bags and thus may in-terest the cash-lean novice backpacker.

Features of frame rucksacks: The beginner should avoid the very heavy and expensive rucksacks (assum-ing he is looking at them at all, possibly enchanted by their fierce aspect) and focus on those obviously in-tended for trails.

Much the same range of materials and other features are found in frame rucksacks as frameless. The main difference, of course, is the frame. The tubular steel frame was originated, or at least popularized, by Ber-gan of Norway in the years before World War II; such frames are rather heavy and rigid, designed for sub-stantial loads, and some are really a variety of pack-frame. Next in support are frames of steel slats or wooden staves and a flexible steel backband, and after that, staves of steel or rods of fiberglass inserted for moderate rigidity. In some designs the frame is built-in and cannot be removed, but in others it is exterior and readily detachable. For comfort, some frames have padded backbands which keep the stiffness from pressing the flesh.

The size ranges roughly from a child's sack of 11 inches by 15 inches by 6 inches to a serious climber's 17 inches by 24 inches by 7 inches. The weight, in sacks that interest the hiker, goes from about one to three pounds, and up to four and one-half pounds in climber's models—obviously reflecting a wide variety in capacity, sturdiness, and special features. The price extends from around $10 to $30 or so.

Packframe and Bag: Details of Construction

Man really is not well-designed to walk on his hind legs at all, and placing a heavy weight atop the precariously erect skeleton definitely goes against nature. Yet for a very long time man has been doing so, and the history of packing would in itself make a book— the basket or pot carried on the head, the pole balanced on the shoulder by loads at either end, the blanket roll slung over one shoulder and tied on the opposite hip. These are only a few of the ways in which man has turned himself into a donkey (another poor beast never intended to carry burdens).

Over the centuries and over the miles, many a suffering soul has mused upon possible alternatives. Among the designs that evolved in America before World War II, the most widely accepted and acclaimed was the famous Trapper Nelson, with a wood frame somewhat contoured to the body in the horizontal dimension (though not the vertical), a canvas

Representative Rucksacks Recommended for Hikers

Many models, many variations are available. These suggest the range in which the adult hiker should make his initial choice.

Style	Approx. Comfortable Load (lbs.)	Size (in.)	Weight (lbs.)	Approx. Price
Frameless nylon bag	10-15	15 wide, 16 high, 5 deep	1	$ 9
Frameless cotton bag			1⅛	$ 7
Framless nylon bag, leather bottom	15-20	14 wide, 18 high, 7 deep	1¾	$17
Frameless nylon bag	15-20	13 wide, 21 high, 6½ deep	1¼	$17
Frameless cotton-canvas bag, nylon bottom			2¼	$13
Wooden-stave and steel-backband frame, cotton-canvas bag	20-25	17 wide, 19 high, 6 deep	3⅛	$19
Wooden-stave and steel-backband frame, nylon bag	20-25	15 wide, 21 high, 5 deep	2⅜	$25
Same frame, cotton canvas bag, nylon bottom			3¼	$20

back, and a canvas bag attached to the frame by steel wires running through eyelet screws in the frame and grommets in the bag. The Trapper Nelson, rugged and inexpensive (currently somewhat less than $20), lives on, as do various other relics of the past, but nowadays is carried mainly by sentimentalists.

The Bergan rucksack (actually a packframe) with a tubular steel frame, also from the pre-World War II era, perhaps started the trend to metal, especially when thousands of the army adaptation (the notorious "kidney-killer") were released onto American trails in the great age of war surplus. Frames of tubular aluminum began to appear, lighter than steel but still not compromising much with the human back and with a tendency to fall apart when sneezed at, as they frequently were. Then Kelty and other pioneers inaugurated modern packs.

A time may come, perhaps ten or twenty years from now, when field-testing by millions of hikers will have sorted out and simplified the options. At the moment, though, packframes and bags are in flux, and the backpacker may develop a hostility toward manufacturers and their incessant picky-picky tinkering with this fine detail and that. However, he should thank them even when they confuse him; they have provided a degree of comfort inconceivable to oldtimers bent over under the torture racks they accepted as just retribution for sinful lives.

The following quick review of the alternative materials and constructions available in contemporary packframes and bags will not satisfy the serious student of the subject, who should read many (one or two

won't do) catalogs of mountain shops and manufacturers and then listen in on a scholarly, gentle-
manly, but passionate debate. The beginner, when his
mind goes numb even with the following oversimplified
survey, should skip to the next section on how to
choose a packframe and bag.

The Packframe

The contemporary standard is a packframe of tubular
metal contoured to the body, rigid but flexible enough
to absorb shocks, suspended by straps from the
shoulders by a yoke harness, with a waist strap that
can transfer as much as 75 percent of the weight
from the shoulders to the strong close-to-leg muscles
of the hip area. It allows heavy loads to be carried
with the body in an upright position, not forcing
the forward lean necessary with older designs (Trapper Nelson). The weight is carried high, in a direct
vertical line with the axis of the body, yet the waist
strap places some or most of the load on the hips if
desired, bypassing the back muscles and relieving them
of strain and discomfort.

One of the most expensive and sturdiest constructions is from high-grade aluminum alloy, heli-arc
welded for strong, perfect, smooth unions between
parts (Kelty). Others are high-tensile-strength aluminum alloy, bolted frame (Gerry); aluminum alloy,
weldless, joints connected by plastic couplings (Alpine
Designs); aluminum alloy, no-weld construction,
curved in a unitized frame (Jan Sport). Some frames

are of welded magnesium alloy (certain Camp Trails models).

The typical frame has two backbands, most commonly nylon (nylon mesh allows ventilation), sometimes cotton, for the back to rest against; some are padded. One or both bands may be adjustable up or down for personal fit; short-waisted or long-waisted hikers may need to experiment to find the best position. When both bands are fixed (Kelty) particular care should be taken to buy the right size frame. In any case the lower band should cover the lower crossbar so it does not press against the spine. The bands are tightened by cords or turnbuckles and must be kept absolutely taut to prevent the bars from touching the back; with heavy loads several tightenings a day may be required.

Some designs have a crossbar at the top for added rigidity and for a lashing point when gear is to be carried outside the bag. Some are designed for addition of extension bars to the upper frame for hauling very bulky, tall loads.

In some designs (REI Cruiser) the lower crossbar has a very slight curve and may tend to rub against the backbone; a padded hip belt (see below) may be needed. Others (Kelty) have an exaggerated curve, a comfort for people with more bones than flesh.

Shoulder straps are adjustable for length by buckles at the bottom, and on many designs at the top for exact placement (close together or far apart) to fit the individual shoulder width. Straps generally have built-in plastic padding, which in the best models is a heavy, dense foam and in cheaper ones is light and mushy. Stitching along the center keeps the foam from shifting inside the strap. Extra pads that slip over the straps may be added for more comfort.

Most frames have an attached waist strap of nylon webbing or cotton. For safety reasons this should have a quick-release buckle; a hiker may have to jettison the pack in a hurry when fording streams, walking logs, and making similar tricky maneuvers (the buckle should always be opened before beginning such passages). Since the strap is the device that transfers weight from shoulders to hips, in ordinary travel it is kept tight. Some heretical hikers find the waist strap uncomfortable and never use it, or if they do, wear it loosely merely to hold the pack on the body and minimize side-to-side sway. Most, though, take full advantage of the strap, which is especially beneficial for people with back problems—and most old backpackers develop back problems. If the pack is properly adjusted to put weight on the hips, one can easily slide a thumb between the shoulder strap and the shoulder.

A padded hip belt that supplements or completely replaces the lower backband and waist strap is particularly appreciated by people of slight build, vulnerable to pressure of frame on backbone, or by any hikers carrying heavy loads. The belt also should have a quick-release buckle.

The Bag

Though bags can be purchased separately from frames, most are not interchangeable between brands; usually, therefore, the bag and frame must be of the same brand

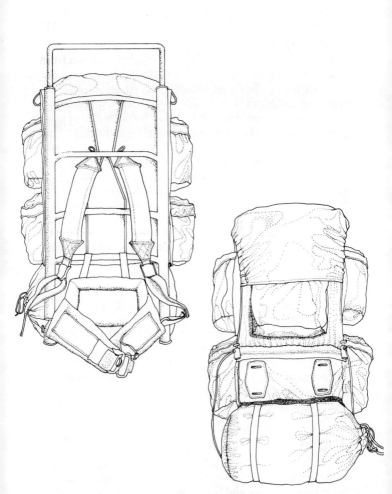

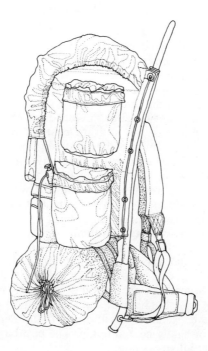

The packframe and bag is one of the more expensive pieces of camping equipment you will buy, so you should select it with great care. Get one that is appropriate not only for your size, but for the sort of camping you do. Unless you are planning an extended wilderness expedition, it doesn't make much sense to purchase a large, expensive pack. Conversely, if you are going to disappear into the backcountry for weeks at a time, it is a good idea to pay for such special features as padded waist band, extra outside pockets and additional inside compartments. You will have your backpack for a long time, so shop around.

unless specially adapted to each other by drilling new holes in the frame (making sure to avoid joints) or some such procedure.

The best bags are of very strong nylon, extremely abrasion-resistant and virtually impossible to tear. Some are water-repellent nylon duck (Kelty); these breathe moisture out and are best for relatively dry climates; in downpours they may require an added rain cover. Others are waterproof nylon duck (REI Cruiser), better for wet climates; however, interior water cannot breathe out and thus if wet clothes are stowed inside they dampen the rest of the gear; with such bags it is especially important to place all items in individual plastic bags. (Actually there is no such thing as a completely waterproof bag; even if the material is, the seams and zippers aren't; interiors of "waterproof" bags may get as wet as those merely "water-repellent.") Some bags are cotton duck, quite durable and lower in price but heavier and absorbing water readily.

Some bags have a reinforced bottom, perhaps of leather or heavy-coated nylon. The best bags are reinforced at all stress points.

The highest-quality bags are stitched with synthetic thread throughout, since cotton thread eventually rots; they are also double- or triple-stitched for added strength. In any carefully made bag the threads are kept away from the edges of the fabric to avoid fraying. Among other features of high-quality bags are covered zippers for rainproofing and rustproof hardware.

The bag may be attached to the frame by clevis pins and locking wires for very easy detachment of bag from frame, or clevis pins on the sides and straps at the bottom. (The clevis pin is a stud that goes through a grommet in the bag, then through the frame, and is prevented from slipping out by a split ring or some other variety of locking wire.) A few (Gerry) snap onto frame-mounted studs.

Bags intended for massive loads, as on expeditions, extend the full length of the frame. In the majority but not universal opinion, better for the average backpacker is a bag extending two-thirds of the frame length; with this style the sleeping gear is carried outside the bag, strapped to the bottom of the frame. However, in some designs (Kelty) the pack bag may be attached in either of two positions—at the top normally, or at the bottom to keep the weight low for better balance in rough terrain.

In an undivided bag the interior is a single large compartment; about half of all current hikers prefer this style for the general ease of stowing gear, especially bulky items. The other half likes the convenient division of the load and the easy access of a compartmented bag and don't mind the stowing problems. There may be two or three upper compartments, separated by vertical panels, and a lower compartment with separate outside access via a zipper. Another style (Gerry) has four or five horizontally-layered compartments, each reached from the outside by separate zippers. One (Jan Sport) has an all-around zipper so the entire bag can be opened wide.

A metal hold-open frame at the top supposedly allows easy packing and maintains the bag in proper contour. Other bags are simply closed by drawstrings; a toggle, a spring-loaded clamp, is useful for locking the strings.

The flap may be tied down by straps and buckles or cords and toggles. Outside pockets, most frequently zipper-closed, range in number from none to six, in various positions. Extra pockets may be purchased and sewed to the bag if desired. A few bags have a map pocket in the flap with Velcro ("sticky tape") closure.

Some shops offer a bag with shoulder straps attached for removal from the frame and use as a rucksack. Extra straps with buckles may be purchased for lashing gear to the outside of the pack.

Stuff Bag

With the most-favored packbag style, extending two-thirds the length of the frame, the sleeping bag and perhaps sleeping pad normally are lashed to the bottom of the frame. These being light by comparison with dense food and stoves and cameras, the method helps keep weight high on the body.

Particularly in wet climates and in brush or rough terrain, the sleeping bag should be stowed in a stuff bag. The best for all purposes is abrasion-resistant waterproof nylon, with a drawstring closure and a weather flap to cover the opening; weight, about five ounces. A laminated polyethylene stuff bag, one to five and one-quarter ounces, is less practical because of its tendency to snag and tear but serves well inside the packbag, where one may also use light nylon stuff bags, about one to one and one-half ounces, or poly bags in various sizes weighing a fraction of an ounce. Cotton stuff bags are cheaper but weigh about one pound and are not waterproof. A compressor stuff bag has outer lacing to facilitate squeezing to tiny size.

The stuff bag is attached to the packframe by two straps with buckles, 36 to 40 inches long (or longer if tarp, poncho, or whatever also is to be carried here), wrapped around the two lower horizontal frame bars and outside the two vertical center bars. Elastic shock cords are not recommended; they may catch on brush or rocks and pull away from the pack, possibly letting the stuff bag escape and certainly throwing the hiker off balance.

Duffle bags are not for backpacking as such, but are useful on long trips to the trailhead by public transportation—airplane, boat, train, bus—when heavy loads in the pack could subject it to severe strain, such as while being tossed around in baggage compartments or from boat to dock. It's discouraging to arrive at the start of a North Cascades trail and find the packframe has been destroyed by a baggage-butcher somewhere between Chicago and Stehekin.

Choosing a Packframe and Bag

The waters being now thoroughly muddied, time for an important announcement: Despite the staggering array of options, it's hard to go far wrong in choosing a packframe and bag from the stock of a reputable outdoor outfitter. There is not, for each person, one and only one pack exactly right with all others hopelessly wrong.

The years of inventing and field-testing and refining and tinkering have established a standard, upheld by all the principal manufacturers whatever variant paths they have taken toward the Ultimate, that is very high indeed. Some trail veterans become fussy about straps and pads and zippers and toggles, and even novices often are fascinated by intricacies of compartment design and stitching; manufacturers love to correspond with such connoisseurs—it makes them feel appreciated. However, the ordinary hiker can be perfectly happy with any of the excellent models on the market, so long as it's the right size.

Nor is frame size critical for the "average" body. (Bag size is another matter and depends on how much gear the hiker plans to carry—and can carry.) People with exceptionally short torsos, narrow shoulders, or thinly covered bones must take more care in choosing a frame, but even they can rather easily accommodate pack-to-back by various adjustments of straps and backbands and/or by adding pads here and there. Large mountain shops generally have a rental service, allowing the novice to try one or two typical packframe-bag combinations, a help in deciding what to buy.

With all due respect to your friendly neighborhood Handy Dandy Super- Thrifty Discount Drugs and Surplus, which usually has genuine bargains in certain articles of hiking gear, the packs sold by retailers of this ilk must be viewed with suspicion. For example, the $5 "aluminum-frame, Scout-type" packs have not been field-tested for present purposes; simply to look at these misery boards sends shooting pains up and down the spine. Nor have the $9 "cruiser-style packs" been examined except in fear and trembling. However, wearing such packs for short trips and light loads probably would not be permanently crippling.

Mass-merchandisers are starting to carry the economy models of certain of the respected manufacturers discussed here, as well as imitations that are inexpensive but of dubious durability. In the future there surely will be a variety of strong, comfortable, economy packs of modern design; the short-money hiker thus may wish to shop around the mass-merchandisers—but warily, very warily.

The ordinary hiker, though, does not long delay purchase of packframe and bag. Assuming he visits a mountain shop or other trusted outdoor supplier, he is—to repeat—unlikely to make a very big mistake. No single shop stocks more than several brands, but most offer a fairly complete range of sizes and styles which among them can fit any body and taste. The only caveat is this: many mountain shops stock nothing but the highest-price packframes and bags; relatively few offer economy models. (The reverse is true of discount houses.) Space is not available for encyclopedic discussion of all the brands and styles of high-quality contemporary packs (for that, see the catalogs) but several of the better-known may be mentioned here.

Kelty, originator of the body-contoured, aluminum packframe and a host of other features now widely emulated, makes frames and bags of the highest quality, as does Gerry, another pioneer and noted innovator. In the same quality and price class, with individual characteristics, are the products of Alpine Designs, Sierra Designs, Mountain Master, and Trailwise. Jan Sport also offers a wide range, from medium price to super-deluxe. New builders are appearing on the scene every year, each with inventions worthy of consideration. In addition, some mountain shops have packframes and bags built to their own specifications and offer them under house names, as in the case of the REI Cruiser.

Not to recommend any pack but merely to suggest the alternatives, following are descriptions of several representative examples in different price categories.

Light-duty packframe and bag (under $20): Exemplifying the lowest price category is one of an increasing number of quite similar Japanese imports, the Alpine Pack. The lightweight frame is of aluminum, 14½ inches wide and 33½ inches high, with a top bar, padded shoulder straps, and nylon backbands. The divided nylon bag has a 13-inch upper compartment and a nine-inch bottom compartment with zipper opening, has a hold-open frame, drawstring closure, map pocket in the flap, five outside pockets, and attaches to the frame with clevis pins. All in all, the Alpine looks to the quick-scanning novice like a "$17 Kelty." The total weight of frame and bag is three pounds and the price is low—roughly the same as current offerings of the old-style but much more durable and trustworthy Trapper Nelson.

In occasional use, say several short hikes a summer, and with light loads, say 35 pounds maximum, the Alpine may hold up fairly well, given very careful treatment. The low price may appeal to beginners who aren't sure how devoted they will become to backpacking.

Heavy-duty economy packframe and bag ($25-$30): Virtually alone at present in its price-quality

Two Representative Packframe-Bag Combinations
REI CRUISER

Style		Approx. Weight of Frame and Bag (lbs.)	Approx. Price of Frame and Bag
Frame	Bag		
Junior (15″ × 26½″)	Junior, undivided	3½	$24
Youths and small adults	Junior, divided	3⅝	$28
Senior (15″ × 31″)	Senior, undivided	3⅞	$26
	Senior, divided	4	$29
Average adults	Expedition	4⅛	$28

KELTY

Size (both frame and bag)		
Small Frame (14½″ × 27″) For men under 5′3″ women under 5′4″	3¼	$48
Medium Frame (14½″ × 29″) For men 5′3″—5′7″ women 5′5″—5′8″	3½	$48
Large Frame (15½″ × 31″) For men 5′7″—6′ women 5′8″—6′	3¾	$48
Extra Large Frame (15½″ × 32½″) For men and women over 6′	3⅞	$48

class is the REI Cruiser, selling in various frame-bag combinations for about $25 to $30.

The frame is of tubular aluminum alloy with an extra top bar for rigidity and strength and has heavy nylon backbands, padded shoulder straps, and a heavy nylon waist strap. The bag, attached by clevis pins, is of eight and one-half ounce waterproof nylon, one of the heavier pack cloths available, and is reinforced at all wear points.

The frames come in two sizes: Senior (for the average adult) and Junior (for youths and small adults).

The bags are Senior, undivided; Senior, divided (identical except the bag is in two horizontal compartments accessible by outside zipper); Junior, undivided; Junior, divided; Expedition, undivided (and the bag extending the full length of the packframe). All Senior models have five outside zippered pockets; Juniors have three. The various combinations of frame and bag weigh from three and one-half to four and one-eighth pounds.

The rugged REI Cruiser has been used to satisfaction from rain-forest jungles to the summit of Mt. Everest, has earned a reputation for being dependable if not fancy, and currently is the best-seller among all packs.

(Speaking of Everest, the Kelty also has been to the top—via the West Ridge. Speaking of the "roof of the world," in 1932 the Trapper Nelson was on Minya Konka, then the highest summit attained by Americans.)

Heavy-duty packframe and bag ($45-$60): Most of the contemporary-design action is concentrated in the $45-$60-and-up category, with Gerry, Camp Trails, Jan

Sport, Alpine Designs, Sierra Designs, Himalayan, Universal Field, North Face, Trailwise, Adventure 16, Mountain Master, and more, all having splendid entries.

Though some of the others have rather different characteristics, the Kelty deserves by seniority to be cited as the representative example. The heli-arc-welded aluminum alloy frame is virtually indestructable and its contours are very comfortable. The water-repellent nylon bag is extremely tough and durable. Without going into minute detail, no expense is spared in any element of material and construction, and improvements are constantly being devised (the same, of course, being true of competitors).

Kelty is particularly notable for the wealth of size options—among them is the right fit for practically anyone. Two frame styles are offered: the Mountaineer, with an extra crossbar on top for strength and for lashing gear; and the Backpacker for lighter loads. Each frame style comes in four sizes: small, medium, large, and extra large.

Kelty has four bag styles: The A4, with an upper compartment vertically divided into three sections by nylon panels and a lower compartment accessible by outside zipper; the D4, identical to the A4 except the upper compartment is undivided; the B4, without compartments; and the expedition-style BB5, also undivided but much larger than the B4. The BB5 has five outside, zippered pockets and the others four (some older Keltys have only two pockets). The range in weight for various frame-bag combinations is three and one-eighth to four and one-quarter pounds.

Packframes and bags for children and small adults ($5-$25): The above packs serve persons from around five feet three inches upwards. People shorter—or somewhat taller with unusual torsos—must look elsewhere.

Jan Sport has two models easily adjustable to "grow" with the kids and well-liked also by small adults. The Mini is for loads up to 25 pounds or so. The frame is 25 inches high; the bag has two outside pockets. Total weight is two and one-quarter pounds and the price about $20. The Scout, for loads up to 35 pounds or so, has a 29½-inch frame and a bag with three outside pockets. Total weight is two and three-quarter pounds and the price about $25.

The very large and comprehensive Camp Trails line includes two models for youngsters. The Bobcat, one and three-quarter pounds, has a cotton duck bag spacious enough for everything a five-to-ten-year-old can carry and sells for about $15. The Tracker is intermediate in size and price between the Bobcat and the Junior REI Cruiser.

The Kelty Sleeping Bag Carrier (not a packframe) consists of a pocket large enough for lunch and cup and a toy, shoulder straps attached, and bottom straps for lashing on a sleeping bag and/or clothing. The device, good for the four-to-seven-year-olds, weighs three-eighths of a pound and costs about $5.

Any child being brought up as a backpacker, either because the parents think it's good for him or because they can't afford a babysitter, should be introduced to load-carrying almost as soon as he or she descends from daddy's or mommy's shoulders onto his or her own feet. Besides, at this age the kid generally demands a pack, imagining it to be some sort of daddy-mommy-type toy; before long the sorry truth is realized but by then the old folk have precedent working for them.

Often the first load is toted in a small rucksack, bought new or handed down through the family, the straps shortened to keep the bag from dragging.

Next may come a Kelty Sleeping Bag Carrier, or a retailored frame rucksack dating from the parents' half-forgotten free and simple past.

Finally arrives the time to buy the first packframe and bag—a Jan Sport Mini, a Camp Trails Bobcat, the smallest Trapper Nelson, or whatever. In a large or extended family or a wide circle of friends such a pack may serve many children over the years. Definitely, parents who love their kids must not yield to the temptation to saddle them with $5 drugstore torture racks, not if they want to keep the family together on the trail.

Bed is a Bag

From *Backpacking: One Step at a Time.*
By Harvey Manning

Many a backpacker with some way to go before total
decrepitude remembers when the setting of the sun
was a poignantly sad event—not for symbolizing the
death of day, but for reminding him that the hour
would arrive to leave campfire warmth and begin the
night-long ordeal by shivering. To be sure, there were
rumors of better equipment available to those of
immense wealth, but the ordinary hiker carried a
rectangular wool or kapok sleeping bag that weighed
a considerable fraction of a ton and never kept out the
chill on a summer night in alpine meadows. At that he
felt luckier than his poor comrades who couldn't
afford a bag and wrapped up in blankets. Boy Scout
troops of thirty-odd years ago often ended by morning
as a circle of tight-packed bodies coiled around a fire.

World War II, which in its aftermath released a
deluge of surplus gear to civilians at a tiny fraction
of original cost, introduced a whole generation of low-
income Americans to the down sleeping bag, formerly
the raiment of princes and magnates, and to the reve-
lation the night need not be miserable.

Unreconstructed veterans scorn modern refinements and survey the stock of mountain outfitters with
hostility. They feel today's youth is being robbed of the

full wilderness experience, that man ought to shiver at night for the good of his soul.

But as has been said, "The past is a foreign country: they do things differently there." The backpacker now accepts as inalienable his right to sleep warm, and with contemporary bags there is no reason he shouldn't, most of the time, if he makes a proper selection.

There, again, is the rub. The sleeping bag is a very important garment, in which a hiker spends roughly a third of his life on the trail, and must be chosen with care. It is also one of the three costliest items every backpacker must own, and unlike boots and pack, which at large mountain shops can be rented, must be purchased outright. But a single shop may stock 25 or more distinct bags and the number available from American outfitters runs into the hundreds. The beginner, having wrestled with the major problems of buying boots, then a pack, now must face the third of the "Big Three" decisions.

However, it's not really as complicated as portions of this chapter make it out to be. First, for any average person planning ordinary summer backpacking, many different bags of various designs and prices will serve quite well. After a few years a hiker may become fussy about fine details, but if a beginner were to walk into a mountain shop blindfolded and grab a bag at random the odds would favor his getting one satisfactory for his purposes.

Second, many bags can be ruled out simply on the basis of weight. The person of average size and metabolism should sleep warm, in typical trail conditions, in a bag weighing less than five pounds and perhaps as little as three. Bags of much more than five pounds are designed either for car-camping or high mountaineering (or winter) and should be ignored.

Third, it is not necessary to wipe out the family fortune for a night's sleep. There are luxury bags offering lavish refinements in every detail of material and construction, but also economy bags that never would win blue ribbons at international expositions yet provide comfort enough at reasonable prices.

Fourth, beware of strangers bearing gifts. Mass-merchandising emporiums having recently noted the dimensions of the backpacker market, have taken to staging great big sales offering bags at astonishing prices. The bargains may or may not be genuine; the beginner, unless guided by an experienced, discerning friend or unless the retailer has an established reputation for good values, has no way of knowing.

So much for general preface. Time now to dig into the guts of the bag and see what it's made of, and why.

Construction

A sleeping bag is an article of clothing that retains body-generated heat by trapping innumerable tiny pockets of dead air. Not the components of the bag themselves but rather the air (a poor conductor and thus a good insulator) provides a barrier between the hot body and the cold, cold world.

The warmth of a bag is determined by several factors: (1) the kind and amount of insulating material—down, polyester, or foam; (2) the structure—the shape of the bag and the manner in which insulating material is compartmented; (3) the bag closure—by zippers and draw-strings; and (4) to a much lesser extent, covers and liners that may be added.

Insulating Material (Filler)

Far and away the best sleeping bag filler identified is down, the fluff growing next to the skin of cold-climate waterfowl. Down traps air better than any other readily available substance yet allows moisture from the body to breathe out; compacts into a small bundle for carrying yet is extremely resilient, quickly expanding when released; and withstands thousands of compression-and-expansion cycles before getting too bent and broken to rise to the occasion.

Eider down: Of mainly historical interest but mentioned for its fame is eider down, gathered from Arctic nests of the eider duck—along with tiny twigs and bits of excrement too closely intermixed for removal. Eider is reputed to be the finest of all downs but the matter is academic; the total world supply is perhaps 100 pounds a year and the current price some $40 a pound.

Goose down: The accepted standard of top quality is goose down from domestic fowl raised for food, the plucking done in early winter when the down is thickest and sturdiest.

Not all down is top quality. First, geese are grown in many climates and plucked at every season; an Alabama goose disrobed in July offers little to brag about. Second, laws regulating the manufacture and labeling of bedding are more or less stringent from state to state; depending on the state, products advertised as "goose down" include varying percentages of feathers and miscellaneous materials (floor sweepings). Third, each down supplier sells a number of grades, including blends, designed for a variety of commercial needs.

To further confuse the issue, suppliers do not agree on what is, in fact, the best sleeping-bag down. For example, all down has from 8 to 20 percent feathers and miscellaneous, since hand-separation of down from tiny feathers (and miscellaneous) would make a prohibitively expensive product. Some suppliers believe the higher the down percentage the better the insulation. But others point out that a certain proportion of feathers is essential for the strength and resiliency they contribute.

The subject is altogether too arcane for a layman to comprehend. It surely is folly to attempt to solve the puzzle on the basis of state laws, assuming that because Utah (say) has stricter laws on bedding than Mississippi (say) that the only trustworthy down comes from Utah firms (if any) and the products of Mississippi (if any) are to be scrupulously shunned; the laws are too tricky for any but experts to understand—and besides, nowhere is it written that a company necessarily sticks to the minimum standards enforced by the state of its location. The Federal Trade Commission, which until 1971 allowed "down" products to contain up to 40 percent feathers and miscellaneous, now has ruled that at least 80 percent of the fill must be down. Again, no reputable firm is affected by the decision.

The average hiker does well to abandon his attempt to pursue consumerism to the last percentile of perfection in this matter and simply patronize trusted outfitters, whose standards far exceed those set by state or federal law. Their bags usually are described as containing "prime goose down" or similar phraseology, perhaps with a brand name given. This only means the filler is whatever blend the shop or supplier considers "prime." Though every supplier feels his top grade is supreme, there is relatively little difference between any of the brands of "prime goose down" used in bags stocked by reputable shops.

The color of the down—white or gray—has no effect on insulating value or overall quality.

Duck down: Only under a microscope lens can duck down be visibly distinguished from goose down. It is not quite so springy and thus a bit less warm, to the extent of about 5° per pound of fill, and has somewhat less longevity because it does not tolerate as many compression/expansion cycles, but the quality difference is too slight, perhaps 5 percent, to be detected by the average person. In Canada a distinction usually is not made and both are mixed in "waterfowl down"; eventually this may become the rule everywhere.

A good duck is better than a bad goose, but the bags stocked by mountain shops employ only prime down of each kind and thus the goose bags are in a higher warmth and price range than the duck.

Mass-merchandisers advertise inexpensive bags filled with "duck down" or just plain "down." The price is low because the down comes from warm-climate areas of Asia or North America and is of very poor quality compared to the cold-climate down used by mountain shops. Cheap the bags may be, but no bargains.

Old polyester (dacron, fortrel, kodel): Polyester, a synthetic fiber, now comes in two quite different varieties. The older material has much less springiness (air-trapping capacity) than down and therefore provides substantially less warmth for equal weights; it also is less compressible, making for a comparatively massive piece of baggage.

The great advantage is low cost. Polyester-filled bags, though heavier and bulkier than those of down, are warm enough for most outdoor living and many are light enough for backpacking—perhaps at the cost of an occasional night of shivering.

Further, polyester is more water-resistant than down and unlike down does not totally collapse, de-loft, and lose all insulation value when wet.

In addition, a few people are allergic to down and feathers or to dust that collects on fibers; for them polyester bags are the only alternative since the fiber is nonallergenic and can be washed regularly to get rid of dust.

Second-generation polyester (Dacron II): New from Dupont in 1971 is a second-generation polyester, Dacron II, or Fiberfill, soft, resilient, and very resistant to matting, distortion, and lumping.

The manufacturer says that unlike the older polyester, the new product compresses easily for stowing in a stuff bag; when released it quickly springs to full loft, giving for equal weights of filler some 85 to 90 percent the insulation of down.

Further, the new fiber absorbs so little moisture (less than 0.4 percent) that even when soaking wet the bag can be wrung out and give a warm sleep—a claim that cannot be made for down.

Assuming certain production problems (inherent with any new material) are solved, the claimed advantages may well give Dacron II a good share of the backpacker trade, but because the price is higher it will not eliminate the older polyester—henceforth there may be two grades (and two price ranges) of polyester bags.

Experimental bags entered the market in 1972; extensive testing will be required to eliminate present problems and determine whether Dacron II does, indeed, represent an attractive alternative to down.

Rayon, foam, and whatnot: A very dim view indeed must be taken of fast-buck artists who advertise a $4 bag (filled with God knows what) as "good for up to two weeks" and promote it as "disposable—don't pack it back." Ditto for the "seven-day disposable bag" priced at 99 cents. Such irresponsibility toward back-country littering leads one to wonder about the integrity of these merchandisers and the quality of their offerings.

At upward steps are bags of "Thermo-Cloud fiber fill" for $6, "CelaCloud acetate fiber" for $9, and "acrylic-filled" for $18. All these are cheap substitutes for polyester, usually rayon, and have little if anything to recommend them but low price. Warm and durable they are not.

Recently introduced and now undergoing field-testing with the jury still out, but quite promising, is a polyurethane foam filler which has the air-trapping capacity of down, breathes well, is nonallergenic and easily washable by rinsing in a bathtub. The foam holds its shape and thus warmth when wet, unlike down which coagulates and compresses, and does not flatten under the body as down does, thereby eliminating the need for a sleeping pad. On the debit side, foam is heavier than down for equal warmth, relatively incompressible and thus bulky to carry, soaks up and wicks water like a sponge, and in present designs does not hug the body (one sleeps in air chambers) and buckles when the sleeper cinches up drawstrings, creating avenues for air to pass in and out. Polyurethane foam is far less expensive than down and the current bags cost somewhat less for equivalent warmth —though not as much less as one has a right to expect. Further experimentation may lead to improved designs which eliminate many of the disadvantages.

Structure of the Bag

The insulation value of a bag is determined partly by the kind and amount of filler and partly by various aspects of the structure. In order of importance as affecting warmth are (1) the shape of the bag; (2) the method employed to compartment the filler; and (3) the construction of the inner and outer shells (the fabrics which hold the filler).

Shape: Other things being equal the smaller the bag the warmer, since there are fewer interior air spaces to be heated and more of the insulation is near the body rather than off in distant corners. The configuration of the upper opening, where the sleeper extends some

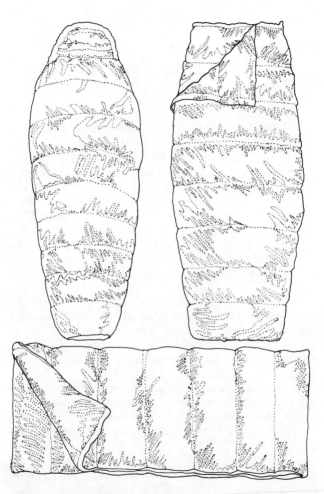

Mummy, barrel and rectangular bags.

portion of his face or head out of the bag, also is significant; the brain receives 20 percent of the body's blood supply and thus the head area can radiate a great deal of heat.

The warmest design is the mummy bag, contoured to the body and closed at the top by a drawstring that completely shuts off breezeways, leaving exposed, when desired, merely the sleeper's nose and mouth.

Though most mummy bags are substantially roomier than was once customary and some have a flare at the bottom for foot space, claustrophobics tend to prefer a barrel bag, which rather than tapering from head to foot bulges outward at the midsection to let elbows and knees maneuver. The design adds weight as well as comfort. Generally barrel bags are square-cut at the top with drawstring closure for sealing off the outer chill.

Roomiest and heaviest are rectangular bags, usually with no top closure, thus allowing heat to escape and breezes to enter; at low elevations and in warm climates this is, of course, an advantage. A tapered rectangular bag maintains the ease of ventilation and saves weight at the foot.

As a rough generalization, in bags of comparable filler and baffling (see below), barrel bags are about 10° colder than mummy bags and somewhat heavier; rectangular bags are about 20° colder and considerably heavier.

Compartment (baffling): To trap air and thus do its job the filler must unwind, expand, fluff up. The bottom-to-top thickness of the unoccupied bag when spread flat, fully fluffed and ready to go to work, is called the loft; obviously, the more inches of loft the more trapped air. A shop which stresses this method of measuring insulation value may state that its down bags for ordinary backpacking have from five and one-half to seven inches of loft and cold-weather and expedition bags nine or even 11 inches.

Such figures may be useful in comparing bags offered by any single manufacturer. However, there are nearly as many ways to measure loft as there are manufacturers. Therefore, some suppliers ignore loft, feeling that until an industry-wide standard is agreed upon statistics can be misleading.

It seems safe to assume that in any bag stocked by an established mountain shop the manufacturer has gotten the maximum loft possible from the filler. Thus, a more dependable all-around guide to the insulation value of a bag is first, the amount of filler, and second, the manner in which it is compartmented.

If filler were merely stuffed between an outer and inner shell it would soon lump up in certain spots, leaving others unprotected. Therefore, some compartment system is required to hold the filler in place. The aim of a designer is to get the most loft for the least weight of filler and compartmenting fabric; another consideration, especially in economy bags, is to do so at the least cost. Compromises are necessary on several counts and are evidenced by all backpacker bags.

The simplest and cheapest construction is sewn-through (stitch-through), where inner and outer shells are stitched directly together. The stitching lines offer no insulation and are "cold spots." This method is employed on down bags intended to be placed within outer bags for extreme cold and also on polyester bags where the goal is an inexpensive product light enough for backpacking.

Most bags are built with panels (baffles) sewn to the inner and outer shells. Almost always the compartments run around the bag (circumferential, or the variant "chevron cut") instead of in a line from top to bottom (longitudinal), in which pattern the filler tends to collect at the foot.

The panels commonly are of a nylon netting which is light, inexpensive, easy-breathing, and gives maximum compressibility. A few manufacturers prefer nylon cloth, a bit heavier and more costly but preventing movements of down between compartments.

A step up from sewn-through construction and eliminating cold spots is the box, in which the panels form right-angle compartments.

Generally considered the most efficient design for down bags is the slant tube (slant box, slant wall, parallelogram), providing maximum loft for minimum panel weight and, in the judgment of a majority of experts, the greatest warmth per pound of total bag weight. When released the parallelogram walls straighten into rectangles, thus letting the down loft better than in ordinary boxes. Though construction expense is the same as with the box design, more baffle material is required, adding a bit to weight and cost.

The overlapping tube (diaphragm tube, V-tube) method holds the down very closely in place but somewhat restricts loft, thus giving slightly less insulation than the slant tube for equal amounts of filler. Also, construction expense is greater and the extra paneling

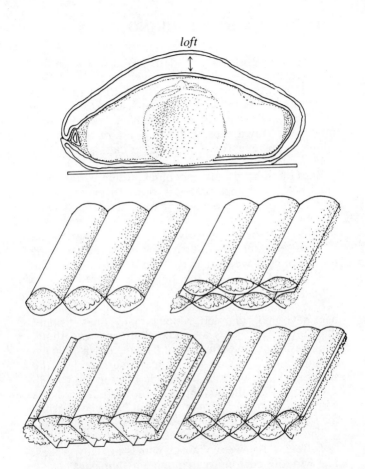

Baffling: Top: Sewn-through and laminated. Bottom: Slant wall and V-tube.

increases weight and cost. (In the quest for perfect down control it is possible to "over-panel.")

A laminated bag has two sewn-through layers stitched together in an overlapping fashion to eliminate cold spots. Because of the weight of the additional fabric, few down backpacker bags are of this design, which is, however, used in polyester bags intended for cold weather.

Bags often have a channel block, a side-baffle opposite the zipper that prevents down from migrating around the circumference—and for that reason disliked by many hikers. They point out that down beneath the body is compressed virtually to zero thickness (thus the need for a sleeping pad, discussed later); before going to bed in cold weather they "chase" down from the underside of the bag to the upperside where it can do some good.

The shell—outer and inner: Nearly all backpacker bags have shells of nylon, which is many times stronger than any other readily available cloth, easy-breathing, wind-resistant, and effective at keeping down from escaping; on the inside the slippery surface lets the sleeper revolve without the whole bag turning.

Cotton offers the advantages of lower cost and less vulnerability to campfire sparks, but being heavier for the same strength is mainly used for car-camping bags.

The nylon may be either taffeta or ripstop.

Taffeta, a flat-weave fabric, comes in many grades. The varieties customary in mountain-shop bags have a somewhat higher thread count than ripstop and thus are about the same strength. Taffeta has a softer, more comfortable texture, and for what it's worth is widely considered to have a more pleasing appearance.

Ripstop, which has extra-heavy threads every three-sixteenths to one-quarter inch that stop tears from running and form a reinforcing web which distributes stresses widely, also comes in many grades and weights. The cloth used in backpacker bags ranges in weight roughly from 1.5 ounces or less per square yard to two ounces; obviously the former is lighter and the latter more durable. Lightweight ripstop loses its calendar (the flattening and pore-sealing given during manufacture) after repeated flexing and bending and thus rather early on starts leaking down (actually, the feathers usually escape first).

Though ripstop can be stronger than taffeta for equal weights, perhaps the main reason for its current dominance is the magic-word factor; ripstop is "in." Reputable suppliers use both fabrics in high-quality bags and the average backpacker is unlikely to discern any important difference.

Pages of precise logic and passionate rhetoric are devoted by mountain-shop catalogs to debating the optimum way to cut the shells.

Many bags are differentially cut (concentric cut), which is to say the inner shell is smaller than the outer. The theoretical advantages are that the filler is permitted to loft more freely and that sleepers (especially those who thrash around a lot with knees and elbows) cannot so easily press the inner shell against the outer and create cold spots. Proponents claim such bags are warmer for equivalent amounts of filler.

Some manufacturers disagree and use a space-filler cut, with inner and outer shells the same circumference. Their theory is that the inner shell folds around the sleeper and fills air pockets. Proponents claim such bags are not only simpler and less expensive to make but have less inside air to heat and thus are warmer. They also say that in any event the concentric cut doesn't prevent cold spots as claimed. Innocent bystanders suspect it doesn't make any difference how the shells are cut.

The body gives off not only heat but water vapor; while retaining the former the bag must freely breathe out the latter. Though beginners often ask for a waterproof sleeping bag, if such existed it would sweat the sleeper like a Turkish bath. Unwary hikers have been known to ruin bags by applying waterproofing compound.

Zipper and Drawstring

Insulating material and structure have much to do with the warmth of the bag; the method by which it is closed (to freezing blasts) and opened (to cooling zephyrs) also affects warmth, and the overall comfort and convenience as well.

Incidentally, so much moisture is exhaled in the breath that even on the coldest nights a sleeper should try to keep his nose outside the bag to avoid dampening the interior. In extreme cold he may wish to protect the nose from freezing by breathing through a sweater.

As noted above, the head of the bag is a particularly critical area and thus may be treated first, followed by a discussion of zippers.

Drawstring: Rectangular bags ordinarily are wide-open at the top, though some have a drawstring.

Mummy and barrel bags usually have a drawstring closure to shut the airway. There may be a drawstring at the shoulders plus an extended hood which can be left flat in warm weather or drawn tight around the face with another drawstring. Or there may be a single drawstring around the top to form a hood.

For easy opening, to avoid a trapped feeling, a hiker does well to use a toggle, a spring-loaded clamp, on the drawstrings.

Some manufacturers offer a down hood, or collar, which either can be sewn to the top of any bag or attached by Velcro tape. Also available is a completely detached hood that can be worn with any bag— or without one, as far as that goes.

Zippers: Very light bags dispense with a zipper altogether (the more zipper, the more weight) and the sleeper wriggles and slithers in from the top.

Some designs have a center or top zipper. Partisans claim these advantages: the sleeper can lie on either side without being atop the zipper and can zip and unzip while on his back; the bag can be spread flat to use as a quilt; and when two top-zipped bags are joined the zipper is on the outside rather than in the middle.

Others have a side zipper, which may be on either side (left-opening or right-opening). Partisans claim as advantages that ventilation is most easily controlled and hoods can be used when two bags are joined.

Those hikers (perhaps a majority) who flop around a lot in the night find no important difference between top-zipped and side-zipped bags.

Mummy bags often have half-length zippers some 36

to 40 inches long, extending about halfway down from the top; as a general rule the less zipper the less of a cold spot and thus the warmer the bag.

Other mummies and barrels and most rectangulars have a full-length (70-inch or so) zipper. Some have a zipper running the full length and across the foot for complete temperature control in warm weather, or full-length zippers on both sides.

Hikers who travel mainly in warm climates prefer a lot of zipper to avoid night-long stewing in their own juices. Cold-country hikers generally want much less zipper: when a full-length zipper fails (which occasionally happens even with the best) the sleeper is faced with either a shivering night or a massive hand-sewing job by flashlight; when a short zipper fails the comparatively small opening can be adequately closed with several safety pins or by clutching the fabric with the hands.

Two bags with full-length zippers can be joined—if the zippers are compatible—to make a double bag. Many couples like to have this option, either for the theoretical warmth of snuggling or simply for togetherness. (Wildland swingers, mindful of the adage that "a bird in the bag is worth two in the bush," check zipper compatibility when playing the trail version of the dating game.) Another advantage is that a small child can be accommodated, saving the weight of an extra bag. However, some couples (old marrieds) declare that in cold windy weather so much heat is lost through the top that a double bag is like no bag at all, and that sleeping with a squirming, kicking infant is no sleep at all.

Bags of different styles—mummy, barrel or

rectangular—can be combined for versatility (again, if the zippers are compatible). For example, if a couple has one bag with two pounds of down, another with three pounds, the two can be joined with the two-pounder on top for warm nights, the three-pounder for cold ones. Similarly, a polyester and a down bag can be combined, the former on the bottom since polyester compresses less and gives better ground insulation, and the down on top for its better air insulation.

The best zippers are nylon (a polyamide plastic) or Delrin (an acetal plastic), which unlike metal do not conduct heat, freeze, or rip the shell fabric when snagged. The highest-quality bags have "oversize" or "heavy-duty" zippers for greater dependability.

As with all special features a two-way zipper adds expense but is convenient in allowing the bag to be opened from either the top or bottom; in warm weather, the feet may thus be ventilated without chilling the shoulders.

Since the zipper is a line of zero insulation, in the best bags it is covered by a down-filled tube to prevent heat loss. (Incidentally, when buying two bags not the same model that are intended to be joined, make sure the insulating tubes overlap; otherwise the zipper will be uncovered, a full-length cold spot.)

Covers and Liners

A separate sleeping-bag cover of cotton or nylon may be slipped over the bag to protect it from wear, to keep it clean when cooking and eating while storm-bound in a tent, and for extra warmth. Covers are used mainly by climbers and winter hikers; few back-packers find the added protection worth the weight.

A sleeping-bag case of ripstop nylon with a coated bottom, built-in foam pad, and drawstring hood is designed for extreme cold, such as sleeping on snow, and is of little interest to the average hiker.

Many hikers insert a light liner of nylon, cotton flannel, or cotton-polyester to keep the inner shell of the bag clean or because they prefer to sleep within snuggly cotton rather than slippery nylon. A liner adds a bit of extra warmth; during the night it also twists into interesting tangles.

Selecting a Sleeping Bag

The preceding section gives some notion of what dedicated, ingenious, idealistic, argumentative manufacturers are up to and the range of options and opinions they offer at every point. If, contrary to prior advice, the novice has ventured into that swamp, doubtless his indecision and anguish are now acute. Therefore, from motives of humanity, time for plain and simple talk.

There is no single sleeping bag ideal for everyone in the whole wide world. Choice of this intimate garment depends on very personal needs. Thus, a few questions and answers:

Do you plan to use the bag for non-expedition backpacking? If so, rule out those weighing more than five pounds.

On the other hand, will the bag be carried short distances, infrequently? If so, weight doesn't matter that much. Or often, and long distances? Weight then matters a lot.

Will you be camping mostly at low elevations and/or in cold climates? The "warmth rating" is critical and a mummy or barrel design with minimum zipper probably best.

On the other hand, do you have a history of sleeping cold, or warm? A cold sleeper may shiver on a tropic night in a bag designed for the South Pole, while a warm sleeper wrapped in an old horse blanket may snore up a storm on an icecap.

Will you be sleeping in a tent or under a tarp? Tarp-campers need more bag insulation; even ignoring the influence of wind, the interior of a closed tent is usually about 10° warmer than the surrounding area.

Most important of all, how are you fixed for money? There are magnificent bags priced at $100 and up, and up, halfway to the Moon. But there are also polyester bags weighing as little as four pounds, warm enough for summer conditions, selling for $25 and less. As far as that goes, a Handy Dandy Super Surplus 99-cent special "good for seven days" probably is no colder or heavier than the average Boy Scout bag of 30-odd years ago.

On the other hand, you do well to buy the highest-quality bag you can afford; with proper care a well-made down bag can outlast and thus be more economical than a series of make-do substitutes—not to mention the difference in comfort and convenience at all those camps, through all those nights.

Hopefully, the above catechism, now ended, has

oriented the novice in a general way. Next, two specifics about choice of sleeping bag.

Bag Length

First, body length/bag length. Bags come in various lengths and obviously the bag should be long enough to contain the entire body, keeping in mind that a six-foot bag is insufficient for a six-foot sleeper; the body is longer when lying flat than when erect, and also extra inches are essential to let the toes flex and the neck stretch. However, for reasons of warmth, weight, and expense, a person should buy the smallest bag into which he fits comfortably. [*Exception: Winter back-packers often purchase a size longer than height requires, allowing extra space for the boots. In the morning they come out warm, dry and closer at "foot."*] A complicating factor is that some suppliers list the inside

Recommended Sleeping Bag Lengths

Body Height	Approximate Bag Length (outside measurement, in inches)		
	Mummy	Barrel	Rectangular
Up to 4 ft.	52	58	58
Up to 5 ft.	63	70	70
Up to 5 ft. 8 in.	78	78	78
5 ft. 8 in.-6 ft. 1 in.	84-86	76	74-78
Above 6 ft. 1 in.	94	84	82-86

length of their bags, others the outside; at any shop, therefore, one must ask which system is used and what bag lengths are recommended for various body lengths. (When in doubt, better to choose a too-long bag than suffer cramped knees and neck.)

Rectangular and barrel bags, not intended to include the head, are shorter than mummies for the same body height.

Warmth Rating

Second, the warmth rating of sleeping bags (or minimum temperature rating, or comfort range), which is a matter of controversy, argument, no industry-wide standard, and much nonsense. For example, a few suppliers state an "upper comfort limit"—as if the sleeper were too stupefied to open up the bag to cool off. More to the point, what scientist has investigated sleeping with the thoroughness devoted in recent years to more interesting bedtime activities? Who has precisely measured the difference in cold toleration between fatties and bare-bones? Still in all, warmth ratings are widespread in the literature and the catalogs and with due warning will be used here.

The ratings, intended to suggest the lowest temperature at which a bag will provide reasonable comfort, are very approximate. They assume a dry bag, untouched by wind, and a roof to minimize radiation heat loss. They are for the average person who sleeps neither extraordinarily cold or warm and thus can differ $10°$ or more for an individual. In summary, the ratings are better than nothing, but just barely.

Representative Sleeping Bags Recommended for Adult Backpackers

These are examples only; innumerable variations are offered by outdoor outfitters

Material	Filler Amount (in lbs.)	Shape	Baffling	Length for Persons up to Approx. 6 Feet Tall (outside meas. in inches)	Warmth Rating (minimum comfort)	Weight (lbs.)	Approx. Price
Polyester (Dacron, Fortel, Kodel)	3	mummy	sewn through	86	32°F	4	$24
	3½	mummy	laminated	86	20°F	4¾	$29
	3	rectangular	sewn through	77	32°F	5	$28
Dacron II	?	mummy	?	86	?	?	$36
Duck down	2	barrel	box	76	25-32°F	3½	$40
	2½	barrel	box	76	10-20°F	3¾	$46
	3	barrel	box	76	0-10°F	4½	$50
Goose down	2	mummy	slant tube	86	20°F	3¼	$58
	2½	mummy	slant tube	86	0°F	3¾	$67
	3	mummy	overlapping tube	86	-20°F	4⅜	$79
	3	rectangular	slant tube	78	10°F	4¾	$72

Representative Bags

Against this background, following paragraphs describe several representative bags. The key word is "representative"—these are a few points on a continuum of hundreds of bags and in a particular mountain shop the hiker may find nothing exactly matching the examples and certainly will observe many variations in details, many distinct composites of compromises. However, from most suppliers a person can obtain comparable bags suiting personal needs and ability to pay. (To qualify that statement, some mountain shops stock only bags of the very highest quality while others cater to a broad spectrum of hikers, offering economy as well as luxury models.)

Middle-class sleeping bag—goose down ($67): The next category includes bags that provide the optimum combination of warmth, durability, and lightness for habitual backpackers who sleep often in alpine altitudes or other cold conditions, carry loads long distances, and don't have all the money in the world. A representative example is a mummy bag generously cut to avoid the mummified feeling, with half-length (40-inch) nylon zipper covered by a down-filled tube, drawstring closure that forms a hood, inner and outer shell of ripstop nylon, and slant-tube construction filled with prime goose down.

In the 96-inch length (for people up to six feet one inch), with two and one-half pounds of down, the warmth rating is 0°F, bag weight three and three-quarter pounds, price about $67. It may be noted that this warmth rating of 0°F is the most versatile choice for backpackers who sleep sometimes in valleys but often in high meadows, mainly in summer but frequently in wintry conditions that come with chilly spring and fall nights or strong winds anytime.

In the same basic bag, two pounds of down give a warmth rating of 20°F and three pounds (with overlapping-tube compartments) of −20°F—for winter and high-altitude use and for people who sleep cold.

Bags of 94-inch length (for people over six feet one inch) have one-quarter pound additional down for the same warmth ratings and cost and weigh a little more. For those who wish to join two bags into a double, the same design is available with full-length zipper; weight and cost are somewhat greater.

Upper-middle-class sleeping bag—goose down ($100): A substantial jump in price leads to a class of bags with a variety of special features for extra comfort and convenience. A representative example is a mummy bag with shaped foot area for roominess, integral hood formed by the drawstring, full-length, two-way, heavy-duty nylon zipper covered by a down tube, ripstop nylon shell, and slant-tube construction.

The 86-inch length (for people up to six feet one inch), with two and one-half pounds of prime goose down, has a warmth rating of −10°F; bag weight four and one-half pounds, price about $100. As in previous examples, more down and greater length increase the weight and cost.

Luxury sleeping bags: "Luxury" is really the wrong word to describe products of manufacturers who refuse to place their names on anything less than what they consider to be the finest possible combination of comfort, convenience, and durability, and hang the expense.

Actually, bags made by these scrupulous people overlap in price with the previous two categories (special features add cost even when the amount and quality of down are the same) and vault upward and beyond to the region of $150. Though the beginner must again be cautioned not to buy more bag than he needs, for the experienced hiker of refined taste these supreme-quality bags may be worth every penny.

No representative example will be described here; see the catalogs of mountain outfitters, look in the $90 and up price range, and admire, perchance dream.

However, a word of caution—some of these "luxury" bags are purely and simply overpriced. The "upper-middle-class" bag described above, costing $100, is identical in every respect to certain other bags selling for $135.

Special sleeping bags: Double bags, mummy or rectangular, may appeal to couples certain they always will want to sleep together; for equivalent weights such bags are warmer than two singles united; of course, they lack the separate-bed option.

A barrel bag with no zipper, a drawstring top, sewn-through construction, one pound of prime goose down, weighing only two and one-eighth pounds, is intended for cold-weather use inside another bag; alone it means a few shivers on chilly nights. This and similar bags keep the load light, which may be desired on long rambles where comfort is less important than covering ground.

The "elephant's foot" ("half-bag" or "footsack"),

extending on the average adult from feet to stomach, is designed as a climber's bivouac bag to be used in combination with a down parka. Again, a hiker in a hurry may appreciate the combination; a typical "foot" weighs only one and five-eighths pounds. It can also do duty as a child's bag.

Economy (very) sleeping bag—old polyester ($25); Dacron II ($36): For summer backpacking and slim budgets, a representative example is a mummy bag with half-length (38-inch) nylon zipper and drawstring hood, nylon shell, sewn-through construction, and a warmth rating of 32°F, which means occasional shivering in alpine camps. The 86-inch length, for persons up to six feet one inch, contains three pounds of polyester. Total bag weight, four pounds; price about $25. (For taller persons the 94-inch length has three and one-half pounds of filler in the 86-inch length; total bag weight four and three-quarter pounds, cost about $30.)

For mild climates and hikers who want to join two bags, an example is a sewn-through rectangular bag with full-length zipper. The 77-inch length (for persons up to about six feet) has three pounds of polyester; total bag weight five pounds, price about $25, warmth rating 32°F.

Though limited distribution has begun of experimental bags filled with Dacron II, the designs similar to those using the older polyester, it is premature at this writing to go into details.

Economy (considerable) sleeping bag—duck down ($46): A representative example in the next price jump up from polyester, and good for all but the chilliest summer nights in alpine meadows, is a barrel bag, box construction, nylon taffeta shell, full-length nylon zipper (allowing two bags to be joined) backed by a down-filled tube, hoodless drawstring top.

In the 76-inch length (for persons up to six feet), and filled with two and one-half pounds of prime duck down, the warmth rating is 15-20°F, the total bag weight three and three-quarter pounds, and the price about $46.

The same length with two pounds of down, warmth rating 25-32°F, total weight three and one-half pounds, sells for about $40; with three pounds of down, warmth rating 0-10°F, the bag weight is four and one-quarter pounds, price about $50. Bags 84 inches long, for people taller than six feet, have one-quarter pound more down and weigh and cost a little more for the same warmth ratings.

Sleeping bag kits are available from Frostline. The pieces are precut and come with detailed instructions for assembly; the purchaser does the sewing and stuffs the down in the tubes. It is not a project for the novice seamstress but requires little skill, the major problems being that of jockeying the voluminous amounts of material into proper position for stitching. Typically for an expenditure of $50 one may obtain a $90 bag.

Two new sleeping bags, not yet widely available, deserve mention as innovations that may become popular in years ahead. One has polyester filler on the bottom, where its resistance to crushing is an advantage, and down on the top, where its lofting capacity can be realized. The other has polyurethane foam on the bottom, in effect a built-in sleeping pad, and down on the top.

Sleeping bags for children: One reason many married couples buy sleeping bags that can be zipped into a double is to make room for little kids. The weight of an extra bag is saved and the kid (or kids) can snuggle between mommy and daddy—which is perhaps the only place they will sleep in the strange environment of the wilderness.

Family togetherness is, however, a disaster for everyone concerned if the kids kick and squirm all night. In any event, beyond a certain size the child cannot snuggle with parents and needs a separate sack. Long-time hikers with a basementful of old gear often take a worn-out bag, chop off the bottom, patch as needed, and thereby make a child's bag with no cash outlay.

When a bag must be purchased the same rules given above apply. Children, though, being smaller and generally having better circulation, don't need bags with so much insulation or weight (or expense) as adults to gain equivalent warmth ratings.

One representative example is a mummy bag with nylon shell, 36-inch nylon zipper, filled with one and one-quarter pounds of polyester, 52 inches long (for people up to four feet), warmth rating 32°F. Bag weight two pounds, price about $14. A similar bag 63 inches long (for people up to five feet), same warmth, weighs two and three-quarter pounds and costs about $20.

A goose-down bag of the design described above as "Middle Class," in a size for people under five feet eight inches, with two pounds of down, warmth range 0°F, weighs three and one-quarter pounds and sells for about $56.

An almost identical bag but filled with two pounds of prime duck down, rated 0°F, of a size to fit people under five feet, weighs two and one-quarter pounds and sells for about $36. Finally, the elephant's foot, with three-quarter pound goose down, drawstring closure, weighing one and five-eighths pounds, selling for about $31, is a fine bag for children up to four feet—or in a more expensive design, up to four feet nine inches.

However, many parents consider it extravagant to buy expensive mini-bags which will serve only several years. Instead, as soon as a kid can carry a bag they buy an adult size and let him grow into it.

Important note: down bags should be used for children only after they are potty-trained; repeated cleaning destroys the loft (see below).

Care of the Bag

There is no formula for predicting the life span of a sleeping bag. Every-night use for months on end, as during an expedition, may pretty well finish it off. If slept in only a few weekends a summer, it may last years. However, more important than the amount of use is the manner of use. Proper care can greatly extend a bag's life, and carelessness can kill it while still new.

The nylon shell of the typical backpacker sleeping bag is strong but very thin and thus must be protected from wear and especially snagging. Therefore—and also to keep the bag dry—a layer should be placed between bag and earth, such as tent floor, sleeping pad, or ground sheet, and the bag should be carried within a stuff bag. The hiker's repair kit should include a roll of ripstop tape for patching holes through which down might escape.

Nylon shells must be scrupulously guarded against fire; even a tiny spark instantly melts a hole in the fabric—and could kindle a smolder in the filler. Using an unprotected bag as a seat cushion for campfire seminars usually leads in the course of an evening to several holes per cushion, despite constant cries of "Spark! Spark!"

Even more perilous is steaming out the residue of a rainstorm. All fillers require some time to dry and down takes forever, and during the long process spark holes are inevitable. And patience becomes exhausted, one moves closer to the flames, the fabric is scorched and disintegrates, and it's time to buy a new bag. All the more reason not to let the bag get wet in the first place.

Down bags should never be stored in the stuff bag between trips. The more time the down spends tightly compacted the more it bends and loses resiliency and thus loft and warmth. Instead, the bag should be loosely rolled, or better, hung on a wall or draped over a line in the basement or a hanger in the closet.

By the same token a down bag should be thoroughly fluffed before it is slept in. The rule is, as soon as camp is reached and the tent or tarp rigged, the bag is unrolled, shaken vigorously, and placed under the shelter to finish attaining full loft.

Any bag, but especially down, should be air-dried after each trip to avoid mildew and rot and to prevent the filler from matting. Indeed, on multi-day hikes the bag should be aired every day or two, weather permitting, to dry body moisture breathed into the filler at night.

Your sleeping bag should be kept clean, not only for reasons of hygiene and social acceptability but to prevent the shell from rotting or being nibbled by small creatures (in the mountains or in the basement) which lust after salt and oil. Further, some people are allergic to the dust that collects on filler.

With polyester bags there is no problem; they can be safely washed in warm water with a mild soap either by hand or in a front-loading ("tumble") machine adjusted to the gentle or delicate setting. Polyurethane foam bags can be rinsed out in the bathtub.

Down is something else. Experts unanimously agree that more down bags are ruined by improper cleaning than all other causes combined, including long, hard use. Beyond that experts separate into three factions, each passionately defending its position and attacking those of the others more or less vigorously.

Tolerate dirt and save the down: Suspicious conservatives declare absolutely: never clean a down bag! Spot-clean the shell, yes, by gently sponging with water and mild soap, then plain water to remove the soap. But washing turns the down to string and dry cleaning can be fatal to the sleeper; if the bag gets too dirty for fastidious tastes, buy a new one.

Conservatives sardonically advise the hiker who insists on converting his down filler to string at least to slow the process by washing very rarely and then only in cold water with mild, cold-water soap; even plain warm water, they say, de-lofts down.

Wash the down—but gently: Some manufacturers and mountain shops think the best method for cleaning a nylon-and-down bag is washing and feel damage is minimal if the job is done carefully. They advise as follows:

Washing should be done with a very mild soap and warm water, never hot, and thorough rinsing to remove soap residues which can mat the down. (Incidentally, all down is washed in detergent by the processor to remove the natural oils, which stink.)

Never—repeat, NEVER—lift or hang or shake a soaking-wet bag—the weight of the saturated down will instantly tear out the baffles and for all practical purposes the bag is at that moment a dead loss.

Hand-washing is safest—some experts declare it's the *only* safe technique, that any machine mats the down, tears the baffles, and rips up the shell if the bag snags on moving parts. Other experts say an automatic machine of the "tumble" (front-loading) type can be used—but never an "agitator" (top-loading) machine, which will destroy the baffles in seconds and before the cycle is over perhaps the nylon shell as well. Put the machine on the gentle, or delicate setting—with warm water only, with mild soap. Rinse at least twice.

The bag can then be dried, say these experts, in an automatic machine, set on warm—never hot. Run it through as many cycles as necessary, maybe three or four. (A tip: throw a pair of clean sneakers in with the bag; the combination of rubber and nylon hastens the build-up of static electricity necessary for full loft and the sneakers break up clumps of wet down.) If possible, air-drying should follow. Air-drying used exclusively may take several days—and must be done with caution to avoid destruction of the baffles.

Other experts scoff at the "three or four cycles" and say a bag never is thoroughly dried by an automatic machine except by dozens of cycles. They recommend gently squeezing water from the bag, then air-drying it for a week, frequently massaging the down to break up clumps. There are dangers in the neighborhood laundromat—the previous user of a machine may have employed bleach and if any lingers it will discolor or spot-hole a nylon shell. Before using a public (or perhaps even a home) machine, run it through a cycle empty to flush out residues of bleach and detergent.

Dry clean the down—but afterward breathe with care: Because of the above problems a third faction recommends dry cleaning, which all agree is much simpler and safer (for the bag) than washing. However, great care must be taken to completely air-dry the bag afterward—for at least a week. If cleaning-solvent residues linger they will attack the down. Also, the solvents are toxic and have killed sleepers in the night; the U.S. Bureau of Standards warns against dry cleaning as altogether too risky. Partisans say there is no danger of poisoning once the solvent odor is gone.

Cautious convervatives ask who's to know what solvent is used—the petroleum-based compounds some experts claim are okay or the chlorinated hydrocarbons generally agreed to be bad for bags and living creatures? Regarding the no-odor no-danger rule, conservatives wonder about people with a poor sense of smell. Therefore, trusting their local dry cleaner exactly as much as the friendly used-car dealer they say: better dirty than dead.

Between Bag and Ground:
Sleeping Pad, Air Mattress, Ground Sheet

Disillusioning though it surely is for the beginner to hear, the typical sleeping bag does not provide all-around insulation; especially in the case of down, the protection against cold is almost entirely on the air side, with little if any on the ground side. Nor does the usual bag have significant cushioning value.

If the ground is warm, dry and soft, no matter. But more often the ground is chilly, stealing heat from the body, and/or wet, dampening the bag and speeding heat loss and/or hard or bumpy, unkind to tender flesh and bones.

The bag, therefore, is only one of the three parts of the "sleeping system." Another is the tent or tarp. The third is what goes between bag and ground.

The old-style backpacker sought to live off the land. In high meadows he luxuriated in the grandest of earth's mattresses, a clump of heather. In forests, when ground was wet or snowy, he cut branches from living coniferous trees to build a bough bed.

Farewell, pioneer! There is not enough heather in the remaining wilderness of America, not enough greenery of trees, for these scarce resources to be utilized for sleeping. There is barely enough for looking. As a friend of the Earth, entitled to all the responsibilities thereof, a backpacker must carry a complete sleeping system and not improvise a missing part by attacking the scenery with ax or knife or saw.

For Insulation Mainly—The Sleeping Pad

Though polyester gives some bottom insulation, down crushes flat under body weight; a down bag rated as having six inches of loft really has only three inches of useful loft. With either filler, bottom insulation frequently must be provided by a sleeping pad.

(As noted above, sleeping bags are available with foam bottom and down top. And polyurethane foam bags are in effect all-around sleeping pads.)

The most popular sleeping pad for summer use is ensolite (polyvinyl chloride; Thermobar is another trade name) one-quarter inch thick, 28 by 56 inches (for the average adult), weighing one and one-eighth pounds, and costing about $4.50. The size is adequate for the shoulder-to-hips area where most of the body weight rests against the ground, the weight is small, and the pad rolls easily into a tiny diameter. Ensolite is a closed-cell foam and thus watertight. Ensolite pads come in lesser and greater lengths and widths with weights and prices to match.

Slightly lighter for the same sizes but otherwise virtually identical are polyethylene pads, also of a watertight closed-cell foam. An air cap pad, of a clear polyethylene sheeting filled with one-quarter inch air bubbles, is very inexpensive and lightweight; the bubbles soon puncture so the life expectancy is short. Further, the large bubbles give nowhere near the insulation of the myriad tiny cells in foam. In a 24- by

72-inch size such a pad weighs six ounces and sells for about $1.35.

A one-quarter inch or even a one-half inch pad does little to blunt the thrust of rocks or cushion the hip bone against hard soil. Their role is not as mattresses but as insulation compensating for body-flattening of the bag filler. The above pads also give partial protection against wet ground.

Some hikers prefer a urethane (polyether is similar) pad one and one-half inches thick, giving not only insulation but cushioning. The most popular 24- by 48-inch size weighs one and one-quarter pounds and costs about $3. Urethane is an open-cell foam, much softer and more resilient than closed-cell foams, which eventually fatigue and stay compressed. However, because of the softness about three times the thickness of closed-cell foam is required for equivalent insulation. Also, open-cell foam is literally a sponge, wicks water from damp ground into the bag, and when wet is as cold as a water bed; in damp terrain it thus must be used in conjunction with a ground sheet. (But then, body moisture may condense on the ground sheet and be absorbed by the foam.) Another disadvantage is the major effort required to roll one and one-half inch urethane into a diameter less than enormous.

A covered-urethane pad, the top covered with non-slippery cotton oxford cloth, the bottom with waterproof coated nylon, takes care of the moisture problem but is not only bulky but heavy and expensive. For example, the 24- by 48-inch size in a thickness of one and one-half inches weighs two and three-quarter pounds, costs about $8.

For Cushioning Mainly—The Air Mattress

An air mattress gives more cushioning than a urethane pad and, being deflatable, makes much less bulky baggage. However, despite also giving wetness protection, when used alone its insulation value is minor; convection currents in the air cells efficiently carry heat from bag to ground.

(Cushioning *and* insulation can be obtained by slowly, patiently inserting down into the mattress. As little as two ounces is enough to give a cozy-warm sleep even on snow. The only drawback is that a pump thereafter must be used to inflate the mattress in order to keep the down dry.)

Another disadvantage of air mattresses is the evening-and-morning time needed to inflate and deflate. Another is the aggravating habit of letting the sleeper down in the night, either from a tiny puncture invisible to the naked eye, a valve failure, innate crankiness, or practical jokes by surly companions.

Full-length mattresses are splendid for weekends but too heavy (three pounds or more) for extended backpacks. Long distance walkers whose thinly covered or old bones demand pampering generally are content with a size reaching from shoulders to hips. A 28- by 50-inch nylon mattress weighs one and seven-eighths pounds and sells for about $8.

Cheaper and a bit lighter are vinyl mattresses. A 22- by 46-inch size weighs one and one-half pounds, costs about $4. Vinyl punctures even more easily than nylon, almost at the sound of a harsh word; however, one can carry a kit of cement and patches and while away many an hour in camp, day and night, searching for and repairing holes.

If a mattress is used for comfort an ensolite pad may still be wanted for insulation between mattress and bag. An alternative recommended by snow-camping veterans is to sleep semi-nude and put trousers, shirt, and sweater between mattress and sleeping bag; they swear the method gives all necessary insulation.

A few hikers appreciate an air or polyester pillow weighing five or six ounces, costing a dollar or two. Others improvise a pillow from the stuff bag filled with extra clothing or a boot wrapped in a sweater.

For Moisture Protection—The Ground Sheet

For any sleeping bag—no matter what the filler—to get damp or soaked in the course of a trip is always a minor or major catastrophe, to be avoided by every available manner and means.

Neither pad nor mattress can be trusted to keep the bag absolutely separated from wet ground; during the night a sleeper inevitably slops over the edges. The tarp-camper therefore must carry a ground sheet. (The tent-camper, with a floored tent, needs no sheet to keep his bag dry but may want one to prevent abrasion of the expensive floor.)

Some hikers use a small canvas paint cloth, available at any lumber yard or hardware store. Though heavy, the cloth is very water-resistant without being waterproof—a genuinely waterproof sheet creates a mini-still, condensing body-exhaled moisture on the cold ground-facing sheet and dampening the sleeping bag bottom. However, the distillation is slowed by intervention of pad or mattress, and therefore most hikers prefer a lightweight sheet of polyethylene or coated nylon.

As an example, a polyethylene sheet seven by eight feet, large enough for two or three sleepers, weighs one and three-eighth pounds, sells for about $3.50. Among other sizes, a sheet 12 by 14 feet, sufficient for four or five adult bodies, weighs four and one-half pounds, costs about $7.

Home Is a Tent

From *The Joy of Camping*.
By Richard Langer

There are few experienced campers who set out to meet
the wilderness without taking a shelter of some sort
along. And if it's your first time camping, even for only
an overnight introduction, with beautiful weather
guaranteed by all the forecasts, a tent adds warmth,
comfort and security. You don't have to sleep in it. You
may even set it up, trim and taut and tidy, and then
decide you'd like to slumber under the stars after all.
But it's still nice to have around, in case the wind rises
or the rain comes or you get—just a wee bit, you
understand—jittery about those odd rustlings in the
underbrush. Canvas or nylon walls certainly seem
flimsy compared to those of a house. Yet creatures of
the woods respect their shadowy impregnability (unless
you have food inside the shelter with you).

Many forest preserves and parks offer log lean-tos,
or even cabins for the weary camper. But before you
plan on skipping a tent and slipping somnambulantly
into one of these rustic shelters at the end of the day's
trail, consider the facts. Everybody and his dog head
for them. Chances are the one you arrive at as dusk falls
will be filled to capacity—with campers often not of the
strong, silent type. Even during the mythical out-of-
season period you're apt to find the shelter sadly

overflowing—this time with discarded cans, wrappers, and rotted leftover food scraps. Rumors of ecology are only now beginning to filter down to the layman camper. Most certainly, whatever else is or isn't, there you will find an unsoft carpet of that most foul of modern discards, the snap-top can tab. (I fervently hope the eternal fires of hell are built on these, so their inventor may pace over them barefoot forever.) Then, too, animals have learned to dine regally on man's droppings around these carelessly housekept shelters. And although part of the joy of camping is wildlife, in your food and gear it can be a costly nuisance. Reconsider a tent, and the freedom to pitch it in a quiet, welcome spot.

Which tent is right for you? Well, that depends on what kind of camping you have in mind. The tents available today are a fantastic improvement over those from only a few years ago. Many are of the multiple-use variety. Still, multiple-use tents are, by definition, hybrids, and hybrids can't have everything. Their differences should be considered in terms of function. Summer canoeing is a far cry from winter ski touring, for instance, and some of the gear you need for one won't do for the other.

If you're going camping for the first time, why not rent a tent, to try it out for size? This is a good idea anyhow, considering that your tent will probably be your biggest single camping investment. Most of the larger mountain and camping supply stores today have a rental program. In many cases part of your rental fee can be applied to eventual purchase if you so decide. And if you don't happen to immediately fall in love with one tent, renting gives you a chance to try out several different kinds.

In all likelihood you will start out summer camping. Pick a tent basically with this in mind. Later you may try a second, or even a third, tent, depending on what particular times and places of the great outdoors you get really hooked on. But by then you'll know a lot more about tents.

Three Little Tents All in a Row

Rarely should you consider anything bigger than the two-man tents. You're not trying to take a seven-room house to the woods when you go camping. You're looking for compactness, easy portability, warmth and coziness in cold weather. In warm weather you'll want to be outside the tent. Rain? Well, even a huge pole tent won't keep you from feeling somewhat cooped up if you want out. Buy a couple of good ponchos—rain is one of the elements of the natural world you set out to find when you left the city or suburbs. Listen to it pattering on the rain fly of the tent. It's a soft sound.

Kids go for tents like bees for basswood. Think back to your own childhood, when you were forever busy crawling into little houses (my favorite was the kitchen woodbox) or making a brand new one by hanging a blanket over the table or a set of chairs. Kids like tents so much they'll even camp out in the backyard at home. So why not a tent of their very own for the trail? Besides the privacy and comfort of sleeping only two in a tent, children will usually accommodate parents by playing house with their own tent, sometimes even permitting their elders a well-deserved late snooze in the morning.

The backyard play camp, incidentally, is an excellent way to break children in on sleeping in their tent. If you have the opportunity to let your kids practice before you set out towards the wilds, by all means avail yourself of it.

How young can you start a child out in his or her own tent? Reasons of parental convenience, such as responding to calls for milk or a less soggy diaper in the middle of the night, may dictate three in a tent, but our daughter Genevieve, presented with the opportunity of sacking out in one by herself when 14 months old, seemed to view it as a cozy little nursery, apparently with much more interesting walls, doors and furnishings than the ones at home. Needless to say, when camping with young children, separate tents should be within easy reach and hearing distance of each other—no matter how tempted you may be to pitch yours at the other end of the lake.

The Tarp Tent

The most elementary tent is the tarp. This is simply a waterproof square of material usually somewhere between nine by nine feet and 14 by 14 feet in size. It has reinforced grommets at the four corners, the midpoints, and quarter points of each edge, as well as five tie tapes distributed along the top surface, to permit creation of a wide variety of roofs. It can be slung between two trees, wrapped over a canoe, pitched triangularly from a midpoint grommet, suspended in turn from a suitably high branch, and so on.

Even in tarps modern tent technology has made advances. The first tarp tent I had was a water-resistant ten-by-ten-foot cotton one that weighed all of a ton (actually closer to seven or eight pounds). My present one is a nine-by-nine-foot model weighing a fraction over one pound and fitting into a small outside pocket of my pack. The difference is nylon (through which water goes like a sieve), double-coated with polyurethane (through which water goes not at all).

If you use a tarp, you'll also need a ground cloth, which will add a bit more bulk and weight to your gear, although not much if it's simply a sheet of plastic. You can get away with skipping the ground cloth if you use Ensolite padding and a bivouac cover with your sleeping bag. Or if you carry a poncho, it will double as a ground cloth on smooth ground.

Compactness is not the only consideration in a tent. The tarp's use is quite restricted except for the hardiest of woodsmen. I never use mine in mosquito country. A tarp tent will give you shade, keep the dew off your sleeping bag, add some warmth to your nights, and cut down a considerable amount of wind. It will also protect you and your belongings from vertical precipitation. Notice the word 'vertical.' A good storm will blow the rain in on the most expertly rigged tarp tent.

Take, for instance, the night we spent at Schroon Lake in the Adirondacks (New York State) some years back. It rained, and rained, and rained. Nice and vertical the whole time. But there's such a thing as ground water. We were on a slight slope, and by three o'clock in the morning rivulets were running past our sleeping bags with such force I expected us to float down the hill like Hans Christian Andersen's one-legged tin soldier on his bar of soap. The next day was sunny and bright. The wet corners of our bags dried out by noon. The world was wonderful once more. And I still use a tarp tent on occasion.

You should consider the tarp tent for weekend trips in areas of infrequent rainfall. You should also seriously consider taking a tarp along on day hikes in rough country where there is an odd chance of being stuck overnight unexpectedly. A third reason for having one is to use it as an extra fly, shading and protecting the area between two or more tents when family camping.

If you do get a tarp, make sure it's double coated with polyurethane for best results. There is also one indispensable accouterment, namely, 50 feet or more of lightweight but strong nylon line. The tarp, except when rigged over a canoe—one of its most effective setups, incidentally—needs plenty of line to suspend it from appropriately located trees. Trees have a fickle way of being just two feet farther apart than you have rope to reach. A second item, not indispensable but very handy, particularly if your tarp lacks sufficient ties and grommets, is the tarp garter, or Visklamp. It looks like a combination jacks' ball and shower-curtain ring and works on the same principle a garter does. You put the ring flat against the tarp wherever you wish to attach a line, then you push the tarp through the large end of the ring with the ball and slide the whole thing up to the slim end. Then just tie your line on to the large ring, lead it to the rigging point you've picked out, and you're set.

A last word: the key to pitching a tarp tent is to have a minimum of sag on your roof. To this end, if you are using a nylon line, which tends to stretch, tighten things up before hitting the sack at night.

Security Is a Real Tent

Snakes don't really like best of all to search out a warm sleeping bag for a snooze, honestly they don't. Nevertheless, on rare occasions they have been known to do so. And no matter how remote this possibility is on your camping trip, knowing it couldn't happen in a fully enclosed tent adds a comfortable degree of security to your own snoozing—particularly if it's early on in your camping career.

Let's face it, a bit of nervousness in approaching the wilderness, away from so-called civilization, is natural today. When a society features a way of life in which its members feel they control nature—getting dark? turn on the lights; cold? turn on the heat; need help? reach for the telephone—how could it be otherwise?

There's really little to fear in the wilds for the careful camper. I know I'm safer canoeing down a river in no-man's land than crossing a street in New York. But the fear lingers on subconsciously. Rare is the camper who hasn't been spooked at least once in a while. And when it happens, being able to close yourself off completely in a real tent is a reassurance.

I still vividly remember one moonlit night on the shores of Bora Bora. Susan and I were comfortably stretched out between some bushes far enough from the coconut palms so no milky missiles could drop on us during the night, yet close enough to them for a quick breakfast. Shortly after we bedded down, there began a general rustling accompanied by the castanets of snapping claws—coconut crabs, measuring over a foot from claw to claw, were doing a *danse macrabre* with their mandibles all about us. Now coconut crabs are vegetarians. We *knew* they were vegetarians. Nevertheless, it was a restless night in paradise without a tent. The silver lining, of course, was crab claws sweeter than the best Maine lobster for breakfast.

A Tub for the Floor

The floor of a real tent should be of the tub, or wraparound, variety and preferably seamless to eliminate the possibility of ground leaks. A tub floor comes up and around to form the lower six to 12 inches of the tent sides. This waterproof sill prevents seepage if your gear of sleeping bags happen to touch the lower walls. It also keeps raindrops splattering off the ground from saturating the tent itself, which is not and *should not* be waterproof. A waterproof tent—and there are some being made—will raise a small rainstorm inside the tent while you sleep. Moisture from your breath and body rises to the roof, can't go through, condenses, and drops back over your sleeping body, turning your abode into a miniature cloud chamber. The moisture involved is not just a few drops, incidentally, but up to a full quart per person per day.

A Rain Fly for the Roof

But if a tent isn't waterproof, how is it going to keep you

dry? Simple. You cover the tent with a second roof, one that is waterproof and appropriately named a rain fly. This is suspended anywhere from three to six inches above your tent. Water bounces off this top layer, while inside moisture passes through the tent itself into the space between and then out at the sides. The double layer also keeps a tent considerably cooler during the day and warmer at night.

Tent Fabrics

Although backpacking tents are all made of synthetics, to save on weight, tents for other camping endeavors are often constructed of high-quality cotton. Unlike synthetics, pima cloth is woven so tightly that when the rains come, the minute swelling of the fibers reduces the size of the weave pores to such an extent the water will not penetrate the fabric. However, you can't brush up against it or capillary flows will be initiated. Also in its favor, the tight weave of pima cotton is less wind-permeable than the synthetics. Then, too, because of its porous structure, it accepts water repellents (as opposed to waterproof coatings) readily.

On the negative side, cotton requires more care than synthetics, mainly in that it must be dry before being packed, and it tears more easily than, say, ripstop nylon. This doesn't mean it's going to rip automatically. Most quality cotton tents are of six-ounce-per-yard fabric. A good deal of abuse is needed to rip that.

All in all, old-fashioned, tried-and-true cotton is an excellent tent material except for the weight factor. As a purely personal esthetic aside, cotton just feels good to the touch, as compared with the slipperiness of nylon.

Nylon has one undisputed advantage: its light weight. The material for any good canvas tent will weigh from two to four times as much as its nylon counterpart. Nylon's big disadvantage used to be that it ripped when you looked at it. However, by running reinforcement threads closely throughout the fabric, you get ripstop nylon, which—true to its name—stops rips. Another advantage, though not much of one for campers who normally take good care of their tents, is that nylon is almost mildew-proof, so you don't have to worry about drying it out thoroughly before packing it up and moving on.

The Catenary Cut

A floppy tent may look sloppy from a distance. From inside it can drive you wild. When the winds are high, it's not exactly like listening to a soft military roll on kettledrums but it's close enough. Besides, a wrinkled roof catches snow and rain, and is a strain on the tent in general.

To eliminate sag and looseness, particularly along the roof line, good tents are catenary cut. In this process the fabric is cut on the bias to compensate for the sag between the end support points of the ridge. This means a concavity, slight, of course, is built right into the tent ridge line, and no further slack should develop when you set it up. Hence, no loose fabric and no flapping. It also makes the tent fractionally lower, by the way. Never mind, you won't be spending that much time striving for uprightness in a tent.

Forest Tents

Forest tents, as you might guess from the name, are intended for use primarily below the tree line and are popular multipurpose tents. They need not be as aerodynamically stable as alpine tents, designed for higher altitudes or winter camping.

There are floorless forest tents, but you're far better off with a tub-floor model. You'll have to lug along a ground cloth of some sort otherwise, so there is no real weight saving. Besides, with a floor, and screened doors and windows, or vents, also standard, you can seal yourself off for a good night's rest from mosquitoes and slugs and other crawly things.

There are several one-man forest tents available. They are rarely used, however, since even most loners will lug the minimal extra weight of the two-man model just to have the additional space.

Most two- and three-man forest tents use the A-frame construction recently popularized in inexpensive vacation homes. Double poles at each end add a bit more weight to the overall package than the old single-pole arrangement. However, they do away with the entrance blockage of the center pole and add stability, as well as keeping the tent walls trim and taut, free from flapping.

The Tunnel Entrance

Looking more specifically at tents in the forest category, any list of good ones would include Ski Hut's Trailwise Mountain tent, which, despite the name, is really a forest tent. The double-urethane-coated ripstop nylon floor measures four feet, eight inches by seven feet, five inches and wraps up the sides of the tent, also of ripstop nylon, for 19 inches. Weight, complete with poles, stakes and fly: seven pounds, four ounces. The front opens completely with zippers and has a zippered screen behind it. There's nothing more delightful, incidentally, than parking your tent overlooking quiet, moonlit waters somewhere on a summer's night, and being able to open the tent doors wide to the sounds and the scenery of gently lapping waves or a rushing stream. The only thing more pleasurable, perhaps, is not putting up the tent at all. But back to the Trailwise.

At the rear is a tunnel entrance, which comes in very handy during snow season, both because zippers can freeze up and because it gives you a sheltered space outside the tent itself in which to remove and brush off your boots. However, I would still categorize the tent as a forest model, since some of the other features of an alpine tent (more on that later) are missing.

Aside from its being a plus in snow, I find little to recommend the tunnel entrance. For the most part such appendages are bulky, hard to keep as neat as all the pictures show them and basically a pain to crawl in and out of. But the zippered screening behind the tunnel entrance as well as on the ventilation tunnel above it afford excellent air circulation even in the most bug-infested country.

I'm told there are people who develop an immunity to bug bites after long years of camping. My immunity used to consist of Susan, who drew all the bugs. Now they go for Genevieve. There's bound to be someone in the family interested in the screening a tent has.

The Lightweights

For the really weight-conscious camper who desires a sturdy, breathing, nylon tent with fly, there's the Eddie Bauer High Lite. The two-man model is seven feet, two inches long; five feet, three inches wide at the front; four feet, three inches wide at the rear; and four feet high at the front, with a rear height of only two feet. Mighty cramped for some, yet you'll see plenty of these and similar models around at the far end of the walking trails and on the summits come summertime. Polyvinyl-impregnated floor and fly; insect screen over entrance; weight, complete with stakes, poles, guy lines and fly: five pounds, nine ounces. Can be used in light rain without the fly; then it's four pounds, nine ounces.

One tent I haven't tried but have heard a lot about is Stephenson's Warmlite. Stephenson is somewhat the odd man out in the camping supply business. His catalog photographs are peopled with nude playmates cavorting through the tents and sleeping bags. Design-wise, his equipment tends to be equally unorthodox. The floor of the Model #6 two-man tent is 11 feet long by five feet wide at the front and four feet at the back. The highest point measures 40 inches from the ground. The overall design uses aluminum hoops instead of poles, giving it a covered-wagon look and better wind stability than flat-sided tents. What makes the Warmlite seem definitely worth trying is that for all its room, the two-man model, complete with frame, insect screening and condensation liners, which absorb the moisture from your breath and thus supposedly compensate for the fabric's water impermeability, weighs an incredible two pounds, nine ounces. Not included are the stakes. Again incredibly, there are only three of them used instead of the usual half dozen or so. One of these days I'm going to try a Warmlite.

Fine, you say, but the thought of one of these three- or four-foot-high roofs above your head is already giving you claustrophobia, not to mention a backache when you think about getting dressed in the morning. There are two solutions to this dilemma. First, if you haven't done any camping before, it may all be imaginary. Small tents become very cozy after you've used them a couple of times. We switched from a two- to a three-man tent on one recent extended trip to give Genevieve, then a little over a year old, a bit more maneuvering space. But we did miss the snug womblike warmth of our two-man model.

Larger Models

A second option is to get an altogether different type of tent. There are three specific forest models I have in mind, each with its own special plus. The first is Moor and Mountain's revival and transformation of the classic Baker tent. In the old days the Baker tent was the epitome of a superior wilderness shelter, featuring roominess, quick access, flexibility, and being essentially a giant canvas reflector oven, easy heating. For the modern camper, however, its problems outweigh its advantages, and the Baker tent vanished into obscurity, kept alive by only a few trappers and rangers.

It had no floor, much less insect protection, and the process of erecting it usually called for cutting down five to seven saplings in the eight-year-old bracket, making it not only a tedious setup but a destructive one as well. As an extreme example, consider that in 1972 well over four million people passed through Grand Teton National Park, not exactly one of America's largest. Assuming everyone used an old Baker tent or other pioneer rigged model, even if the poles were reused by different parties all summer, at five poles per tent the park would have lost four to six million trees— which is probably more saplings of that size than are to be found in the whole park. Obviously, *cutting tent poles from trees is out*.

So on to Moor and Mountain's solution. It's called the Norfell Forester, and weighs under nine pounds complete with pegs and poles. It sleeps five, being nine feet wide by seven and a half feet deep, on a urethane-coated, ripstop nylon floor. The back has a foot-high, insect-net-covered window running the whole length for ventilation. At the front there is a three-inch splash and dust sill that helps to keep the floor clean. A storm flap closes around the entire six-and-a-half-foot-high front by means of a nylon zipper. The storm flap may also be pitched out as a dining fly, giving you a roofed-over area exceeding nine by 12 feet.

Manufactured for Moor and Mountain by Hood Sailmakers, one of the best known in the industry, the Norfell Forester is worth serious consideration if you feel you need a big tent, particularly if you're planning on canoe camping or setting up a base camp, in both of which cases weight is not a primary consideration. In heavily forested regions, the lightness of the nylon, as opposed to traditional canvas, permits the tent to be field-hung from trees and bushes, using the ample number of tie points and grommets provided. Without stakes and poles, the weight drops to only six pounds, ten ounces.

Another tent that will give you six-foot headroom and modern tent construction besides is North Face's Cathedral Tent, catchily named after the peak in Yosemite. It's a very stable hexagonal three-man tent with a striking appearance. The floor is four feet, two inches on a side and eight feet across. Using a ridgepole-modified triple-A-frame construction, it has no interior poles, a space-saving convenience that becomes almost essential when camping with young children. A tunnel entrance on one side, a double-zippered door on the other and three screened vents assure that ventilation is excellent and access easy. (Made of 1.9-ounce ripstop, with polymer-coated tub floor and nylon zippers.) Shock-cord-loaded poles that spring into place make for speedy erection. Packed into two separate stuff bags to equalize the weight, the tent, complete with poles, fly, guy lines and pegs, weighs ten pounds.

The Draw-Tite

When I take the family canoe camping, we can carry considerably more weight with us than when backpacking. Weight is even less of a problem for those who want to set up a base camp somewhere in the wilderness, moving out each fine day to explore a portion of the surrounding area and returning to their homey campsite for the evening. In both cases there is one tent that is not yet perfect but sure comes close. It's the Draw-Tite, developed back in the 1930s by outdoorsman Robert Blanchard. Working with lightweight, heat-treated, aircraft-aluminum tubing, he designed a self-tensioned tent frame from which the tent itself was tightly suspended by means of hooks and shock cords. The exterior frame literally pulls the tent out in all directions, eliminating sagging and flapping completely. In addition to always giving you a smooth tent surface, it minimizes wear, since stress is evenly distributed. And it provides an entranceway and interior entirely free of clutter.

Modern tent designs have come a long way since the thirties, and the A-frames give you pole-free entrances and interiors as well. But what no other tent has besides the Draw-Tite, manufactured primarily by Eureka, is freedom from stays, guy lines, and in most cases even tent pegs. It's a truly self-supporting tent. Once you've set it up, if you decide you don't like the location, all you do is pick the tent up and move it. As is. You probably won't do this often. Still, it's a nice feature, as we discovered one dark night after finding we had set the tent up right next to an anthill. The large wood ants couldn't get into the tent, but they were a royal nuisance when we stepped out, particularly since it was beautiful summer barefoot weather.

For years we used a two-man Eureka Draw-Tite. With each trip we became more enamored of it. The modern backpacker may cringe at 13¼ pounds, which is what the two-man model weighs. But for any other form of camping it's unbeatable. The same exterior frame that keeps the tent walls free of ropes and stakes also permits you to set up the tent on sand or solid rock, where other tents are difficult, if not impossible, to erect. And pitching a Draw-Tite is simplicity itself. Identical aluminum sections slip together to make the frame from which the tent is suspended. There are no lines to set or adjust. The whole thing can literally be done blindfolded. We usually have the tent up and ready by the time it would take to figure out where the stakes should go best for a regular tent. Mighty handy when you get caught in a downpour and want to make camp as quickly as possible.

The body of the tent is made of 6.5-ounce-per-square-yard combed poplin with a tight 200-thread-per-inch weave. The newer models have a heavy-duty coated tub floor, seven feet, nine inches long by five feet wide, in the two-man size, which wraps up well on the sides. Our three-man model, eight feet, ten inches by seven feet, has an unfortunate seam across the middle of the floor. However, after sealing it off, we had no trouble with it even during two-month stretches of solid camping.

A rain fly for the small, flat roof, 48 inches and 64 inches at the highest point for the two-and three-man models, respectively, is recommended for snow camping or in areas where continuous rain can be expected.

Ventilation is excellent in the Draw-Tite, with a screened rear window beneath a canvas eave so it can be left open in the severest storms, and three-way zippering screen and storm front flaps set at a lovely rakish angle that shelters the entranceway by its overhang.

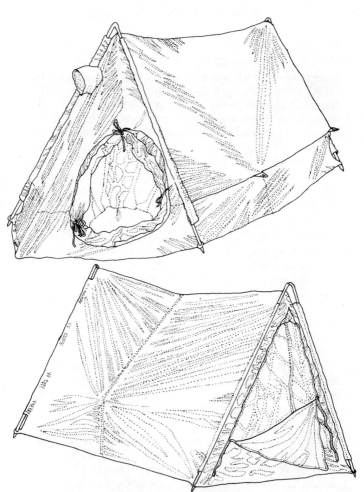

Top: Alpine tent. Bottom: Forest tent.

The zippers, unfortunately, are metal, but hopefully it won't be long before Eureka switches to the self-repairing, snagproof nylon ones.

And since no one is ever totally happy with his tent, there's one more improvement I've always wanted. I'd like the option of fiberglass poles, which would save considerable weight. Also the aluminum occasionally needs straightening out, and it gets mighty cold to handle when temperatures drop down below zero. I'd pay a small fortune for fiberglass poles to fit a Draw-Tite.

Bishop's Ultimate Outdoor Equipment and Eddie Bauer have also come out with Blanchard-design tents manufactured by Eureka. Both are half a foot shorter in the two-man model than the original Eureka canvas version, though slightly wider along the back of the roof line. They are also about 10 to 20 percent lower than Eureka's tent, giving an interior appearance of less room.

The Eddie Bauer model uses 1.5-ounce ripstop nylon. The tub floor and the fly are urethane-coated. Comes in two stuff bags, with a total weight of eight pounds, 13 ounces. Split between two backpackers, it would definitely be worth having even with the extra avoirdupois over the usual hiker's tents.

Bishop's version of the Draw-Tite is essentially the same, except it doesn't have the front and back eaves of the Bauer model. This streamlining adds some additional aerodynamic stability for high-altitude expedition use.

"Expedition model," incidentally, is a term you'll see bandied about frequently in camping shops. Often it's just "in" terminology and public relations work. The Draw-Tite design, however, has been used by expeditions from the Antarctic to Mount Everest.

The Bishop tent is slightly heavier than Eddie Bauer's (nine pounds, three ounces for the two-man model) because it uses 1.9-ounce nylon for walls and floor. Extras available with the Bishop model include connecting and storage vestibules with sleeve entrances (eight ounces for the connecting vestibule, one pound, three ounces for the storage vestibule in the two-man size) and a frost liner for winter camping (one pound, ten ounces cut to fit the same model).

Now all Eureka, Bishop or Bauer have to do is switch to fiberglass poles, add a tunnel entrance to the rear, and a winter cook hole with vent, and we'll be set with a single tent to fit all the seasons.

Alpine Tents

True mountain tents, designed not only for windy, high altitudes but snowstorms as well, have several features not usually found in forest tents. Although they are important under gusty blizzard conditions, these modifications add a not inconsequential amount of weight plus expense to a tent. Equipment fanatics will want them all, no matter what they cost. The more easygoing camper is apt to stick with a forest or multipurpose tent, which will serve him admirably under most winter conditions. However, if you are planning on plenty of high-altitude snow camping, you're in luck, for some of the finest tents are made with you in mind.

There are five essential modifications that distinguish the alpine tent from others: cook hole, exhaust vent, frost liner, tunnel entrance, and snow frock valance. Some of these may be found on the hybrid, or multiple-use tent, of course, but the true mountain tent will have them all.

The Cook Hole and Exhaust Vent

A zippered opening in the tent floor, set well away from the wall for fire safety and convenience, permits access to the ground below an alpine tent. If you must cook in the tent, this is where you will set up your stove. It will also be your garbage pit, either by accident or design. The idea is that when you spill the stew, it falls to the ground rather than sliding slowly and inexorably across the tent floor, past your rucksack, underneath your sleeping bag. Cooking in your tent is a practice not recommended except in really extenuating circumstances until you're comfortably familiar with your equipment. Better to munch on cold gorp. Any extensive inside cooking will cause moisture condensation in the best of tents. To minimize it, alpine tents have a small hooded closable tunnel vent half a foot or more in diameter at or near the cook hole to permit an updraft exhaust of the moisture-laden air.

The Frost Liner

In weather below 20°F frost lining becomes an essential part of a tent. The removable frost liner is cut from light cotton fabric and attached as an inner wall. In some cases nylon is used; although lighter, it is far inferior for this purpose since it holds comparatively little moisture. Ice crystals forming from tent moisture condense on the surface of the liner during the more extreme temperature conditions rather than falling— especially at night—on your sleeping bag. At a convenient moment you take down the frost liner and shake it off outside the tent. If you don't get a chance to do this before the tent warms up, the ice crystals will melt. But the frost liner will then absorb the moisture rather than letting it drip down your back.

The Tunnel Entrance

Tunnel entrances are another essential in the winter camping conditions the alpine tent is designed to meet. Zippers are prone to freezing, jamming or breaking in extremely cold weather, rendering the usual tent flaps worthless. Also a flat vertical entranceway is more readily blocked by snow than a tunnel.

As a rule, a tent tunnel entrance is roughly three feet in diameter, with a three- to four-foot sleeve that can be pulled out and suspended to a guy line or attached to the tunnel entrance of a second tent to make a cozy set of twins during long heavy rains or severe storms. It certainly makes for easy tent-keeping. With the tunnel extended, it's not difficult at all to enter a tent unaccompanied by blowing snow even in a determined blizzard.

The Snow Frock Valance

A last modification found in the alpine tent is the exterior snow frock valance or flaps. Pieces of coated

fabric of the same material as the floor extend out from
the base of the tent to lie flat on the ground. Usually
about a foot wide, the flaps can be covered with a thick
layer of snow and then stomped down thoroughly to
keep the wind from slipping under the tent floor. Not
only do they add warmth, but in the case of a severe gale
they prevent your tent from breaking its mooring and
drifting off like the *Hindenburg*.

Maybe a Vestibule

An additional plus you may want to look for in an alpine
tent is a vestibule or two. One or both ends of the tent,
instead of being made flat, are curved out to give you
extra cooking and maneuvering room when you're
tent-bound. Avoid tents with unfloored vestibules unless they have sills to keep the dirt from being tracked
into the main part of the tent. If a sill is provided, the
bare-ground vestibule makes an excellent cook hole.

Do You Really Want All That?

There are several good alpine tents. Among the best are
Gerry's Himalayan, Sierra Design's Glacier and North
Face's St. Elias. Gerry's Himalayan, weighing 13
pounds, eight ounces with the works, has a seven-by-
five-foot floor space with an additional two-foot vestibule at each end. Fiberglass wands curve the main
walls out, making the interior even roomier.

The Sierra Design Glacier is less to tote at nine
pounds, eight ounces complete. It has a floor space four
and a half by seven and a half feet, including an alcove
with sleeve door set rakishly off to one side.

Lightest of the lot, at six pounds, 12 ounces, is North Face's St. Elias, identical to their forest tent except for six inches extra width and the addition of a frost liner and snow flaps.

The choice among these and other alpine tents should be made carefully, since they represent a considerable investment. Perhaps the first question you should ask is whether you'll really do enough extreme winter and high-altitude camping to justify the expenditure. For an occasional frolic in the snow your Eureka Draw-Tite, North Face Cathedral or other quality forest tent will do fine. Also, for an occasional winter outing, renting is a good option. But assuming you need a winter tent, what you should look for besides the alpine features is the same as with any tent, quality of craftsmanship.

Checking Out a Tent

The thread used to stitch a tent together should match the material: nylon thread with nylon, cotton thread with cotton. Cotton is really the best of all threads because it swells when wet, sealing the stitch holes. However, when it is used on nylon tents, owners tend to treat the whole tent as if it were a nylon tent. This induces premature rot in the cotton thread, materially lessening the seam life of the tent.

Seams preferably should be lap-felled and double-stitched for maximum strength, particularly with lightweight fabrics. Horizontal seams should lie so that the folded-over part dips towards the ground on the outside. Otherwise the seam will tend to hold water like a rain gutter. The stitching should be evenly spaced and neat. Remember, neatness does count.

Nylon, even ripstop, is susceptible to unraveling. All nylon edges should be heat-sealed. Most tent makers hot-cut their fabrics, effectively binding off the edge as they snip, all in one process.

Peaks, corners, pole sleeves, and particularly pull-outs and grommets should be reinforced. Any part of the tent to which a line is going to be tied should be strengthened with a patch to spread the stress. Set the tent up and check all stress points while it's raised. That's the way you'll be using it.

Zippers are best made of nylon, the coil variety being the most desirable of all, with nylon teeth in second place. Following these are the old brass zippers. Aluminum teeth come in a far distant fourth. Check out not only the quality of the zippers, but their arrangement as well—always with these questions in mind: How convenient would this particular setup be for me and my party when we're inside? Is the door easy to work? Can the window be closed if the gear is at the back under it? And so on.

Making Your Own

If you're handy with a sewing machine, consider making your own tent during those dark days when you're by the homeside hearth. Not from scratch, unless you're both a fanatic and equipped with the necessary, fairly technical engineering know-how, but with a kit from Frostline or Carikit. Several styles come with precut, prelabeled parts to be put together in a stitch-by-number fashion. Instructions are clean and easy to follow, so if you've sewn at all you don't need to acquire any additional skills. Neither do you need an industrial sewing machine. A home model will do fine. And you save about 50 percent over equivalent models of finished tents. That's true of Frostline's and Carikit's other camping gear, too.

The Frostline Sun-Lite two-man, in nylon, is a cozy little forest tent with a ridge height of three and a half feet, a urethane-coated floor seven feet, one inch by four feet, three inches, and mosquito netting at each end. The front and back ends close from the bottom using Velcro tape, a product I personally haven't gotten used to yet. Snow tends to pack into the hairs so they close poorly. The completed tent, including a waterproof, urethane-coated fly and poles, but not stakes, weighs five pounds, four ounces.

Mending a Tent

Speaking of water, any tent can and may develop a small seam leak, particularly along the edge of the floor and in corners. A little squeeze bottle of Neoprene sealer complete with pointed nozzle should be kept in your tent bag to remedy the situation quickly and painlessly. Make a mental note of any spot that leaks—when it leaks. Otherwise you may not find it till the next rain. Seal it before you leave the tent for the day, first making certain all possible vents are open. Sealer sure doesn't smell like pine boughs, and it can give you a nasty headache as well. But after two or three hours the smell will be gone along with your leak.

Besides sealer, a small repair kit put together with your particular tent in mind is handy, indeed almost essential. Canvas tents will rip on occasion. The new nylon tents are very susceptible to fire damage. They won't burn. They simply melt, a fact of which one tent salesman up around Hudson Bay has quite graphic proof. He'd been trying to sell the Crees, who live in the traditional canvas wall tents, on the new nylon tents. Sales resistance was running so strong he literally couldn't give one away. Finally, after much bargaining, he talked Jim Went-Out-Spring-Goose-Hunting-And-Got-Stuck-In-The-Mud (I'll always remember the English translation of his name if nothing else) into trying one out. Jim promptly cut a two-foot-square hole in the roof, led a stovepipe through, and finished it off with the usual flashing holding the tent in place. As dinner was cooking the tent roof melted and oozed into the stew. So much for nylon tents up around Hudson Bay.

Now obviously you're not going to lead a flue up your nomadic tent. And your fire, if you have one, should not be close enough to permit sparks to land on your tent. Still, accidents of various kinds do happen. Remedy? For a nylon tent, a few inches of two-inch-wide adhesive ripstop nylon. The same kind of tape, but waterproofed, should be used for the floor and fly.

If you have a canvas tent, a couple of elbow-sized patches, sturdy thread, and as fine a needle as two thicknesses of the material will allow can do the job. As always, it's a good idea to apply sealer to the seams.

Stakes

Pegs or stakes are often not included in the complete

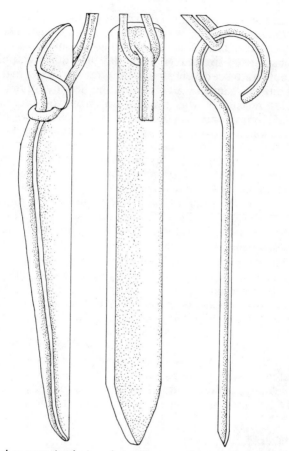

Stakes vary in design depending on the terrain for which they are intended.

tent package because terrains vary vastly and so do the suitable stakes. Luckily stakes are cheap. The curved aluminum models nest together (use a rubber band to keep them that way). Medium length ones (eight and a half inches) are a good all-around compromise in that they will hold well either in forest or meadow land or driven into sand, where shorter ones would give way. High-impact plastic stakes, usually in nine-inch or 12-inch lengths, are very durable and do not bend as aluminum sometime does. Their primary use is in sand, and there the somewhat large holes they leave behind are easily filled in. Skewer pegs of chrome-moly steel 10 to 12 inches long are favorites for pebbly ground.

Mother Nature is accommodating. Most of the time you should be able to lead at least some of your guy lines to trees or bushes, which offer strong, problem-free moorings. Happiest of all, of course, is the camper who has a self-supporting tent and thus can pass up the pounding, line-tightening ritual altogether. He'll be studying the stars or lazily answering the coyote pups practicing their yipping just that much sooner.

Good Eats

From *Pleasure Packing*.
By Robert S. Wood

Backpackers, like armies, travel on their stomachs. Food can make or break a trip. Most seasoned backpackers can recall trying to read complicated recipes by flashlight while nursing a smoky fire after an exhausting day; or endlessly chewing cold and tasteless food in the dark. Even with the marvelous foods now available, mealtime for many people means tepid, unappetizing dishes that yield neither energy nor satisfaction. One of the principal causes of this grief is the impulsive but mistaken attempt to reproduce meals in the wilds that look, taste and nourish like those we are accustomed to enjoying in the city.

To eat well and happily in the wilds, one must set aside the rigid and ritualized habits of urban eating (like the stricture to eat three square meals and not to snack between them) and adopt, instead, an entirely different set of rules. For instance, the principal purpose of wilderness eating is to keep the body fueled and fortified and capable of sustained effort. Energy production, ease of preparation and lightness of weight must all take precedence over flavor. Actually, a rehydrated stew at the end of a strenuous day often tastes better than a juicy steak in the city.

A backpacker's tastes usually change in the wilds. The body's needs are altered by heavy exertion and prolonged exposure to the elements, and these needs frequently are reflected in cravings for carbohydrates and liquids and a disinterest in other foods (like fats, meat and vegetables).

Individual meals lose much of their significance. To keep the body continuously fueled, the backpacker should eat, or at least nibble, almost constantly. Many snacks and small meals provide better food digestion, which means better utilization and energy production, than several large meals. A backpacker who makes it a rule not to let an hour pass without eating a little something will enjoy more energy and less weariness and hunger.

I start nibbling soon after breakfast if I am hiking, and on a long day I eat two lunches, one before noon and another in mid-afternoon. Some hikers I know go one step further: to avoid the bother of fixing meals, they dispense with them altogether, eating every hour and fixing a larger snack (or a hot one) when they feel the need.

A hiker living outdoors in a dry climate should drink at least as often as he eats. Since his body may easily lose a gallon of fluid in a day, and since the dehydrated food he eats will absorb additional moisture, a backpacker can scarcely drink too much—provided he takes only a little at a time. Severe dehydration can result if most of the lost fluids are not replaced every day. Although I sip from every brook I pass, and drink with every meal, I often consume another quart of water, tea or lemonade between dinner and bedtime. Since water loss means salt loss, backpackers benefit by salting their foods liberally and taking salt tablets if water loss is extreme or if nausea, aches or cramps signal a salt deficiency.

Every experienced backpacker knows that hot food must be cooked, served and eaten one course at a time if it is going to reach the stomach before turning cold. Nevertheless, it is a common sight to see frantic cooks trying desperately to serve two hot dishes simultaneously and equally frantic eaters trying to finish them before they get cold. Where exertion is great or the climate cold, hot—really hot—food is psychologically important.

Veteran backpackers usually rely on a pot of steaming soup for dinner, followed after an interval by an equally hot one-pot dinner that can best be described as stew. In warm weather, food preparation can be reduced by curtailing cooking. More than a few backpackers avoid cooking altogether, especially on short trips. They find the saving in time, labor and weight (stove, grill, pots) more than makes up for the absence of hot food.

A truly varied diet in the wilds is usually a luxury. But the ingenious person can increase his variety by the clever use of spices. The latest pre-cooked, freeze-dried dinners make it possible to dine differently each night with a reduction rather than an increase in preparation.

The importance of easy preparation can scarcely be overemphasized. After a long hard day the weary, starving backpacker cooking over an open fire on the ground, perhaps in the cold and wind and dark, needs all the help he can get. Steps that seem trivial in the city kitchen become difficult operations under wilderness conditions. In the wind, cooked food may be five times as hard to prepare as uncooked food. A recipe that calls for milk may be twice the work of one that requires water. At high altitude, raw dehydrated food might take ten times as long to cook as a pre-cooked, freeze-dried dish.

Many of the dishes offered specifically for backpacking in mountaineering shops, while perfectly good to eat, are patterned after city meals and require an unreasonable amount of preparation. If the directions run more than a sentence, or if more than one pot is required, I quickly lose interest. Two dishes designed to be eaten at the same time I pass over quickly. Dinners with low caloric yield are also rejected. Packages that contain three or four separate containers do not interest me.

Despite my disappointment in some of them, backpacking foods form the nucleus of my diet. But the shopper who knows what he is looking for can find a growing number of ideal foods in supermarkets, health food stores and Oriental markets. And the return of interest in organic foods is a boon to backpackers. It is possible (at least in Berkeley) to completely provision a backpacking larder without recourse to mountaineering shops, at no great sacrifice in quality and at a significant saving in cost per meal.

Calories

Since backpacking is one of the more strenuous activities and since it is sustained for days and weeks at a time, it is hardly surprising that the body's fuel intake must increase significantly in order to keep up with the increased energy output. The body's energy requirements and the energy production of food are both measured in calories. It takes twice as many calories to walk on a smooth surface at sea level at three mph as it does at two mph. And it takes two and one-half times as many calories to gain a thousand feet of elevation as it does to walk at two miles per hour on the level for an hour. Rough terrain, cross-country travel and the weight of a pack increase the caloric requirements considerably.

A variety of studies have shown that—depending on innumberable factors involving distance covered, terrain and the weight of the individual—it takes somewhere from 3,000 to 4,500 calories a day to keep a backpacker properly fueled. Long-distance hauling of heavy loads, or climbing, may require 5,000 calories, or more. Leisurely family trips may burn only 3,000. By comparison, the U.S. Army allows 3,500 a day for semi-sedentary garrison duty and 4,500 for strenuous work. For those who wish to compute the energy content of their menus, 4,000 calories a day should be adequate.

Backpackers who take in fewer calories than their systems need will find that the body compensates by burning fat to produce energy. Stored fat is efficiently converted to fuel at the rate of 4,100 calories per pound. The backpacker who burns 4,000 calories, but takes in only 3,590 (410 fewer), will theoretically make up the difference by burning a tenth of a pound of body fat, although individuals vary widely where fat conversion is concerned.

Backpackers unaccustomed to strenuous exercise will usually lose weight, but probably not from lack of caloric energy. Exposure to the elements results in water loss, and the change from the high bulk diet of civilization to low bulk dehydrated foods tends to "shrink the stomach." For most people, a little hunger and weight loss is beneficial to health and need not be construed as the first signs of malnutrition—as long as energy levels remain ample.

An understanding of the caloric yield of various foods is necessary, if only to avoid overeating. There is a tendency, even among experienced backpackers, to eat until they feel full, forgetting that concentrated low bulk foods yield far more power than a high bulk city diet. It is common to see a hungry hiker eat up two days' supply of the community lunch at one sitting, because he knows he needs fuel and because he is accustomed (in the city) to eating until he is full.

Packaging

To avoid depleting the larder, it is often a good idea to package each day's lunch separately. Eating concentrated food until the stomach is full often causes nausea and cramps. If the food is dehydrated and insufficient liquid is supplied, bloating and dehydration will result as the food absorbs moisture from the body. The backpacker must exercise restraint, have confidence in the caloric production of his food and remember that the semi-empty feeling in the stomach after eating reflects a healthy lack of bulk, not a dangerous lack of fuel.

It goes without saying that food must be light and resistant to spoilage in any kind of weather. Weight and bulk can usually be saved by repackaging food into plastic bags and jars. Menus can be devised that provide the needed 3,500 to 4,500 calories per day at weights anywhere from one and one-half to two and one-half pounds per day per person. Averages are only reliable for parties of four for a minimum of a week. Two people on a three-day trip can (and usually will) carry half again as much.

The most desirable foods on the basis of low water content are freeze-dried and dehydrated (usually 3 to 5 percent water) and air- or sulphur-dried (as much as 25 percent water). Food packed in glass or tin cans—quite apart from the weight and possible breakage of the containers—is seldom worth carrying, even if repackaged, due to its high water content and vulnerability to spoilage.

A Balanced Diet

Food is divided into three major components: fats, proteins and carbohydrates, all of which are essential to the backpacker's diet. The ideal proportions are essentially unknown and vary according to the temperature, individual, environment and type of activity—but a rule of thumb suggests that caloric intake be roughly 50 percent carbohydrates, 25 to 30 percent protein and 20 to 25 percent fats. There is a myth that the more strenuous the activity the greater the protein needed, and many backpackers go to great lengths to load their diets with the common proteins: meat, cheese, milk and eggs.

Actually, protein requirements are unaffected by activity. Excess protein can be a liability in that it is comparatively difficult and slow to digest. Large intakes are poorly assimilated and provide no immediate energy. Furthermore, protein at 1,800 calories per pound provides less than half as much energy as a pound of fat (4,100). Most protein-happy hikers would do better to switch their enthusiasm to fat, in which they probably are deficient.

Fats are no easier to digest than proteins, but they supply more than twice the energy and release it gradually over a long period of time. The principal fat sources for backpackers are oil, butter, margarine, nuts, meat

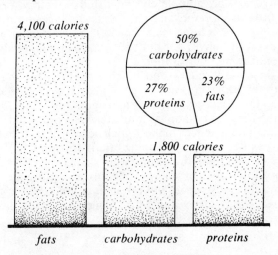

fat and cheese. The digestion of protein and fat demands the full attention of the body's resources for a
considerable period of time. Consumption should be
limited to small amounts at any one time, i.e., intake
should be spread through breakfast, lunch and snacks
rather than being concentrated in a heavy dinner. Even
relatively small amounts should not be eaten before or
during strenuous exercise. The blood cannot be expected to circulate rapidly through exercising muscles
and digest complex food in the stomach at the same
time without failing at one function or the other.

Carbohydrates may conveniently be thought of as
pure energy. Digestion is rapid, undemanding and efficient and the energy is released within minutes of consumption. But fast energy release means that carbohydrates are completely exhausted of their power in
as little as an hour, and more must be ingested if the
energy level is to be maintained. The backpacker who
lives on carbohydrates must eat almost continuously to
avoid running out of fuel.

Since trail snacks and lunches tend to be chiefly
carbohydrates, it is not a sign of gluttony to eat all day
long. Or as Harvey Manning aptly puts it in *Freedom of
the Hills*, "As soon as breakfast is completed the
climber commences lunch, which he continues to eat as
long as he is awake, stopping briefly for supper." The
nature of carbohydrates digestion makes clear why fats
(for slow efficient energy release) and proteins (for
constant body repair and rebuilding) are necessary to
balance the backpacker's diet. The common sources of
carbohydrates are cereals, fruits, sugar, starches and
candy.

With the exception of vitamin C (which is a natural antibiotic and prevents infection and is best taken in pill form), vitamins and minerals can usually be forgotten since they are provided in adequate quantity by any reasonably balanced diet. Even though storage is comparatively small, there would be virtually no effect on the body for at least a month if vitamins and minerals were absent.

In recent years, there has been considerable study and experimentation in an effort to produce maximum work capacity in climbers, backpackers and cross-country skiers. Dr. Per-Olof Astrand (*Nutrition Today*, June 1968) suggests that work capacity can be increased as much as 300 percent by careful dietary preparation. His studies show that a carbohydrate-rich diet several days in advance of heavy prolonged exercise greatly improves the body's respiratory quotient (oxygen supply) and thereby improves capacity for prolonged hard work. (Utilization of carbohydrate depends on the rate at which oxygen is supplied to working muscles.)

The most startling increase in work capacity, however, comes from emptying the body's store of glycogen about a week in advance, then building up a fresh store just a few days before the trip. Glycogen is a starch normally stored in the body in small quantities. It can be quickly converted into glucose to answer sudden energy demands upon the body. The higher the body's glycogen content, the greater its work capacity. By flushing the glycogen from the system a week ahead of time by heavy prolonged exercise, and keeping it low with rest and a carbohydrate-free diet for four days

before building it up again with a heavy dose of carbohydrates, a substantially higher level of glycogen
storage is achieved and work capacity is therefore
greatly increased.

Dr. Astrand found that a man who could do one hour
of heavy work on a fat-protein diet could do two and a
half hours of the same work after that diet had been
heavily supplemented with carbohydrates for three
days. When the man flushed the glycogen from his
system a week in advance and followed the same diet,
he was able to produce up to four hours of work.

So the backpacker who wishes to start a trip on
Sunday with the greatest possible capacity for prolonged exertion should, the Sunday before, load up a
pack and take a practice hike that thoroughly tires him
out. Then on Sunday, Monday and Tuesday he should
eat fat and protein exclusively to keep his glycogen
down—avoiding carbohydrates—get plenty of sleep
and limit his exercise to a walk around the block. On
Wednesday, Thursday, Friday and Saturday he should
"gorge" on carbohydrates while continuing to consume ample protein and fat. On Sunday he should be
admirably prepared for the most strenuous hike.

Food Planning

Food planning must be taken seriously if the menu is to
provide plenty of calories, lightweight, a good balance
between fat, protein and carbohydrate, maximum ease
of preparation, and no waste, spoilage or surplus. Beginning hikers will find it easy to spend many hours in
menu planning, shopping and packaging for the sim-

plest trip. But the alternatives—unappetizing meals, complicated preparation, insufficient fuel, hunger, heavy loads, etc.—make the preparation worthwhile. And gradually, as proficiency grows, the task becomes easier.

In order to learn from each trip, before I leave I list all the foods I am taking and their weights or amounts. Then, immediately after I return, I note on the list after each entry: how much I brought home, how much more I should have taken, foods to be forgotten, and unfilled cravings or needs. Such a list becomes invaluable in planning food for the next trip.

Food planners should be able to make distinctions between food requirements for different types of trips. There is no satisfactory all-purpose menu. For instance, when I go on an easy, leisurely trip with my wife, daughter and Saint Bernard, we take a greater variety of foods and worry less about preparation: we are likely, for instance, to carry lemons and a frying pan for trout, more and softer bread, popcorn, avocados, and so on.

If I am going on a cross-country ridge walk with a friend, foods are chosen for the energy they provide and ease of preparation. Variety is forgotten. The food list that follows lies somewhere in between. Weight is not as critical for four days as it is for two weeks, but must still be watched carefully where, as in this case, the hikers expect to cover about 30 miles, move every day and travel cross-country as well as by trail at relatively high elevation in the California Sierra. Four days should lie close to the length of the average recreational backpacking trip.

It has been the habit of a good many writers on backpacking to dismiss or scarcely mention freeze-dried foods because of their expense. In my view, backpacking is so inexpensive as vacations go, and freeze-dried food so cheap when compared with restaurant meals, that its slightly greater expense is hardly worth considering. Backpackers spend such a relatively short time in the wilds (during which they would have to eat anyway) that to skimp on quality seems foolish. I have spared no expense in the food list that follows, yet the cost per man per day is $3.83—less than the price of dinner in a modest city restaurant.

Dinner

Maggi and Knorr soups yield one and one-half to two cups per person, the first step in replacing liquid lost during the day. Half of the remainder of the day's allotment of butter and Bacon Bar (originally four and one-half ounces respectively) goes into the pot. So does any leftover milk or jerky. There is nothing to do but boil soup in a quart of water, then simmer until ready. The four freeze-dried dinners, each of which comes packed in a foil pan, are even easier to fix. Each produces at least a pound of casserole.

At sea level I peel back a corner of the foil top, pour in the prescribed cup and a half of boiling water, reclose the top and keep the pan close to the fire or at least out of the wind. Since I am fond of mushrooms, I add a quarter-ounce packet of freeze-dried slices to the dinner every other night when I add the hot water. At 6,000 feet and above, since the soaking-cooking time is more than twice the five minutes suggested, I forget the pan and empty its contents directly into the remains of the soup for easier reheating. Just before serving, I stir in a pinch of spice mix and a tablespoon of butter.

I am fond of cottage cheese served cold with salt and pepper, but only take it when I am sure of a snowbank or icy rill in which to chill it. The package makes an easy side dish in a plastic bag for one or two meals. The applesauce, strawberries and fruit cocktail (each of which serves four) are half for dinner and half for breakfast. The choice of the evening is cooked in a tea pot.

After half of it is eaten the remainder goes in a heavy plastic bag so the pot can be rinsed and water put on for tea. The pudding (for dessert every other night) requires no cooking and is made in a plastic bag. The ice cream is for the other two nights. All courses are eaten successively. On cold, late nights, the casserole and soup are cooked together in the big pot. We often finish off the day's allotment of a quart and a half of lemonade in the evening, perhaps with a slice of buttered bread and jam, or a succulent pineapple ring.

Breakfast

In the city, I rarely eat breakfast at all. In the mountains, I have little interest in the traditional cooked breakfast foods (bacon, eggs, oatmeal, etc.). But I get off to a good start, nevertheless, with a cup of cold fruit, a cup of Birchermuesli with milk and sugar, and a cup or two of tea.

Birchermuesli, based on the formulas of Swiss dietician Dr. Bircher-Benner, is an ideal dry cereal from the backpacker's point of view. I have tried half a dozen different brands and found little variation. Familia, the best known, is composed of oat flakes, apple flakes, wheat and rye, millet flakes, dried raisins, unrefined sugar, honey, crushed almonds, and wheat germ.

Three-quarters of a measuring cup provides the three ounce allotment for breakfast. To this, we add at least a tablespoon of dry milk powder from the plastic squirter bottle, along with about half a teaspoon of sugar (Birchermuesli is quite sweet and sugar is not needed, except for its energy value). After stirring in enough water to produce the desired consistency, and adding as much of the cold, stewed fruit as the cup will hold, breakfast is ready. Birchmuesli has been computed to yield about 1,600 calories per pound, a quarter of which probably comes from protein and fat. I like it best with freeze-dried strawberries mixed in.

To assure an ample supply of fat to last me through the day, I rely on Sherpa tea, the drink that is a staple in the diet of Sherpa porters who carry enormous loads at extremely high altitudes in the Himilayas. Sherpa tea is simply strong, milk-rich, sweet tea with anywhere from a teaspoon to a heaping tablespoon of butter (or margarine) stirred into the boiling water in the cup. The result is hot buttered rum with tea instead of rum. I know of no easier, more palatable way to ingest fat in the wilds—especially early in the morning.

Lunch

Lunch usually begins about an hour after breakfast—if

I am carrying a pack—with a square of rum fudge or mint bar followed by half a stick of jerky. By sucking first one then the other, I manage to make the snack last half an hour. If the day is strenuous, we may stop twice for lunch to thickly spread slices of pumpernickle with butter, jam, cheese and crumpled bacon bar, and to make up a pint of lemonade in a wide-mouthed container. Our four ounce daily allotment of pumpernickle means three generous slices each, and we share a cube—four ounces—of butter each day. The pound and a half of cheese is divided into four six-ounce chunks to prevent overeating. Dessert is mint or fudge bar, or a piece of dried pineapple.

Gorp is likewise eaten during lunches, but it is also extremely handy in the afternoon, along with fudge bar, as the body begins to slow down. By late afternoon, I am interested solely in the quick energy of carbohydrates and I rely entirely on squares of mint bar slowly melting in my mouth to keep me going until dinner can revive me. On layover days or when activity is light, I generally reduce my intake of snacks and settle for a single lunch, saving the excess for climbing or carrying days.

There are too many foods available for backpacking for anyone to list, much less try, them all. The notes that follow are limited to common items and those with which I have had some experience. Listings are alphabetical.

Apricots (*dried*): (Also peaches, dates, figs, prunes and other sun-dried fruit.) The trouble with this otherwise excellent source of carbohydrates is that the 25 percent water content makes it too heavy where power per ounce is concerned. Agricultural Handbook No. 8 (the source of most of the figures in this section, available for $1.50 from *Composition of Foods*, U.S. Government Printing Office, Washington, D.C., 20402) rates dried apricots at 260 calories per three and one-half ounces whereas dehydrated apricots offer 332 calories and only 3.5 percent water content.

Apricots (*dehydrated*): (Also any other vacuum or freeze-dried fruit.) Excellent raw on the trail, stewed, mixed with cereal, baked in bread, etc. Banana chips, date nuggets, freeze-dried peaches and strawberries are all delicious. The increased cost per pound becomes immaterial when water content is considered.

Apples, applesauce, apple slices: The apple is the most widely available, generally most pleasing, dehydrated fruit, and it has the highest calorie count (353 per three and one-half ounces) of the common fruits. Instant applesauce merely requires opening the poly bag, adding water, fastening it shut and shaking. Some brands come with cinnamon, sugar and lemon crystals for added flavor. Applesauce eaters know the daily sugar allotment per person depends on whether or not their sauce comes pre-sweetened. I often add cinnamon and nutmeg to the package beforehand. Vacuum or freeze-dried, not sun-dried, products are recommended.

Bacon: Long a delicious backpackers' staple, bacon yields 665 calories per three and one-half ounces —when completely consumed. But when all of the fat, representing more than 500 of those 665 calories, is not eaten, bacon becomes an impossibly wasteful, inefficient food (protein being only 8.4 percent by weight).

Most backpackers throw away all or most of their bacon grease. Bacon addicts know that unsliced bacon keeps best, but no bacon keeps forever. Canadian bacon has double the protein, and a quarter the fat of cured bacon, but only a third the calories and a very high (61.7 percent) water content. Furthermore, both kinds of bacon are (by my standards at least) troublesome and messy to prepare. Hot bacon grease is not easily captured, stored or reused. Being a bacon-lover, I faithfully carried it (pouring the grease—most of which I never used—in a plastic bottle which I had to throw away after every trip), until I gratefully discontinued it in favor of Wilson's Bacon Bar.

Bacon Bar (*pre-fried bacon*): Like Wilson's meat bar, Bacon Bar is a nearly ideal product from the backpacker's point of view. Its three ounces of precooked, cured bacon is equivalent to 12 ounces of raw bacon, but there is no preparation, waste or spoilage. Bacon bar offers a compressed, conveniently packaged, palatable fat and protein combination with great flavor; I find it useful in all three meals, snacks and emergency rations. It is the closest widely available approximation to the fabled pemmican, which is simply lean, dried beef mashed into suet (animal fat).

Baked foods: A great many people enjoy baking biscuits, cornbread, gingerbread, bannock, coffee cake and the like, and freshly baked breads are extremely welcome, even craved, after a number of days on the trail. Bakery products can provide considerable power, especially the sweet ones that are cooked with (or eaten with) butter or margarine. Small backpacking parties can seldom justify carrying even the lightest reflecting ovens, but a pair of featherweight pie pans held together with spring stationary clamps makes a durable oven.

Surprisingly good baked food can be produced with foil, frying pan and the leftover pans from Tea Kettle Casseroles. Conventional supermaket mixes need more water and additional flour, and they rise higher at high altitude. Mixes packaged for backpackers are becoming less temperamental, but the chef who has never baked anything should not expect immediate success in the wilderness. Pre-baked products (bread, cake, doughnuts) are seldom practical for backpacking trips, being unusually mangled and squashed into an unrecognizable paste.

Beans: A staple for travelers since the beginning of time, beans provide a fair source of carbohydrate and bulk and a popular starch base for many one-pot dinners. The raw bean is virtually uncookable at high altitude. Only precooked dehydrated beans should be considered. I like Seidel's sweet Boston Baked Bean Mix with half a crumbled Bacon Bar. A packet of freeze dried meat turns it into a fine dinner.

Bread: The problem with breads is bulk, spoilage, ease of crushing and drying out. Generally speaking, the harder and darker the better. Pumpernickel, rye, oatmeal and German black are all good, yielding about 250 calories per three and one-half ounces. A variety of small unsliced exotic loaves are now available at organic and health stores, but one must beware of labels that brag of the absence of preservatives, for mold will quickly grow. Many backpackers, especially the more stoic, find bread too much trouble and substitute crackers.

Bouillon: Virtually weightless, ageless foil-wrapped cubes are ideal for flavoring soups and casseroles and for impromptu broth when the body is too tired for food or a sudden storm makes a hot drink at lunchtime desirable.

Butter (*margarine*): Only oils and animal fats surpass butter and margarine (about 720 calories per three and one-half ounces) as a source of fat. Served in Sherpa tea at breakfast, on bread or crackers at lunch, and in soup or stew at dinner, butter palatably provides an ideal source of high yield, long-lasting energy.

Candy: Since candy is always a welcome, rich source of calories (about 400 per three and one-half ounces) and carbohydrate energy, it becomes an ideal staple of the backpacker's lunch and snack bag. Tastes change slightly in the wilds, but mountaineers are usually fond of lemon drops, toffee, coffee, caramels, butterscotch, sour lemon and bitter orange. Nonmelting hard candies or those wrapped in cellophane are most popular, but I often carry juicy, sugar-coated orange slices for variety.

Canned foods: Many a backpacker still carries canned tuna, corned beef, Spam, sardines, Vienna sausage, etc. to serve as the base of his dinner, and many of the cans unfortunately remain in the wilds. Given the heavy use of wilderness and the availability of a great variety of uncanned foods, it is hard to find a reason why cans still need to be carried. Makers of mountaineering foods have found that lighter, more compact, more easily carried out plastic and foil packages are far more appealing than the lightest aluminum can.

Casseroles (*prepared*): Makers of backpacking foods

are gradually abandoning complicated city-type meals in favor of easily prepared one-pot casserole dinners. The leading producer, in my view, is Oregon Freeze Dried Foods. I have used every one of its foil packed Mountain House dinners and pan-packed Tea Kettle casseroles and found them all exceptional in flavor, weight and ease of preparation. Cost runs a reasonable 60 to 70 cents per portion in one- and two-man packages, but drops much lower when No. 10 cans are purchased. Other manufacturers offer casseroles I like almost as well, but do not match OFD's overall consistency and excellence. A gob of butter fortifies and flavors any casserole.

Casseroles (*homemade*): Opportunities for constructing casseroles from scratch have never been greater. Small packets of freeze-dried beef, pork, turkey or ham are easily combined with pre-cooked dehydrated starches, mixed freeze-dried vegetables, soups or gravy mixes and spices. Cost savings can be significant for larger groups. Heavier, cheaper, one-pot meals can also be produced from recipes shown in Appendix 2 of *Freedom of the Hills*, published by The Mountaineers, Harvey Manning, editor, and the Sierra Club's *Food for Knapsackers* by Hasse Bunnelle.

Cereal (*cold*): Birchermuesli is easily the king of dry cereals on the basis of energy yield (about 350 calories per three and one-half ounce average serving) and compactness. And it can easily be fortified by the addition of applesauce powder, banana chips, date nuggets, more raisins, wheat germ and crushed nuts—in addition to sugar and milk powder. Competition like Granola and organic store concoctions are also excellent and far superior to old staples like Grape Nut Flakes and Raisin Bran. Corn flakes and its cousins are bulky and nutritionally worthless.

Cereal (*hot*): Many hikers feel the need of a hot breakfast, believing that heat somehow adds energy to the food. Actually, cooking reduces the potency of grains. The favorite hot cereals are instant oatmeal, Wheatena, Wheathearts, Farina, Cream of Wheat or Rice, all of which may be fortified in the same way as Birchermuesli, but which also permit the addition of margarine or butter. On frigid mornings, I sometimes make my Birchermuesli with boiling water from the tea pot.

Cheese: Deservedly a mountaineering staple because of its high energy output (almost 400 calories per three and one-half ounces for cheddar—divided about equally between protein and fat), cheese, nevertheless, produces little more than half the energy per ounce of margarine. And even relatively dry cheddar and Swiss have a very considerable (34 percent to 40 percent) water content. Soft cheese like jack, edam and blue are often more than 50 percent water. The driest cheeses are Italian Romano, parmesan, provoloni, Kasseri, etc.

Chocolate: Unsweetened chocolate provides more than 50 percent fat and 10 percent protein and yields about 40 percent more calories per ounce than plain sugar or sugar-type candies. Because of its high fat content, chocolate is far more difficult to digest than other candy and should not be eaten in large amounts during (or just before) strenuous activity. Many people fail to make this distinction between chocolate and other candy, and the result is often a queasy stomach instead of a burst of energy.

Cocoa mix: Though higher in carbohydrate than chocolate, cocoa mix still yields about 20 percent fat and protein and is therefore a comparatively powerful drink. Mixes like Swiss Miss which contain sugar are handiest. Some cocoa-coffee addicts make their mix at home with the proportions of cream and sugar they like.

Coffee: The old rituals of settling the swirling grounds with cold water or egg shell have disappeared with the emergence of freeze-dried coffee, and the saving in weight and preparation have been enormous. Maxim and Oregon Freeze Dry produce ideal products, except that sugar and milk powder must still be added by those of us who cannot drink coffee black.

Crackers: Hard biscuits and crackers, hard-pan, pilot biscuit, Triscuit and the like, though subject to breakage, are preferred by many to bread because of the reduced bulk and water content and freedom from slicing or spoilage. Wheat thins, rye saltines, Ryecrisp, Melba toast and Zweibach all have their fans. Fig Newtons, though heavy, have always been popular. My current favorite is Lillie's Muesli Fryit Biscuits which combine all the Birchermuesli ingredients into a hard, mildly-sweet all-purpose cookie-cracker.

Drinks (fruit): Wyler's lemonade and other flavors, and similar drinks by a number of imitators, come in foil envelopes weighing three and one-half ounces, including sugar, that make a quart of imitation, but refreshing lemonade with a few shakes of the poly bottle. Also popular are fruit juices made from citric powders, orange and grapefruit crystals, Tang, Kool Aid and Fizzies, although the last two require the addition of sugar. Artificially sweetened drinks are lighter and less bulky, but without sugar's quick energy. Canned fruit juices are popular on deserts or climbs where water is absent and must be carried, but should not be considered for ordinary backpacking.

Eggs (*omelet*): Powered eggs have come a long way since they gagged the foot soldier in World War II; they now are available from every food manufacturer in a variety of highly edible forms. Omelete fanciers and those for whom breakfast is not breakfast without eggs, can easily find a different featherweight dish for every morning of the week packed in foil or plastic, usually with ham or bacon bits. Calorie content is very substantial (usually upwards of 600 calories per three and one-half counces). Whole eggs, if they must be carried, should be broken into tripled plastic bags, the air squeezed out and the bags packed in wide-mouthed bottles. Even so, they must be kept cool and eaten promptly. Hardboiled eggs are 73.7 percent water, but I like them with salt on day hikes.

Honey: Although sticky and heavy, honey is only 17.2 percent water and offers fine flavor and quick energy (300 calories per three and one-half ounces). It may be used as a spread, dessert, syrup or frosting; it is most easily carried and squeezed from Gerry tubes.

Instant Breakfast: At face value, Instant Breakfast and its relatives like Tiger's Milk should be ideal for backpacking, but my friends and I have reluctantly abandoned them because they dependably produce diarrhea within an hour if we are hiking. I have not tried them on inactive layover days, but I suffer no ill effects in the city where fresh, rather than powdered milk is used.

Jam: Like honey, jam and jelly tend to be messy and should be packed in reusable Gerry tubes. They offer slightly fewer calories and are nearly 30 percent water, but are extremely welcome in the wilds.

Jello: Many people swear by jello as a drink, hot or cold, but the weight per serving is far higher than for other powdered fruit drinks, even though the calories per ounce of carbohydrate is high. Chopped dehydrated fruit mixes and vegetable mixes are packed in gelatin powder by Dri-Lite and are extremely useful dishes as salads or desserts where there is snow or cold water to assure prompt jelling.

Meat (fresh): For years I carried a fresh, juicy steak to broil the first night out. Gradually I discovered that it was my city-oriented association with steak, not the steak itself, that seemed appetizing. On that first night in the wilds, steak usually has less appeal for the weary hiker than soup, starchy stew and cold lemonade. Hamburgers and hot dogs are more satisfactory, but I prefer a freeze-dried casserole like OFD's Beef Almondine. In most climates, fresh meat (50 percent water) should be eaten within two days to prevent spoilage.

Meat (dried): Wilson's Meat Bar, though far less flavorful and fat rich than Bacon Bar, is useful for all meals, snacks and for emergency rations. Beef jerky is a tasty trail food, but cannot be reconstituted and is therefore unavailable for cooking. (It will flavor soup, but bouillon is better and cheaper.) Dry salami, though 30 percent water, yields 450 calories of fat and protein per three and one-half ounces and keeps very well unsliced inside its skin. Chipped beef spoils quite quickly as many people have learned to their sorrow.

Milk: Like dried eggs, dehydrated milk has gradually come to taste almost like the real thing, especially when allowed to stand 15 minutes, and served cold. Most convenient are four-ounce foil packages of Milkman instant, low-fat, dry milk product, which make a quart with a few shakes of the poly bottle. The flavor is better than that of whole, skim or non-fat milk products. A few drops of vanilla or a little coffee or cocoa mix help mask the slightly artificial flavor. Malted milk powder and milkshake mixes are favored by some, but the latter, including sugar, seems excessively heavy. Milkman probably yields over 400 calories per three and one-half ounces.

Molasses: This raw, crude liquid sugar, though nearly 25 percent water, quickly converts to energy and is used like honey or jam by those who like the strong sweet flavor. And a teaspoon or two works beautifully as a gentle natural food laxative—often necessary after a change from city fare to a steady diet of low bulk, dehydrated food.

Nuts: Dried, roasted, salted nuts (almonds, walnuts, pecans, peanuts, etc.) contain very little water and yield 525 to 700 calories per three and one-half ounces, divided roughly into two parts fat and one part each of protein and carbohydrate. Nuts are an ideal snack and a perfect complement to high carbohydrate candy, fruit and bread. Peanut butter, though sticky, is a fine source of protein and fat when it can be carried in the handy Gerry squeeze tube.

Oil: For frying pancakes or fish, oil is sometimes carried in addition to margarine or butter. Salad fanciers also take it, along with vinegar, for dressing. A few drops of Vegalene in frying pans keeps food from sticking. Weight-conscious hikers, noting that oil is unexcelled in number of calories (884 per three and one-half ounces), have tried to subsist on periodically ingested oil capsules and little else.

Pancakes: I shudder when I think how many hours I have spent cooking pancakes in the hot morning sun and then cleaning out the gluey batter pot. Pancakes, in my view, belong to the dark ages of backpacking on the basis of preparation alone. They do, however, provide an adequate source of carbohydrate, especially when sweetened.

Pemmican: The legendary wonder food on which the mountain men of the early West lived almost exclusively, takes some getting used to and is therefore not ideal as a steady diet for recreational backpackers on comparatively short trips. A balanced diet, strong on carbohydrates, will produce more energy and contentment. True pemmican is half lean, dried meat, half cooked animal fat, with the two mashed together into a paste. Recipes for pemmican and jerky are widely available.

Potatoes: Like beans, potatoes are a favorite base and source of bulk in one-pot dinners. Instant potato powders easily produce genuine-tasting mashed potatoes, and the leftovers can be fried for breakfast.

Potato cubes are great in stews, hash and french-fried.

Puddings: Satisfying desserts that contrast well with sweet trail snacks can be a problem in the wilds where sweets are craved. Puddings (like Jello Instant) can be bought cheaply in the markets and shaken with milk powder in a plastic bag (later burned); since they set promptly without regard to temperature, they are a boon to backpackers. Mountaineering shops offer a number of excellent puddings, as well as strudels, cobblers, pies and cheesecakes.

Spices: Amateur cooks tend to know very little about spices and would be well advised to experiment at home, not on the trail. Too much of the wrong spice can seriously impair the edibility of dinner. Judicious use of spices, however, can sometimes transform unfortunate concoctions into savory eating. Spice Islands' Fines Herbs, a mixture of thyme, oregano, sage, rosemary, marjoram and basil, is a safe all-purpose seasoning when used at the rate of half a teaspoon for four servings. And, unless I add it at home, I take a mixture of three parts cinnamon to one of nutmeg for applesauce and other fruits.

Salts: Individual shakers for various salts and peppers are a nuisance to open and close in the dark. After struggling with various clever designs, I have returned to a single shaker loaded with two parts salt to one each of pepper and onion, garlic and celery salt. This all-purpose seasoning is just as good on eggs or stew as on trout; my companions have yet to complain. With my salt mix in one shaker and Spice Islands, Fines Herbs in another, I am well equipped with flavor.

Miscellaneous starches: Beans, potatoes and pancakes, spaghetti, noodles, rice and macaroni form the heart (and provide the bulk) of a backpacker's casserole. Kraft Dinner, which served me in Boy Scout days, is still a good bet, especially when cooked with a packet of freeze-dried chicken, slivered almonds, sliced mushrooms and the above mentioned herb mix. Pre-cooked rice is the quickest of starches to prepare, but pasta has more protein and a shade more calories.

Vegetables: Few backpackers will bother with a side dish of hot vegetables; the flavor and calorie output (around 300 per three and one-half ounces) fail to justify the extra preparation. As components of the one-pot dinner, however, vegetables are indispensable. In order of preference, I like dehydrated mushrooms (check Oriental food stores), onions, celery, carrots and peas and tomato flakes. I also enjoy chopped, mixed vegetables in gelatin (Dri Lite's Sierra Salad). Green salad addicts take along oil and vinegar to make rehydrated vegetable salad, hoping they can find wild onion and miner's lettuce. There are doubtless a good many delectable dishes of which I know nothing.

Pleasure Packing Food List
(two adults, four days)

Brand	Quantity—Item—Packaging—Serving	Wt. (in ounces) Pkg. for Carrying	Total Cost
Tea Kettle	(1)Beef Almondine—foil pan—serves 2	4.1	$1.25
Tea Kettle	(1)Tuna a la Neptune—foil pan—serves 2	4.4	1.50
Tea Kettle	(1)Turkey Tetrazzini—foil pan—serves 2	4.0	1.25
Tea Kettle	(1)Chunk Chicken—foil pan—serves 2	4.5	1.50
Co-op	(2)Sliced Mushrooms—poly bag—serves 2	0.6	1.10
Maggi	(1)Oxtail Soupmix—foil bag—serves 2	3.0	.30
Maggi	(1)Mushroom Soupmix—foil bag—serves 2	2.7	.30

Knorr	(1)Leek Soupmix—poly bag—serves 2	3.5	.40
Knorr	(1)Green Pea Soupmix—poly bag—serves 2	3.6	.40
Richmoor	(1)Cottage Cheese—poly bag—serves 4	3.1	.95
Richmoor	(2)Applesauce—poly bag—serves 4	9.2	1.20
Richmoor	(2)Fruit Cocktail—poly bag—serves 4	12.2	1.80
Mtn. House	(1)Strawberries—foil bag—serves 4	1.2	1.00
Mtn. House	(1)Ice Cream—foil bag—serves 4	2.1	1.10
—	1 lb. Butter—alum. can	18.0	.85
Familia	¾ of 2-lb. box—Birchermeusli—poly bags	24.3	1.50
Wilsons	(2)Bacon Bar—foil bag	6.4	2.20
—	2 lb. loaf Pumpernickle bread—poly bags	32.3	.85
—	Gorp—poly bags: 1/3 dry raisins		
	1/3 salted almonds		
	1/3 M & M's	32.3	1.50
Atkinsons	1½ bars—Mint Bar—poly bag	9.1	.75
Atkinsons	1½ bars—Rum Butter Candy—poly bag	9.1	.75
—	Cheese—Gouda ¾ lb.		
	Cheddar ¾ lb. alum. can	26.0	1.25
—	Salt & pepper mix—metal shaker	2.0	.50
	Spice mix—metal shaker	2.0	.40
Milkman	1 qt. pkg.—Instant Low-fat Dry Milk—		
	poly squeeze bottle	4.5	.25
—	Sugar—poly bottle	9.0	.25
Wylers	(6)Lemonade Mix—foil bags	19.8	.90
—	(12)Tea bags—English & Oriental—		
	alum. can	1.5	.50
Richmoor	(1)Toasted Coconut Pudding—poly bag—	5.7	.50
	serves 4		
—	Trout mix—poly bag	2.0	.25
—	Strawberry jam—squeeze bottle	8.4	.40
—	8 sticks Beef jerky—poly bag	4.2	2.15
—	8 dried pineapple rings—poly bag	8.0	.85
		282.8*	$30.65

*Total food weight includes 17 ounces of packaging.

Recipes

[*Ultimately, every backpacker misses the cozy city kitchen he left behind. The dishes it bakes, fries, poaches and broils are too heavy and perishable, and take centuries to reproduce in the woods. Robert Wood has suggested that practically anything packs on a brief and easy excursion. But for the longer and semi-rugged expedition, the best idea is to supplement your normal diet with treats such as the following standard calorie-studded recipes to be made at home and packed out. Cook them all in quantities and they will supply several trips. My thanks go to Appalachian and Adirondack mountain club chefs who have perfected and offered them for use in this book. Ed.*]

Art's Granola

Mix:

    4 cups rolled oats
    1 cup raw wheat germ
    2 cups chopped nuts (raw cashews and almonds are great)
    1 cup sunflower seeds
    ¾ cup sesame seeds
    1 cup ground, roasted soybeans
    ½ cup bran
    1 cup shredded, unsweetened cocoanut

Heat:

    ½ cup oil (safflower, soy or sesame)
    ½ cup honey
    ½ teaspoon vanilla

Combine all ingredients and spread on oiled cookie sheet. Bake at 300° for about 10 to 11 minutes, stirring frequently. Remove and add raisins to taste. Improvise as much as you like, eliminating or adding to the list of dry goods. Granola will keep for several months providing it is stored in an air-tight container.

Judy's Mountain Bars

Mix:

> 2 cups crushed vanilla wafers
> 1½ cups finely chopped nuts (your favorites will do)
> 2 cups powdered sugar
> ½ lb. finely chopped dates
> 1 cup finely chopped dried apricots
> 1 cup seedless yellow raisins

Combine separately:

> 2 tablespoons light corn syrup
> 6-8 tablespoons honey
> ½ teaspoon vanilla or maple flavoring

Combine all ingredients in a large bowl. Add liquids and knead to mix. A tablespoon of water helps if the mixture resists easy kneading. Press and shape into small log rolls about two by five inches. Roll in powdered sugar and wrap in plastic. No cooking is required. Store in refrigerator until you're ready to pack up.

Gary's Walnut Sticks

> 2 cups whole wheat flour
> ½ teaspoon salt

2 tablespoons brown sugar
4 tablespoons oil or melted butter or margarine
$^1/_3$ cup finely chopped walnuts
$^1/_3$ cup cold water
$^1/_3$ cup honey

Mix the dry ingredients and drip oil over them. Mix well and pour in water and honey. Blend into a stiff dough. Knead on board and press out with hands until one-quarter-inch thick. Cut into one-half-inch by three-inch pieces. Place on a greased cookie sheet and bake for one-half hour at 325°. Turn over once during baking. Store.

Guy and Laura's Logan Bread

1¾ cups water
2 pounds whole wheat flour
$^2/_3$ cup melted shortening
$^2/_3$ cup sugar
¾ cup honey
¾ cup dark molasses
¼ cup milk
½ teaspoon salt
1 teaspoon baking powder
1 cup chopped nuts

Mix dry ingredients together and add milk, water, honey and molasses. Fill two or three small loaf pans two-thirds full and bake at 300° for one hour. Cool loaves enough to remove from pans and replace on rack in oven, letting loaves dry out for several hours at very low heat with door ajar. When the bread is as hard as a rock it is done. Cool, slice and store in refrigerator.

Gorp

> 2 12-ounce packages of semi-sweet chocolate bits
> 2 8-ounce packages of butterscotch bits
> ½ cup honey
> ½ cup yellow raisins
> ½ cup chopped, dried apricots
> ½ cup shredded coconut
> ½ cup cashews
> ½ cup walnuts
> ½ cup wheat germ
> ½ cup uncooked oatmeal
> ½ cup Birchermuesli

Melt chips in top of double boiler, adding honey. Pour over rest of dry ingredients in large bowl. Mix well. Pour mixture into greased pans and cool. Cut or break into hand-sized chunks. Wrap tightly in plastic. Store in refrigerator until needed. (This recipe may be substituted by the simple, uncooked mixture of M&Ms, Spanish peanuts and raisins.)

The Wilderness Kitchen

From *Pleasure Packing*.
By Robert S. Wood

For a majority of backpackers, wilderness cooking must be classified as work—work which hunger and weariness, darkness and wind, can easily elevate to the level of misery. Comfort in the kitchen often depends on starting dinner while the sun is still high—after a healthy snack to ward off approaching hunger. It certainly depends on the selection of tasty, easy-to-prepare food. But it also depends to a large extent on carrying good cooking gear and knowing how to use it.

The first decision the cook must face is whether or not to carry a stove. Twenty years ago stoves were eccentric devices used only by serious climbers bivouacked above timberline. Nowadays, they are much less eccentric and commonly used by backpackers. For many years, even when I was climbing, it did not occur to me to carry a stove. Now, I would not think of going off without one. I like a big campfire to sit beside in the evening as much as anyone. I feel deprived if I have to do without one. But the scant wood supply in the high country is fast disappearing, and my conscience is easier if I cook on a stove. Firewood has grown so scarce in heavily traveled areas that wilderness managers may soon ban wood fires altogether and require all parties to carry stoves.

But stoves do more than conserve scarce firewood. They provide dependable, even, controllable heat and a liberation from greasy, soot-blackened pots. (In my pre-stove days I generally returned from a weekend trip looking like an overworked chimney-sweep.) The convenience of a stove allows the indulgence of a craving for hot soup at lunch or a cup of tea in mid-afternoon. Instead of digging in the ashes to rebuild a collapsed fireplace, or blackening fresh rocks, one can perch the stove conveniently at waist height on a sheltered ledge or boulder and cook without stooping or squatting. Lastly, there is no fire to feed feverishly, no leaping flames to subdue, no smoke to fight and no fallout of ashes in the tea.

Stoves, of course, have disadvantages, too. The small single burner means only one dish can be cooked at a time, and the first course will not stay warm while the next is cooking (except with a cooker). The small concentrated circle of heat makes cooking on large surfaces (frying pancakes or trout) difficult. No stove works well, if at all, if not well sheltered from wind. A shelter must be built if none can be found. Then there is the fiddling with fuel, the assembling, priming and preheating, and, of course, the weight of the stove and fuel. But I view the lack of a second burner as a blessing rather than a limitation; it forces me to employ one-dish dinners or eat in courses, which enormously simplifies meal planning and automatically rules out fussy, difficult-to-prepare city-type meals.

A good many backpackers have never purchased a stove because they look so intricate, because they are rumored to explode or simply because the catalogs and shops offer such a bewildering assortment. With as many as two dozen models to choose from, how does one know which is best? The guidelines that follow should reassure the buyer as to intricacy and safety and help him narrow the field to not more than two or three models.

Types of Fuels

Stoves, first of all, may be divided on the basis of fuels. Kerosene (or coal oil), though slightly less potent, ounce for ounce, than gasoline, is the cheapest, most generally available fuel. It produces more odor and soot than gasoline but it does not explode. Since it is difficult to light without a wick, kerosene stoves normally require a more volatile priming fuel (alcohol, gasoline, etc.) for the necessary preheating.

White gasoline or Coleman fuel, though of maximum potency, is capable of exploding. Unlike kerosene, spilled gasoline lights readily on clothes or hands. Its cost is reasonable, it is generally available, and it tends to be clean smelling, oil-free and produces less soot than kerosene. Preheating is necessary, but since white gas lights readily, a separate priming fuel is not required. Though instructions call for "un-leaded" gas, the "no-lead" and "low-lead" gases contain additives that make them unsuitable for stoves.

Butane and propane are compressed gases sold in pressurized metal cartridges. The liability of explosion is low providing used cartridges are not thrown in the fire. Both fuels are considerably less potent than kerosene or gasoline, comparatively expensive and the least readily available. But both are clean and soot free. Since butane and propane stoves require no filling, priming or preheating, they are unquestionably the easiest and most convenient of backpacking stoves.

Despite a relatively low heat output, alcohol for many years was the traditional stove fuel, due largely to its cheapness and availability in Europe. (Virtually all stoves are of European origin.) But with the development of butane and propane as stove fuels, it has sunk to fourth place and need no longer be considered. Sterno (canned heat), heat tabs, and even candles, can be used to cook food, but these fuels, like alcohol, are too inefficient for serious consideration.

Kerosene and white gasoline stoves work on nearly identical principles; in fact, conversion kits are available for some models. Both fuels must reach the burner in a vaporized (gaseous) state before the stove will function properly. Fuel is vaporized as it passes through a chamber called a generator located between the fuel tank and the burner. The necessary heating is accomplished by filling a small bowl just beneath the generator (called the spirit cup) with an easily lighted primer fuel (white gas, alcohol, benzene, lighter fluid) and lighting it—with the stove turned off.

Flames envelop the generator for perhaps half a minute to preheat it. Just before the flames die, the operator turns on the gas. If the generator is hot enough, the fuel will vaporize and the vapor will be lighted by the last of the flaming primer. Once the stove is lighted, heat from the burner keeps the generator working.

The process is considerably simpler than it sounds. After an hour's experimentation in the backyard, most purchasers of a new gasoline or kerosene stove will be sufficiently experienced to take it on a trip. Those people unwilling to master the procedure can join the growing thousands who rely on effortlessly operated butane and propane stoves.

Kerosene expands less than gasoline when heated and therefore all kerosene stoves have small hand pumps to force the fuel to the burner. They do not, however, have valves to control the flow of fuel. Flame height and intensity are controlled solely by pump pressure. Extra pumping keeps the flame at maximum; opening the air vent reduces the pressure and therefore the flame. But a low flame (for simmering or warming) tends to be difficult to maintain.

Kerosene stoves are favored for expeditions because fuel purity is not critical, kerosene is available in almost any country, and the stove will not explode no matter how it is handled. Expeditionary technique circumvents the need for a separate priming fuel by capitalizing on the fact that raw kerosene will light if fed through a wick. A twisted square of toilet paper placed in the kerosene-filled spirit cup provides an easily lighted wick. Kerosene stoves are equipped with either 'silent' or 'roarer' burners; the fiercer flame of the latter is slightly more resistant to wind. In below zero weather, kerosene stoves perform especially well, largely because fuel pressure can be maintained by pumping.

The smaller white gas stoves have no pumps; they

depend on the heat transferred from the generator and burner to the fuel tank to expand the highly volatile fuel and force it toward the burner. To provide room for pressure buildup, the tank must never be filled more than three quarters full. With these stoves, preheating must accomplish two things: vaporizing the fuel (as in the kerosene stoves) and generating pressure in the fuel tank. Spring-loaded pressure-relief safety valves located in the tank caps protect against explosion, but occasionally are sources of pressure leaks.

Since white gas lights well, neither priming fuel or improvised wicks are required. The manufacturer suggests that, with the vent closed and the valve open, the warmth of one's hands wrapped around the tank will develop enough pressure to force gas out through the burner and down into the spirit cup. Of course, if the stove has been sitting in the sun with the valve open, hand temperature will not warm it, and this method fails. Increases in altitude also create pressure which causes the gas to flow; by filling the stove at sea level one is assured of pressure at the first use in the mountains.

The cooling of a stove after use creates a vacuum in the tank. So does a decrease in altitude. The vacuum must be relieved by momentarily loosening the tank cap or the stove cannot function. The surest way to extract gas from the stove to fill the spirit cup under all conditions is with an eye dropper. Plastic droppers, from old medicine bottles or the drugstore, tuck comfortably in the housing of most stoves. A still quicker method is to put one's mouth to the tank opening and blow.

Butane and propane come in pressurized cartridges or tanks. Empties must be carried out, and most butane cartridges must not be disengaged until they are entirely empty. Butane and propane are notoriously poor in exceptional cold, when tank pressure drops to cause sluggish flow and the lower temperature of the flame becomes apparent. Butane is worse than propane, but I have more than once used a Bluet S-200 in the snow, when the temperature was ten degrees below freezing, with perfectly satisfactory results. Lighting butane and propane stoves is no different from lighting a kitchen stove that has no pilot. One simply holds a lighted match to the burner an instant *before* turning on the gas.

For lighting kerosene stoves, the rountine goes as follows: (1) open vent in tank cap; (2) fill and light spirit cup to preheat stoves; (3) just before flames die, close vent in tank cap, and (4) quickly take two or three quick strokes on the pump; (5) if burner fails to ignite from the spirit cup flame, light it with the match set aside for that purpose. If the flame burns blue the stove is ready to use; if it burns yellow—signifying raw fuel rather than vapor—open the vent to shut off the fuel and preheat again.

For pumpless gasoline stoves the lighting procedure is slightly different: (1) open, then close, the tank cap to relieve any vacuum in the tank; (2) after closing the shut-off valve, fill the spirit cup and light; (3) just before the flame dies, open the shut-off valve wide— only a quarter turn. (4) If burner fails to ignite from the spirit cup flame, light it with the match held ready for that purpose. If the burner flame is blue the stove is ready to use; if the flame burns yellow, shut off the valve; when flames begin to die, open the valve again and hope for a blue flame. Continue this process until vaporized fuel burns a constant blue.

Types of Stoves

Stoves may be further divided on the basis of size, weight and heating capacity. Most fall into one of two classifications: backpacker stoves capable of cooking for one to three people in pots of up to two quarts, and expeditionary stoves built to handle groups of four or more and heat pots of two to five quarts. Backpacker stoves usually weigh one to two pounds, while expeditionary models run two to four pounds. Two burner stoves weigh six to twelve pounds.

The number of models to choose from shrinks considerably with the discovery that the Primus, Svea, and Optimus stoves are all made by the same company and are often identical except for name. For instance, the Primus (P) 71 is the same, except for label, as the Optimus (O) 80. The dozen stoves listed below are the most popular, most readily available I know. There is no "best" stove. The best choice for any individual depends on the importance he chooses to assign such considerations as weight, convenience, burning time, heating capacity, price, etc. All gasoline stoves listed have safety pressure relief valves to prevent explosion and should be considered safe in the hands of adults familiar with their operation.

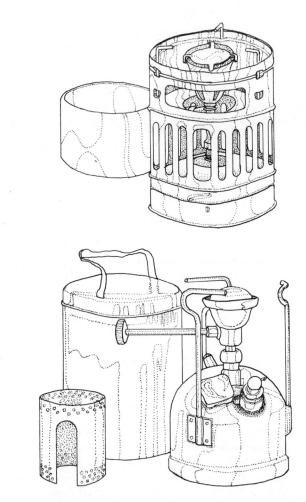

Top: Svea backpacker stove. Bottom: Phoebus expedition-ary stove and carrying container.

Backpacker Stoves

P-71 (0-80). Probably best known and most popular model, this pumpless gasoline stove weighs 20 ounces, burns well over an hour, comes in a rectangular box-stand-windscreen, and costs $9-12.

Bluet S-200. This French butane burner is the easiest, simplest stove to operate, weighing 19 ounces and costing $9-10 (including vital windscreen). Ten-ounce cartridges burn two to three hours and cost $4-5 per case of six. Not powerful enough for heavy or winter use.

Svea 123. The lightest gasoline stove at 18 ounces, the pumpless Svea comes with tiny pot, gripper and two-piece windscreen for $10-13. Burning time and convenience rate slightly behind the P-71, but wind resistance is better.

P(O)8R. This newer pumpless gasoline stove offers a self-cleaner, gravity gas feed to the burner and a low center of gravity. Burning time ranks between the P-71 and Svea 123. Comparatively heavy at 27 ounces, the stove costs $12-14.

P (O) 96L. Equipped with a pump, this kerosene stove with silent burner comes in a box and must be assembled for operation. At 32 ounces it is the heaviest, safest, longest burning (two hours), and the cheapest to operate stove in its class. Cost is $15.

Primus Grasshopper. A 30-ounce propane tank makes the third leg of this easy-to-operate, stable 12-ounce stove. Tanks burn six hours, cost $1.50 each and may be removed when partly full. Stove costs $8-9.

[*Editor's Note: I've recently tested the excellent new Backpacker Stove, Model 9, manufactured by Mountain Safety Research (631 South 96th Street, Seattle, Washington 98108). This stove is destined to be a winner. Weighing less than one pound it can burn nine ounces of fuel per hour, thus having double the output of most backpacker stoves. It will melt snow to make one quart of water in three minutes, and heat it to boiling in another three. The tiny "sparker wheel" eliminates the need for matches. Your Sigg fuel bottle acts as the tank for the stove. The price is about $12.*]

Expeditionary Stoves

P (O) 111B. A larger version of the 8R equipped with a pump, this powerful three-and-one-half pound gasoline stove costs $20-22.

P-210L (0-000L). This intermediate-sized kerosene stove with roarer burner is the lightest in its class. Collapsible (meaning assembly is required), it burns two hours, weighs two and one-quarter pounds and costs $13-15.

P-100 (0-48L). A larger version of the 210L with silent burner, this stove is collapsible, weighs three and one-quarter pounds, costs $10-14 and burns four hours on a quart filling of kerosene.

Phoebus 625. This powerful Austrian gasoline stove (which can burn leaded as well as white gas) burns one and one-half hours, weighs two and three-quarter pounds and costs $14.

Two-burner Expeditionary Stoves

0-22B. A two-burner version of the 111B with pump and built-in cleaner, this gas-burning stove measures 15 inches wide, burns one and one-half hours, weighs six and three-quarter pounds and costs $30.

P-2049 (0-870). There is some variation between the two models of this deluxe, instant-lighting propane stove. Both use the same disposable tank as the Grasshopper, or any American-made refillable tank. Stoves weigh nine and one-half to eleven pounds, cost $34-40.

Gasoline and kerosene stoves require the purchase of either aluminum bottles ($1.50-2.50) or fuel flasks ($2.00-2.50), both of which come in pint and quart sizes. The flat flasks with pouring spouts pack more conveniently, although the mesh screen must be punched out in order to insert a polyethylene funnel which contains its own filter screen (35¢). The bottles are more likely to leak than the flasks. Plastic bottles are not suitable for fuel. Heavy cloth and plastic bags are useful for packing stoves, especially where a box is not included (or has been discarded). Also needed is a rag for cleaning both stove and cook, and the proper stove cleaning needle.

One of the prime disadvantages of stoves—keeping the first course warm while the second is cooking—can be overcome by using one of two cookers made by Sigg. These ingenious five-piece combinations, beginning at the bottom and working up, consist of a two piece stand-windscreen, two pans stacked one above the other, and a lid-pan. While a casserole cooks in the bottom pan, the soup, just above it, keeps warm. Or, by filling the lower pan with water, one produces the controlled, even heat of a double boiler above.

The Sigg Tourist, built solely for use with the Svea 123, offers two and one-half and three and one-half pint pots, nests with the stove inside to measure only eight and one-quarter by five inches, weighs·two and one-quarter pounds and cost $18-20. The cooker alone weighs one and one-half pounds and costs $10. The Edelweiss comes in three-pot sizes: one quart (solo), one and a half quarts (two man) or two quarts (expeditionary). In each case, both pots are the same size. With one-and-a-half-quart pots and the regular stove, the cooker weighs two and a half pounds. Cookers are somewhat specialized items and are most valuable in winter (for snow melting), in wind, and for expeditionary use.

Grills

The alternative to carrying a stove, of course, is to build one out of native material and gather native fuel to fire it. Ease, efficiency, and effectiveness are generally doubled by carrying a small grill. The smallest and lightest, sold by Camp Trails, measures four and a half by fifteen and a half inches, is made of welded tubular steel, weighs only four ounces, cleans easily, comes in a fabric case and costs $6. It is easily mounted on a modest rock fireplace and will accommodate two carefully placed pots.

Still easier to mount on an uneven surface is the Gerry grill, a-five-by-fifteen inch U-shaped stainless steel rod that weighs six ounces and costs $1.75. A conventional nine-by-thirteen inch steel grill weighs eight ounces, costs $2 and needs a cloth or durable plastic bag for a cover. A Swiss nine-by-ten-inch, one-and one-quarter-pound grill from Co-op has seven-inch legs, costs only $1.50 and avoids blackening rocks.

There are larger grills, some with legs, for ex-peditionary use, at weights of two pounds and more. The cheapest grills are oven and refrigerator shelves and broiler racks from used appliance and secondhand stores. The campcraft books are full of fireplace de-signs and ingenious ways to suspend pots, most of which are far too much trouble for the backpacker, who is likely to choose a campsite late in the day and move on again in the morning.

My favorite cooking fireplace design is the half-dugout. There are two advantages: smaller, flatter rocks can be used to insure a more stable structure, and the fire is easier to light and easier to protect from wind. If I were faced with rebuilding a heap of blackened rocks into an efficient cookstove—assuming the loca-tion is appropriate and safe—I would first clear a circle about four feet across and sort through the rocks in hopes of finding a matched pair about the size and shape of bricks. Such rocks are never to be found, of course, so I settle for the best I can find (concave upper sur-faces are better than convex).

Using the direction of the breeze, the lay of the land and the pattern of branches on nearby trees to deter-mine the path of the prevailing wind, I place my rocks parallel to that path and also to each other—about a foot apart. On the downward end, I place a larger rock (or rocks) to form a chimney, so the resulting structure forms a squat "U." Then, using a sharp rock fragment as a trowel, I excavate about four inches of earth and charcoal from inside the pit. Now I am ready to place my lightweight Camp Trails or Gerry grill across the opening, supporting it on the two "bricks" as close as possible to the chimney. Care must be taken to see that it is solid and will not slide or wobble—or the dinner may end up in the fire!

I like to set my grill about two inches above ground level and six inches above the bottom of the firepit, but the proportions must sometimes be altered. On a windy day, I dig deeper and sometimes have to block the windward end with rocks to control the draft. Where there are no rocks at all and the grill sits directly on the ground, the firepit must be deeper still. Inexperienced stove builders invariably build too large a firebox and set the grill much too high. Increasing grill height from six to ten inches probably triples the volume of wood needed to cook dinner. Small fires are easier on the cook, easier on the wood supply, and heat is more easily regulated. Expert backpackers emulate the Indian and try to cook their food with the smallest fire possible.

Lighting the Fire

The traditional structures for kindling a camp fire are the lean-to (match-sized twigs leaned against a larger piece) or the tepee (a cone of twigs). The most common mistake among fire builders is not having good quantities of dry twigs, tinder, toilet paper and burnables of all sizes within easy reach before the first match is struck. I usually start with three squares of toilet paper loosely crumpled, cover that with a handful of dry pine needles, then build a tepee of the smallest, lightest twigs by tilting against the paper from all sides.

After carefully leaning half a dozen finger-sized sticks against the pile, I crouch low to block the prevailing breeze (if it is strong, I block the entrance to the fire pit temporarily with rocks) and thrust a lighted kitchen match beneath the paper with one hand while I shelter the match from stray zephyrs with the other. Once the paper is lighted, I add the match to the tepee and use both hands to shelter the embryo blaze until all the wood has caught. Care must be taken not to put the fire out by knocking down the tepee with fresh wood, by skipping the intermediate sized sticks and adding heavy branches, or by letting the tepee burn up before adding fresh wood.

Matches: There are differences of opinion, not surprisingly, about matches and lighting fires. Some people carry only paper book matches, others (like myself) take only wooden kitchen matches; wooden safety matches that can only be lighted on the box are a bother in the summer but indispensable in the winter when snow covers the rocks. I have used commercially waterproofed and windproofed matches for difficult conditions and emergency kits and found them excellent, though expensive. Some people dip their matches in parafin or candle wax; others laboriously paint the heads with fingernail polish.

Still others carry all their matches in waterproof matchboxes. My simpler, but probably less secure strategy is to stuff lots of matches in all the water-proof outside pockets of my pack. Another dozen are inside my watertight first aid kit. The climate of the California summer Sierra does not seem to me to demand a waterproof matchbox, and I have never carried one. A handful in a securely closed plastic bag makes a decent enough emergency supply.

In wet country or for winter mountaineering, fire starters are sometimes worth the weight (both for open fires and kerosene stoves). I like "Fire Starter" made by the Bernzomatic Corp. because the styrofoam-like sheets are almost weightless, crumble into any size and pack easily in plastic bags. A seven ounce package costs 60¢. I know some people who disdain matches and carry cigarette lighters and a can of fluid, giving their tinder a squirt of lighter fluid to help things along. And I travel the deserts of the South-west with an old prospector who habitually kicks together some brush and wood, douses it with a cup full of gasoline, and nonchalantly tosses a lighted match over his shoulder as he walks away.

Cook Kit

Twenty years ago, a friend and I assembled a back-packing cook kit very simply. From the pots and pans bin at the Goodwill Store, we first selected the smallest practical aluminum pot (about three cups) and found a lid. Then we hunted down two more pots and lids so that the three would nest with the lids on. At home we sawed off the handles, punched holes and added wire bails, then we fitted a drawstring into a flour sack to hold the kit. For frying we bought a twelve inch square of eight-inch sheet aluminum and turned up the edges slightly in a vise to form a lip. Our set was completed with aluminum pliers, aluminum pie tins, aluminum measuring cups (with the handles taped) and Goodwill silverware.

At that time it was impossible to buy a comparable kit in mountaineering shops at any price. Today there are a number of good cook kits on the market for small groups and a variety of good pots, pans and kettles. But thoughtful backpackers will still be well advised to devise combinations suited to the particular requirements of their menus. And the Goodwill stores and supermarkets still offer bargains and a variety not to be found in mountaineering shops.

Ideal pot design depends somewhat on whether a stove or open fire is to be used. For stoves, pots need small, perfectly flat bottoms of small diameter for maximum stability. The thicker the bottom, the less likely that the small concentration of heat will cause scorching or burning. Heat is not a problem at the handle, bail or lid. Pots for an open fire can be any shape and uneven on the bottom, but lids should be easily removed and handles or bails must be usable when flames envelop them. All pots should have rounded edges and no grooves or seams or cracks to trap food and dirt.

Miscellaneous utensil requirements range all the way from the couple who carry a single large spoon and jack knife between them to parties in which each person has his own knife, fork and spoon, wears a sheath knife, and carries additional utensils for the cook. Obviously, the larger the party, the more cooking gear required. Knife, fork and spoon sets of stainless steel and aluminum are widely available for from 50¢ to $2.50. Old kitchen silverware or Goodwill or dime-store offerings weigh slightly more but are easier to handle.

Mixing pans are a luxury that backpackers must forego. Properly planned menus avoid nearly all special mixing of ingredients; and unavoidable mixing should be easily managed in deep plates, large cups, pan lids, plastic bottles and polyethylene bags.

Most experienced backpackers using easily pre-pared dishes forget about table knives and forks and carry only an extra-large spoon apiece and a good-sized simple pocketknife. In addition, the cook needs an aluminum soup ladle with detachable insulated handle (Co-op, 50¢) for cleanliness and to insure an equitable division of the stew. I sometimes carry a large extremely useful hinged aluminum fork-spoon combination; other times I combine ladle and spoon in one huge (11 inch) solid nylon spoon that weighs one ounce and costs 50¢.

A knife is an absolute necessity in the wilds. Some hikers are not secure without a sheath knife, and though these commonly weigh a heavy half pound, one per party is often useful. The smallest sizes are well worth-while Swiss army knives with their endless assort-ment of gadgety blades also have their adherents. But thoughtful, weight conscious backpackers usually prefer a good-sized, good quality pocketknife with one or two blades. The knife I like best has a big, comparatively blunt tipped blade suitable for spreading crackers and cutting salami—and a shorter, slimmer sharply pointed blade for cleaning trout. Brightly colored handles help prevent loss. If I am traveling alone, I put a tiny single-bladed jack knife in the outside pack pocket containing the first aid kit.

Pot grippers or tongs or pliers may be needed to lift lids and serve as pot handles. Aluminum pot grippers weigh little more than an ounce and cost about 50¢, but the handle is too short for an open fire and the lack of a spring makes operation awkward. Longer, stronger spring-loaded steel grippers of similar design weigh a quarter of a pound. Neither fits all pots. I prefer cast aluminum hot pot tongs (three ounces, $1.25) which, being a large pair of pliers, is a more versatile tool. Many people find an old padded cloth pot holder indispensable.

Every backpacker needs a cup, and the more experienced choose large ones and dispense with plates. The traditional pie pan, whether of steel, aluminum or foil, cools too quickly, is hard to hold and a nuisance to clean. Pan lids offer the same disadvantages, and paper plates, though cleaning is eliminated, are more difficult to hold and do not retain heat. Of course a big cup cannot satisfactorily replace a plate for a city-style meal, and strangers to backpacking may view the lack of a plate as uncivilized and crude, but eating from a cup happens to be eminently practical and efficient for a dinner which proceeds by courses from two cups of soup to two cups of stew to a cup of applesauce or pudding and finally to many cups of tea, coffee, lemonade or water. The cup needs only to be wiped and rinsed clean between courses. I always carry a one ounce aluminum measuring cup as a spare and for mixing.

Using a cup for a plate is especially appropriate when cooking on a stove, because dinner (or any other meal) is only ready one course at a time. Since food cooked at high altitudes never reaches temperatures common at sea level, and since it cools with amazing speed in even the warmest breeze, this arrangement is the most effective for getting hot food to the stomach before it can cool. Cup-style eating may be difficult to appreciate until one has labored long and hard to prepare three dishes simultaneously on a wood fire, then discovered with the first bite that the plate and all its contents were stone cold.

For backpackers not yet ready to eat from their cups—or who cannot abide an oily film from the stew in their tea—a small, deep, unbreakable, boilable polyethylene bowl (25¢, one and one-half ounces) is a greatly superior alternative to metal or paper plates.

When it comes to food storage, plastic bottles, bags, boxes, canisters and jars have all but replaced containers of all other materials. Many containers are so commonly available in markets that some mountaineering shops no longer bother to stock them. I make a habit of cruising the kitchenware sections of supermarkets to hunt for merchandise adaptable to backpacking.

In choosing plastic containers, I shun all but screw-on caps likely to form a watertight seal and avoid corners and recessed seams that will trap food and be hard to clean. And I buy wide-mouthed containers whenever there is a choice. Most big mountaineering suppliers offer small and wide-mouth pint and quart bottles as well as a variety of small ones. The same is true of wide-mouth jars, although markets tend to be a more dependable source. Some of my best containers are recycled. When I spot an unusual bottle around the house, I wait until it is empty and then boil it out and add it to my collection.

Refillable squeeze tubes, made by Gerry (three for $1.25) are invaluable for leakproof, easy dispensing of jam, jelly, catsup, butter, peanut butter—anything of similar consistency. I regularly half-fill two with about a quarter pound each of jelly and jam for use on crackers at lunch. The tubes boil out easily between trips and have yet to leak when properly assembled.

I use a squat, wide-mouth screw-top icebox jar of appropriate capacity (they come in half a dozen sizes) for sugar because it fills easily, is hard to overturn, and because I spoon rather than pour my sugar. Many people who like to pour their sugar and do not object to filling with a funnel, prefer a small-mouthed bottle. Powdered milk presents a more difficult problem. When the wind is blowing the only way to avoid considerable spillage is to squirt the powder from a plastic catsup squirter bottle (available at large supermarkets) directly into the cup.

My squirter holds enough to make a quart. The only positive cap I have found for the spout—to withstand the pressures inside a cinched down pack—is a plug made from a wooden match inserted from the inside. Milkman and other brands come in flat, foil-lined quart packages which are themselves so handy that I carry them as refills for the squirter; in fact I often use them as dispensers by tearing off a small corner and keeping the opened package in a plastic bag.

Salt and pepper shakers come in half a dozen clever designs that weigh one-half to one and one-half ounces and cost 25¢ to $2 at mountain shops. The most popular are an aluminum divided cylinder with screw-on caps at each end, and a more easily operated transparent plastic model with flip-top caps that has side-by-side compartments that both dispense at the top. Unfortunately, all shakers hold enough for only two to three days for two to three persons. Salt companies now offer a variety of prefilled plastic and cardboard shakers which are handy and safe if carried in plastic bags. For many years, I carried an old tin spice can filled with a mixture of three parts salt and one each of pepper, onion, garlic and celery salts. It is still my favorite shaker.

For carrying butter and cheese—an important part of my food supply—I still, out of habit, use aluminum provision cans: squat cylinders containing plastic inserts and gasketed, hermetically sealing inner lids. Available at many mountain shops in four sizes weighing two to seven ounces and costing $1.50 to 2.50, they offer greater protection than squeeze tubes and many plastic jars.

For backpackers who insist on carrying individual fresh eggs, two-, four-, six-, and 12-egg plastic containers weighing one to six ounces are available at most shops for from 50¢ to $1.50. Fresh eggs are more compactly carried, where measuring is not a problem, by breaking them into a doubled plastic bag which is sealed to exclude air and packed into a suitably sized, wide-mouthed jar.

For larger parties or where water is scarce, collapsible jugs and bags are extremely convenient. They range in capacity from one to five gallons and weigh as little as seven ounces for a two-and-one-half-gallon bag. Five quart jugs weigh four ounces and cost about $1.50. They roll up or press flat, and eventually they spring leaks, but if I am planning a dry camp on a ridge I carry a collapsible jug to fill at the highest water.

Though the quart bottle I carry for making lemonade doubles as a canteen in wet country, where water is scarce and must continually be carried, the one quart, rigid plastic, Oasis canteen, with belt clip and attached metal cap, is excellent, although the $2.50 price is more than double that of my poly bottle. Flat plastic flasks for "sportsmen" come in various sizes, but I often use a reclaimed vitamin pill bottle to carry four ounces of brandy.

Clean Up

To keep containerless stoves and fire blackened pots from spreading soot in one's pack means storing them in bags. Even very heavy plastic does not do nearly as well as cloth. The best are of closely woven and paraffined cotton or urethane coated nylon, with drawstrings and square bottoms. Cost runs from 50¢ to $2.50 for sturdy washable bags that will last. Standards of cleanliness vary in the woods, but are dependably lower than at home. Kitchenware must be washed daily to prevent the formation of bacteria that can cause debilitating stomach illness. A few people scrupulously boil everything in soapy water after every meal; many only scrape out pots and pans and rinse in cold water—and cross their fingers.

My procedure lies somewhere in between. For a short two-to three-man trip, I carry a four-inch square abrasive scouring cloth, a three-inch square sponge backed with emery cloth. Both are soapless. Completing my kit are a vial of liquid bio-degradable soap —which is incredibly effective at cleaning skin as well as pots—and a clean diaper or small absorbent hand towel. Old threadbare towels are inefficient. I also carry large, heavy-duty garbage bags, which I double for carrying out trash.

After scraping the food from a dirty stew pot with my big spoon I pour half a cup of hot water from the teapot and add two to three drops of bio-degradable soap. After scrubbing with the scouring cloth and/or sponge, I rinse with cold water and set the pot upside down to dry in the sun and breeze. Fire blackened pots are best wiped with wet paper towels, plastic or cloth bags. Pots rubbed with soap before being put on the fire are comparatively easy to clean.

Cooking, for the majority, may never rival good eating as a source of pleasure, but proper gear, good technique and considerable planning can keep it from becoming a miserable chore.

Camp

From *The Backpacker*.
By Albert Saijo

You have followed up the outlet stream of the lake. A slight trail through alpine willow. As you come to the point where the lake spills over to start the stream, you get an eye-level view of the lake's surface. Then you scramble over the lip of the basin and there's the lake in full surrounded by peaks and ridges. The intense blue of a biologically poor lake. Blue like the sky, but deeper from the depth of the water. A wind with a cold edge sweeps wave patterns over it. The water laps gently against the shore. Red mountain heather. Treeline. Mostly rock. Scattered whitebark pine. Now find your campsite.

Setting Up

What you want of a campsite will depend upon varying conditions, but essentially there are a few things you look for. A level spot for your bed—sheltered if there is bad weather. Access to water. Firewood, if you're using it. It should be off the trail and out of sight and earshot of other camps. You may want it to catch the morning sun—for certain, if it's a layover or base camp.

If you're fishing you want to be close to the fish. The spot must please you.

On a well-traveled trail you'll generally find that someone has camped before you at almost every likely campsite, which isn't surprising since everyone looks for the same things in a campsite, more or less. Don't choose a spot that looks over-used, with ground cover worn down by stock or too much camping. Let that spot rest and renew itself.

Choose a sandy spot, bare ground, rock or duff. Find a spot that will take the pressure of your camp without showing it. You want to be able to camp and then leave with no trace that you've been there. As more people go into wilderness it is imperative that we develop this outdoor style of the ultra-light camp and camping without leaving a trace.

In choosing your campsite, go easy on nature. Don't cut trees, dead or alive, for any reason. Don't build elaborate rock structures, windbreaks, big fireplaces and the like. Don't disturb soil with holes and trenches. Avoid meadows for a campsite; they break down easily. Don't dig into the turf or meadows for any reason. Besides, they're quite often wet and being open bottom land, they tend to dew over heavily mornings and evenings.

It tends to be colder and wetter right next to water. It's warmer among trees and beside large boulders. They soak up heat during the day and give it off at night, as does bare ground. Remember, at night cold air flows down valley, close to the ground. Look for a site that shelters you from it. If you like to watch the stars, camp in the open. Try to avoid camping on fragile vegetation like the creeping Douglas phlox with its tiny delicate flower. We've agreed, wilderness is a shrine.

You want an overnight camp. The wind has stiffened a little so you decide to set out your camp lee side a huge boulder, about 15 feet up from the lake on sand. Others seem to have camped on the same spot, but it's still neat. There is a small fireplace made of three flat rocks about four feet out from the boulder. Don't build fires against big rocks and boulders; it blackens them. For warmth it is more efficient for you to sit between the fire and the backstop rock. Sensing no rain or heavy dew, you dispense with shelter. Start your fire and boil water for your end-of-hiking-day hot drink.

Your Bed

While the water heats, find your sleeping spot. Say you want to sleep somewhat apart from camp and be alone. You know to take a little trouble finding your bedsite. Try to find a naturally level spot. Don't dig or level. Avoid sloping ground, but if you must sleep on a slope, feet downhill is best. Don't get yourself into a side-roll position. Some care finding the right spot may prove the difference between a restful and fitful night. Finally you find a level area just large enough for your sleeping bag, protected on three sides by rock and dwarfed white bark pine, sheared off flat on top by wind. The ground is fine granitic sand. You test the spot, lying down on it. It's perfect, even to the red-flowered penstemon at your head.

Clear off sharp stuff from the sand bed. Spread out your poncho for a ground cloth, then your foam pad.

Take out your sleeping bag, shake it and lay it down so it will loft out before bedtime. Fold the sides of the poncho over the bag if it feels like evening will dew.

Water

It's come to pass that wilderness waters are being polluted at an alarming rate. It is apparent we should do no washing or rinsing of any kind directly in streams and lakes. Fetch water and wash everything far back from stream and lake and be sure that dirty water doesn't drain back. Use soap, *not* detergent. Bathe out of cookpots.

One of the deep pleasures of wilderness is being able to drink of all waters you come across. It's of utmost importance that the purity of wilderness water be preserved.

Firewood

In well-traveled treeline country, wood is being burned faster than it grows. This is also true around campsites and along most well-traveled trails, even through forests. It has become necessary to use wood sparingly or, in many cases, not at all. The big, roaring campfire is out. A small fire or no fire at all. The only kind of wood to be used in wilderness now is down wood—wood lying on the ground. Don't break or cut snag wood off standing trees, live or dead. It destroys the beauty of them. Leave saw and hatchet at home. If there's wood at all, with a little patience, enough can generally be found for a small fire. Use wood like a precious gift.

Twilight

After supper there is time for ambling around camp with a hot cup of tea. You watch trout feed on insects, making that quiet sound between a pop and smack as they break water. An occasional, exuberant, arching leap completely out of water. Plop. Alpenglow. Sunset. Mosquitoes quit for the day. The first star. Westering light drops behind horizon. The air turns chill.

Now it's time for that small fire. Burn trash and garbage. Boil water for tea. Old friend fire. Wasn't this what you came out for? To warm by a pine-wood fire out far back with nothing but stars, air, rock, trees and water around you? Big eye-watering yawn. Fix the fire so it will burn to ash overnight. Put it out if there's a wind.

Sanitation

A proper toilet will be a hole six to eight inches deep. A shallower hole might be dug up by animals, a deeper hole would put your waste outside the layer of soil within which it can be broken down biologically. Carry a digging tool. You can't do it right kicking at the ground with your boot, or using a stick. Do it right and bury it well. Tramp down earth on top. Locate your toilet at least 50 yards from open water and away from trail and camp. Don't use the dry course of an intermittent stream. Don't use potential campsites and likely sleeping spots for a toilet.

Sleep

Stumble off to bed. Take a canteen of water and a flashlight, if you have one. Turn boots and slippers upside-down to keep out the dew. Get into the bag. Cold nylon warms fast. Except in very cold temperatures, a down bag works better if you have on fewer clothes. Perhaps a light shirt to keep the cold off your shoulders. Use folded clothes for a pillow. If you're using the torso-length sleeping pad, you can make your bed more comfortable and warm by putting folded pants, wool shirt or jacket under the lower part of the bag, under your legs and feet. Adjust the bag for ventilation.

At higher elevations you generally will fall into deep sleep at first, then wake up in the middle of the night and experience difficulty getting back to sleep. Don't worry, it's the elevation. Relax. Rest. Sense the night, watch stars—sometimes you can catch an orbiting satellite. Doze off. Nights are longer outback. You will feel rested enough in the morning.

Breaking Camp

You're awake before dawn and you watch it happen. Cloudless. Pure sunrise. Out of warm bag into chilly morning air. Dress. Open out bag, shake it, and set it out to air and dry. Same with poncho and pad—they will be wet on the underside from condensation. Start a pot of water boiling. A pot of hot water is handy first thing in the morning. Morning ablution and morning worship, whatever its form. Breakfast. Kitchen clean-up. Fill canteen. Get everything together and pack.

Now clean up camp.

Carry a plastic bag just for trash and garbage. Carry out everything that won't burn to clean ash. Don't burn plastics; the fumes can be harmful to vegetation. Aluminum foil doesn't burn or disintegrate; it must be carried out.

Hopefully you did not overcook so that you're left with waste. Don't bury garbage. Park and Forest services prohibit the digging of pits. Scatter edible garbage thinly away from camp and trail. Animals will find and eat it. Burn cans, then smash them, and pack them out.

The ideal is not to leave a trace of your stay. Double-check the fireplace. See that the fire is dead out. If the ashes are still warm, wet them down thoroughly. Rake out nonburnable items from ashes, both yours and any left by previous campers. Lay in some clean sand or dirt. As far as you can, make every wilderness trip a clean-up trip.

If this was a virgin camp and you made a fireplace, break it down, put the rocks back where they came from with the blackened side under, and scatter the dead ashes in some inconspicuous place.

You are packed and ready to start the day's walk. You enjoyed this camp. Stand quiet a moment and thank the place. Have you forgotten anything? You are leaving a clean camp and a dead fire. Let wilderness be surrounded by a ring of devotees.

[Editor's Note: Be kind to the trees, the grasses, the waters and finally, to all other backpackers who don't wish to feel the impact of your excursion. Go light on them all. Read and study the following reminders (in addition to those made by Albert Saijo).

1) *Leave your city noise—radios, musical instruments, etc.—at home where they belong. Listen instead to the birds, the wind and the silence.*
2) *Do not take your domestic pets if there's a chance they'll frighten or pursue other animals—or people.*
3) *Do not disturb vegetation (pick flowers, take saplings, etc.).*
4) *Leave all firearms at home. No trail or campground is an appropriate place for target practice.*
5) *Keep your campsite tidy. Don't spread clothing, equipment or food containers on the trail or where it might bother other campers.*
6) *Avoid short-cutting switchbacks and stay on the path. Never hog the trail. It is common courtesy to allow approaching hikers right of way.*
7) *And to repeat, "Pack it out. Pack it all out!"]*

The Littlest Camper

From *The Joy of Camping*.
By Richard Langer

"She's not even a year old, how can you take her camping?"

"She's not even a year and a half old, what do you mean you're taking her up to the Yukon with you? How's she going to live in a tent when there's snow on the ground?"

Those were the softer questions asked of us when we began camping with Genevieve. The fiercer statements threatened to have us locked up for child abuse. You'd think children had always been raised with central heating, running water, and the supermarket around the corner. Yet today's high-quality camping gear makes it almost easier to care for a child, even an infant, in the great outdoors than in the wilds of the city.

For camping purposes, kids can be divided into three distinct classes, depending on their mobility: carry-alongs, anchors, and catch-me-if-you-cans. As infants they ride and even fall asleep in a Gerry or similar kiddie pack with such ease you almost have to force yourself to remember they're there when you duck a low-hanging branch or sit down for a rest and start to lean back against a sun-warmed boulder. Your partner will remember better, since he or she will be carrying most of the gear for all three. I once tried to talk Susan into toting a knapsack behind, the baby in front in the frameless Peterson carrier, to keep nicely balanced all around, but she didn't go for the idea.

The second, or anchor stage, is the only one that limits your mobility to any real extent. Roughly between the ages of two and five, children become both too heavy and too restless to be carried for prolonged periods; at the same time they're not really self-propelled enough for treks over appreciable distances. It's a great time for base or canoe camping, but not for backpacking. (When canoeing, by the way, put the kids in life vests and give them the run of the boat except when you're in white water. They'll get their sea legs before you do. But learn how to swim first, both of you parents. And give the kids lessons as soon as they seem eager for them.)

After the riding-at-anchor stage, it's catch as catch can. Developing a plan of tactical exhaustion simmers things down, but make it one that gives the junior camper a sense of accomplishment and belonging to the group. Don't force your child on, you yourself walking into the trap of bragging. "He's only seven, but he can carry a 20-pound pack all day." Maybe he can, but that's no way to teach him to appreciate the great outdoors.

Start by letting the child assume some responsibility for his or her own gear. Any time a child takes the initiative, encourage it. Genevieve carried a small blue knapsack around camp with her toy lambs in it. Sometimes on her back, sometimes clasped in her hands, no time for very long. But she knew it was hers.

As every mother knows from endlessly emptying out

boys' pants pockets, children collect things. This can be channeled in the direction of gathering twigs for the fire, picking berries, bringing water, and cleaning up the campsite. Genevieve became quite adroit, if somewhat irregular, at wood gathering as soon as she could toddle. Unfortunately, her harvesting spilled over to collecting pine cones, the favorite repository for said prickly bundles being Daddy's sleeping bag. Never Mommy's. I'm sure there's some deep hidden Freudian significance in that, but even when pulling out half a dozen cones in one night, I've never been able to discover it. Besides, she giggles a lot as I make a somewhat extravagant project of mining my bag.

Probably no one knows how much infants who are a year old or younger absorb of their wilderness surroundings. Communication at that age is somewhat elementary. Babies of camping parents we know almost invariably seem to make a leap forward in development both when they arrive in the wilds and when they return home. Maybe it's just the change in environments. Nevertheless, there it is. So if your only reason for not taking the baby camping is a fear he can't adjust to the woods, relax. With a little care and planning, it will be a great experience for all of you.

For a big baby, take a Gerry or similar kiddie pack; a very young or a lightweight baby may be more secure and protected in a Peterson or Snugli model that can be strapped on in front. Start out with short trips to areas you are familiar with before you tackle a long journey. And a small point, but one easily overlooked: backpacking a baby usually lulls the little tyke to quiet murmurings or even sleep, so you may have to remind yourself to check that he's not getting too much sun or wind back there.

The Wilderness Nursery

The Crees have the easiest solution I've heard of to the diapering problem. They use a highly absorbent and skin-soothing variety of tree moss as an all-day diaper liner. Unfortunately I haven't been able to discover where the moss is to be found. So for us the gear still has to include a fair-sized diaper duffel. Some mothers find Pampers a real boon in the city, but in the wilds these diapers are something else again. They can't be buried, since the plastic outer linings don't decay and would be around for at least the next 60 or 70 generations. And burning wet Pampers is not my idea of a cozy fragrant campfire. So you end up lugging a lot of extra plastic out. By the sopping bagful. We use cloth diapers because Genevieve is more comfortable in them. We wash them out by hand as we go, drying them in the sun, which both bleaches and sterilizes them.

Formula should be no particular problem in this day and age, with all the canned varieties—buy in single-feeding size, even though it means more flattened cans to pack out, so you can use up what you open right away.

Unfortunately, there's no getting around the weight factor completely. But powdered formula, and to some extent the concentrated liquid, will save a lot of pounds. And there's always the evaporated and dried whole or skim milks. However, with the liquid concentrates or powders, you'll need a boiled water supply for mixing;

the premixed formula, if you have room for it, saves time and bother. Naturally, as with the baby foods, you want to check with your pediatrician if you have any questions about formula feeding.

The presterilized nursers on the market today make hygiene simple, even though you're packing out the used refill containers. All you have to worry about is boiling the nipples. Mother's milk is, of course, easiest of all.

For the baby just going on solids, a handy pureeing device often available in local infant specialty shops is the Happy Baby Food Grinder. It does almost as good a job as the blender back home, and will save the cook's wrist a lot of busy mashing activity at feeding time.

Through the first day it's fun and games. Everything is new and exciting. Then suddenly comes night and it's time to go to bed. To go *home* to bed, to security. This can be a problem, but need not be if you prepare for it. Take along the littlest camper's favorite lovey, be it the teddy bear, lamb, blanket, or the huge gingham dog with floppy ears you know are going to flap into the cereal. Take several of the next-favorite toys— these can be kept to the small-size variety—on long trips, hiding one for a couple of weeks and bringing it out again as something both old and new.

Even six- or seven-year-olds appreciate having a favorite toy with them. It may be as unrelated to the wilds as a small dump truck or airplane, but it's something to fall back on.

Letting a baby or young child sleep in his own bag at home for a couple of days before you set out will convince him he's got at least a chunk of the real thing with him when he hits the road. If it's a down bag, it will be too warm to sleep inside of in the house. Sleeping on top of it, however, breeds the same familiarity.

Get There Before the Toddler Does

Once a kid is weaned and out of diapers, the adjustments and modifications of your camping routine are pretty similar whether he is in the anchorage or catch-me-if-you-can stage. I trust it goes without saying that you'll childproof your campsite as you would your home, and be especially watchful about where you leave the fuel and stove, matches, ax, first aid items, and all such potential hazards to young children. . . .

There are a couple of suggestions I would make on planning where to go. Keep to familiar areas on at least some of your trips. Children like to go back to favorite haunts, and parents rest easier knowing the lay of the land and its trouble spots. You may want to stalk out the new places before you let the family loose in them, so you'll be aware of any local hazards as well as the convenient rest spots for a hike, the perfect frog pond to camp near, or the spot up in the mountains that has snow banks still clinging on through late spring. Snow and children go together like ice cream and cones. Finding snow when it's totally unexpected is almost as good as having an extra Christmas.

Knowing about an area does wonders to keep kids amused and interested. And if a camping trip isn't fun, what good is it? A couple of lightweight handbooks, such as the Peterson series, which covers nature from mammals to birds, are handy for reference if you're rusty on your flora and fauna and such. Maps and adjunct reports on the geology of the region will have you telling the kids about the massive glaciers that once moved down that particular valley, or the volcano whose fiery lava now lies still and fertile beneath their feet—and it's amazing how fascinated you yourself will become with it all.

Oh, by the way, it pays for you to be familiar with your equipment too. "That's not the way it goes, Daddy," from a three-year-old is no morale booster, especially if he's right.

Through a Small Child's Eyes

Keeping a child busy and active is not much of a problem. The real problem is more apt to be toning things down. I still remember Genevieve, whose animal vocabulary at the time was limited to city creatures, running after a 1,200-pound bull moose that edged toward our camp in Alaska, shouting delightedly, "Doggie! Doggie!"

Almost any child will play for hours with "boats" in a stream or by the lake shore. He'll stick a small leaf into a bigger one and watch the ship sail with its bounty all the way across a pond to China. Again I trust it goes without saying to parents that water play time is a time for keeping noses constantly, vigilantly counted.

But sometimes a child not brought up in the country needs a little help to enter his new world of the wild. Give him a hand, and he'll carry you through with him to a universe you may have long since forgotten. A small, fallen log laid across another becomes a seesaw the likes of which no playground at home can match. And a pile of pine needles, well, have you ever seen such a wonderful cargo for loading in and out of trucks? A few pipe cleaners tucked away in anticipation will turn pine cones into a menagerie. Then there are always snail races, frogs and salamanders found and returned to their proper place, and of course that most wondrous of outdoor Pied Pipers for a child—the willow whistle—to make.

The world's not the same when you're three feet tall. Vistas of Grand Canyon splendor can't compete with walking along a log, carefully balancing so as not to fall over its six-inch precipice, nor the wide Missouri with a foot-wide creek that can be dammed. A winter landscape stretching like a vast vision of Siberia is hardly noticed while a dozen icicles hanging from a low branch to the ground is a magnificent castle. When you camp with children, look at the world through their eyes occasionally. It will turn those frequent rest stops you have to make with them into a delight rather than a chore.

So there you are, all ready to take the kid on his or her first camping trip. Go to it. It'll be a great experience for all of you.

Backpacking in Winter

From *America's Backpacking Book*.
By Raymond Bridge

For backpackers whose favorite wilderness lies deep under the snow during the winter months, cold-weather camping can provide a fascination matched at no other time of the year. Snow camping is also more difficult than bedding down in summer meadows, especially for the self-propelled camper, and far more skill and endurance are required than in milder seasons.

In snow country, winter brings peace and solitude to many areas that have become crowded and noisy in summer. The beauty of the winter landscape is the equal of any other season, and the quiet clarity of the air is unrivaled. Winter brings challenge for the competent and potential danger for the careless, both of a much more serious nature than trials and threats that occur in milder seasons.

Because of its unique rewards and difficulties, deep snow country is a special place for the experienced backpacker, a place where true wilderness can often be found even in regions relatively close to civilization. There is a peculiar exhilaration in the winter wilderness that can be found at no other time of year.

Special cautions must be applied, however. Except in a few particularly harsh environments, the summer backcountry rarely presents any serious danger to any traveler who takes the most elementary safety precautions. A couple of nights out in the woods at most times of year will make you hungry, and if you are not adequately clothed you will be a bit the worse for wear, but that's all, providing you keep your head. Even in the mountains in the summer, a person who is properly equipped can generally spend a night out suffering no more than moderate discomfort. In winter things are not so simple. Adequate clothing, equipment, food, and the skill to use them well are often essential for survival, not merely for comfort.

In summer, I really believe that any reasonably healthy person who has not allowed himself to dissipate completely can manage to go on a successful backpacking trip. He may have to limit his goals at first, and he certainly will need to be careful of his equipment and load if he is not in proper physical condition, but normal good health is the only qualification for easy trips. The victim of the idiot box and the reclining chair may be dog tired at the end of an easy day, but he can manage it, and he will feel good on Monday morning.

In winter this is not the case. Some winter trips are easy, and some winter activities are not strenuous. Backpacking in snow conditions that may change in a few hours is a different matter, however. Physical reserves are required that are not necessary in summer. A typical winter trip will require a heavier pack than a summer one. More clothing, heavier sleeping equipment, more food, a more comprehensive emergency kit, and various incidentals must all be carried, and either snowshoes or skis must be worn. Travelers in winter often have to break trail through powder snow or breakable crust, and this is strenuous exercise. On reaching camp, it may be necessary to stamp a platform before a tent can be pitched and before one can stand without the aid of snowshoes or skis. Days are short, weather can be severe, water may have to be melted. Simply getting up after a spill in soft snow can be quite tiring for the novice to wilderness travel on skis or snowshoes.

This partial catalogue of difficulties is not intended to discourage the prospective winter visitor to the wilderness. It is merely cautionary. A rank beginner may well enjoy easy snowshoe hikes or ski tours on trails, perhaps including overnight trips to cabins, accompanied by experienced companions. True wilderness travel in deep-snow country is not for the neophyte, however. Start backpacking and camping in mild weather, and take to the snowy trails when you feel physically fit and at home in the wilds. If you want to start in winter, begin with short trips of a few hours on skis or snowshoes, *with companions*, or start camping close to home or car. Cold-weather camping, like cold-water swimming, should be approached with caution. It's all right to plunge right in *after* you know you can take it.

Walking in the Snow

Backpacking with a few inches of snow on the ground is not much different from doing the same thing with no snow. You must make sure that your boots are heavy and watertight enough for the conditions and that your clothing is adequate for the weather conditions. Other equipment must also be suitable. With a light autumn snow cover it is usually best to clear a tent site of snow so that the tent can be pitched directly on the ground, but in spring the snow cover is likely to be more consolidated; a bare spot may be so wet that it is just as well to camp on top of the snow.

Occasions when it is practical to hike with snow on the ground may range from relatively mild spring conditions or moderate weather in places which do not receive a heavy winter cover to the extremely severe cold that may be found in midwinter during a light snow year in the north country. Camping techniques range accordingly between regular summer methods and the snow-camping procedure outlined below.

Besides taking special care that they have adequate clothing, shelter, and food, hikers in cold weather must beware of one particular danger, especially when engaged in fall and early winter camping in heavy-snow regions. They must remember that even though there may only be six inches of snow on the ground when they leave, a storm in the backcountry could easily bring a couple of feet or more, making the trip *out* a very different affair from the one going in. On snowshoe and ski trips when a heavy base has already been built up, an additional two or three feet is of no particular consequence and may even make the going easier, but for hikers caught by the first heavy snow of the year, a pleasant autumn hike may easily be turned into a survival ordeal. Backpackers should be wary of this possibility in fall and in early winter, particularly in the mountains, and they should go prepared. On long trips into

deep wilderness, this will probably mean carrying
snowshoes even if they are not needed for the trip in.
Four days of good going can get you a long way in
before there is much snow on the ground, and if you'd
like to be sure of getting out again before spring, think
about what the same trail would be like after heavy
snows and drifting winds.

Snowshoes and Skis

In areas where the snow comes and goes and at times
when the snow is shallow enough or well enough consolidated to allow normal walking, camping and hiking
are simply a bit more challenging than they are when
there is no snow on the ground. When the snow pack
begins to build up, however, travel becomes impossible
without special equipment designed to keep the traveler
on top of the snow. In principle this is fairly simple:
you fasten something to each foot which increases the
area bearing your weight and thus prevents you from
sinking too far into the snow.

There is not adequate space here to go into the
selection of snowshoes and skis in great detail, and I
have discussed this and other winter backpacking sub-
jects in considerable detail in my book on snow camping. Essentially, the choice depends on the sort of country you want to travel. The first choice to be made is
between skis and snowshoes. Skis are the more elegant
form of transportation, and in country where they are
suitable they are much faster. With skis one can slide
effortlessly on downhill sections of a trip, while with
snowshoes one must still walk. Properly chosen and

waxed, skis also allow a lot of gliding on the flat and on gentle uphill slopes, except when breaking trail through heavy snow. By comparison, snowshoes require one to slog along. Finally, on many kinds of steep, open alpine terrain, skis are much easier to use than snowshoes, whether for up- or downhill going.

Before you conclude that no one in his right mind would use snowshoes in preference to skis, though, you should consider the other side of the coin. Skis are very awkward to carry when they are not in use, whereas many kinds of snowshoes can be strapped on the back of the pack so compactly that only their weight will be noticed. Skis require snow deep enough to provide a reasonably clear path, especially on steeper slopes, and to cover rocks and stumps enough to prevent damage to the skis. Snowshoes have considerably more latitude. This difference is of little importance in places like the Sierras which have plenty of snow and open terrain, but can be decisive in regions like the Northeast which have less snow and more brush. Skis are also generally more expensive, less adaptable in use with various sorts of footwear, and demand more preliminary practice.

As a general rule, the hiker who wants to continue backpacking after the snows fall can start snowshoeing almost immediately, and he can become a skilled snowshoer in a fairly short time. Skis take more initial practice and gradual development of skills, especially for steep slopes and alpine conditions. In regions like the Northeast, skiers are more confined in their range. For country with heavy snow cover, though, skis are by far the finest means of transportation in winter.

There are many specialized varieties of both skis and snowshoes, and there is not enough space here to go into detail about choice. For snowshoes the following general considerations apply: (1) longer shoes are faster and more comfortable to wear in open country and on good trails, but they are not good for steep slopes or brushy, rough country; (2) upturned toes are best in light, powder snow and with moderate slopes; straight toes are good for step-kicking on steep slopes, but are a pain in the neck the rest of the time; (3) tails help the shoes track and reduce dragging, but they become inconvenient in brush; (4) the area of the shoe governs flotation; smaller shoes sink deeper, and more body weight or a heavier pack should indicate a bigger shoe; a long, narrow shoe may have the same flotation as a shorter, more rounded one; (5) all snowshoes should be heavier at the back, so that the toes will lift clear of the snow without special effort; (6) the area in front of the foot which actually bears weight determines whether the shoe will tend to "dive"—the smaller the front area, the more dive; a toe-hole close to the front of the shoe will make the shoe dive and will be better for climbing, but the more true this is, the less comfortable the shoe will be for straightforward going; (7) the awkwardness of snowshoes depends mainly on how far apart the legs must spread in walking, and this depends both on the width and form of the shoes— the Michigan and Maine patterns, for example, are wide in the center, but they fit together in a walking pattern so that the feet don't have to spread far; longer shoes will do the same with a long, gliding stride.

Any well-made pair of snowshoes will do in almost

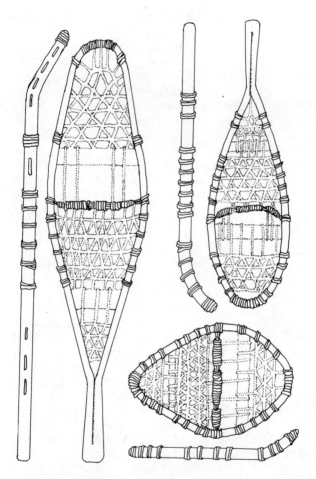

Snowshoes. Front and side views: Alaska (left), Michigan (top) and Bearpaw (bottom).

any country, even though each type has particular advantages. My own preference for general use is the Maine or Michigan design, both of which are rather like the old beavertail styles except that they have toes curved up a few inches. In mountain country I use bearpaws, which have no toe lift at all and which have the toe hole well forward. In regions where the advantages of very long snowshoes are evident I almost always use skis, so my experience with long snowshoes is limited.

Like snowshoes, skis come in specialized versions, but unlike good snowshoes, they are not all equally rugged. Most of the ski-binding-boot combinations used for downhill skiing these days can be dismissed out of hand for wilderness use, but with the increasing availability of Nordic touring equipment, the self-propelled skier still has a vast variety of equipment available. Any skiing gear which will be used on the flat and uphill as well as on downward runs must be adjustable to permit the heels to lift and the ankles to move back and forth. Rigid modern downhill arrangements won't do.

Acceptable equipment for wilderness skiing with backpack can range from Nordic "light-touring" gear to slightly modified downhill equipment. The lighter the equipment, the more enjoyable it is to use, but since safety and versatility have to be major considerations for wilderness skiing, lightness must often bow to conservatism. For most backpacking trips regular Nordic touring skis, 60 millimeters (2¹/₃ inches) across in the center, are the minimum size suitable in durability for backpacking in unbroken snow on varied terrain. Experienced wilderness skiers in suitable terrain can often manage with light touring equipment, but one should be wary of using fragile gear in deep wilderness. For alpine wilderness travel, Nordic mountain skis should be considered the minimum in sturdiness—their steel edges are a necessity on steep and icy slopes. When alpine skis are used they should be fairly soft if possible, since stiffer skis tend to bury themselves in troughs of soft snow. "Deep-powder" types are excellent.

Bindings and boots for wilderness backpacking must be such that the heel will rise easily from the ski during cross-country travel. Boots and socks should be heavy and warm enough for the conditions that may be encountered; neither ultralight Nordic shoes nor alpine molded casts are suitable for the varied demands of the generalist.

My own recommendations would be as follows: for the backpacker on really easy terrain who plans to travel mainly in groups or mainly on day tours with occasional overnight trips in good snow, standard Nordic light-touring equipment with pin bindings and insulated boots; for the person who wants to do a lot of week-long or weekend backpacking on skis, mainly along trails, roads, or rolling country, standard touring skis, Nordic cable bindings, and the best insulated Nordic touring boots he can find; for the mountain tourer who expects to go through a lot of rough country, crusty snow, and icy slopes, but who is willing to sacrifice some downhill speed and control for better mobility, ski mountaineering boots, Silvretta bindings, and mountain touring skis; for the mountain tourer who doesn't want to sacrifice any of the thrills of the down-

hill run, a flexible downhill ski, Ramy or Eckel bindings, and a good ski-mountaineering boot.

Snow Conditions

Whatever your means of transportation, on foot, ski, or snowshoe, the most important thing to remember in planning trips for the snowy seasons is the variability of the snow cover. The experienced mild-weather backpacker learns to judge his capabilities pretty accurately. With some general knowledge of the country and a map he can plan to get from point A to point B with relative confidence. Except for difficult off-trail routes near the peaks, even the weather is not likely to slow him too much. Even the exceptions can usually be anticipated—ridges or valley rims that may or may not turn out to be passable, and so on. Snow upsets all this easy planning: the smooth ski tour of one day becomes a hard three-day slog with different snow conditions; the easy hike through six inches of powder becomes an endurance trial after a heavy night's fall; a little sun changes simple snowshoeing atop a crust into a grueling slog through sticky, wet, soft, heavy slush.

Snow can be deposited rapidly, it can form deep drifts in minutes, and it can change quickly in important ways. This fact, combined with the severity of winter weather conditions and the more isolated circumstances which generally prevail during the winter months, makes it necessary for the wilderness traveler to allow himself much greater margins for error when planning trips. One of the unavoidable consequences is a much heavier pack.

Planning winter trips will depend on your means of transportation and the area where you travel and on information which you must obtain either through experience or research. The depth of the snow cover is often a vital factor in determining what a particular tour might be like, and this will vary with region and year. By midwinter of practically any year you can confidently plan to ski almost anywhere in the High Sierras of California, but that is certainly not true in New England. A late December trip through the Rockies might slide over a snow cover a couple of yards thick or take you up a trail as dry as it was in July.

The most difficult conditions for winter travel occur when there is enough snow to make walking difficult or impossible but not enough to provide a smooth cover over which to ski or snowshoe. The rocks stick out far enough to make skiing impossible, snowshoes take a terrible beating and tend to sink and jam between boulders, and the walker finds himself plunging repeatedly through the unconsolidated snow. In these conditions, all but the most ambitious are best advised to stick to smooth valley trails, where ski touring and snowshoeing are possible long before steeper slopes are filled in.

Depth of snow is relative to terrain. On the plains, fields, and beaches, a few inches of snow makes ski touring with Nordic equipment so speedy and effortless one seems to ski in a dream. Mountain boulder fields will require many feet of snow for snowshoeing and even more for skiing. An open forest floor makes for easy travel with little snow, but brush, small growth, and deadfall take much more snow before easy travel is possible. Whatever your means of transportation, pace

and ambitions have to be adapted to the prevailing snow conditions, and plans have to take into account the possible changes that may precede your return to civilization. A change for the worse will cause you to regret running your supplies down to the end.

The most important special feature of the winter trail is the much greater need for regulation of the body's temperature. Cold air requires that you dress heavily at camp and during rests, but strenuous going forces your body to produce lots of extra heat, and you may find yourself sweating almost as soon as you get going. Normal human frailty prompts most people to procrastinate at each step of stripping down—*don't wait*. Take clothes off before you begin to sweat. Perspiration will soak into your clothing almost unnoticed until you stop, and then the chill wind will remind you that sweat-soaked clothes are poor insulators. Wet clothes in winter are dangerous, and they get wet as often from the inside as from outside.

Clothing is discussed in an earlier chapter, and it is only mentioned here to note that it is important. In summer you can get away with a lot, but cold weather is often unforgiving of such carelessness.

There are several things that summer backpackers are likely to forget when they first hit the trail in the winter. Winter days are short—remember? In summer you may be able to get away with late starts and late camps, but in winter that sun goes down early, and then it gets *cold*. Wilderness travelers tend to become dehydrated easily. You work hard, you may be panting, and you often sweat without knowing it because the perspiration evaporates quickly. Winter air tends to be dry, so that you lose more moisture, and the fact that available water is frozen may make you drink much less than you need. Whether you stop for tea, get lots of liquid at supper, or solve the problem another way, it is important to maintain an adequate liquid intake. Among other things, your body is much more vulnerable to shock in case of injury if it is dehydrated. Also, it is more important to keep the food going into your system in cold weather. If you don't, hard exercise can easily drain your ready reserves, leaving you without fuel for warmth when you need it. Eat fats and proteins for staying power and carbohydrates for quick fuel.

Camping

There are several major differences between cold-weather camping and living outside at milder times of the year. For one thing the harsher climate generally makes shelter necessary. It is possible to sleep out under the sky even in winter with sensible and efficiently designed backpacking equipment, but wind combined with cold often makes this impossible. Such shelter must also do more than simply shed rain. Winter camping in the woods may utilize the cheerful combination of a lean-to tent and a fire in front, but if you plan to venture into windswept regions with sparser vegetation or into forests where fires would be inappropriate, you will have to build a snow shelter or have a closed tent, preferably one with a floor.

A good snow cover at least minimizes the danger of forest fire, so that there is usually no hindrance to building fires on that account. Other problems do con-

front the camper who wants to keep himself warm in front of a cheery fire, though. As a start, he should remember that a cooking fire is quite a different matter from a warming fire, especially when it comes to gathering wood. The mountains of wood that a healthy fire can consume have to be collected a few times before their size is adequately impressed on your mind. An ax or a saw is usually mandatory for those depending on fires for warmth in winter, both because dry wood may have to be split out of logs or stubs and because deadfall is often covered over in winter. For this purpose, emergency tools are not adequate—putting up enough wood for a good night's fire requires adequate equipment.

The problem of justification is just as relevant in winter as in summer. In some areas with plenty of fast-growing woods, fuel is no problem, but in many regions it *is* a problem, and even in heavily wooded areas big fires are unjustifiable if heavy use in the summer leaves no surplus growth. It is important to note that going out in the winter and proving your hardy constitution does not give you special license to cut down live trees where the cutting would be improper in summer. Deadfall may be easy enough to find where the snows don't fall too deeply, but in some places standing dead trees or stubs are the only source of deadwood. These are always good prospects for dry wood, since they will not become wet to the core until they rot out.

Cooking fires don't present the problems of all-night warming fires, and in most forested areas you can get enough wood for cooking from dead branches or deadfall, even without a good ax or saw. Squaw wood *usually* provides adequate kindling, and your pocket knife can be used to make fuzz sticks.

For any kind of fire in winter you will have to worry about the problem of a base. If the snow is only a few feet deep, digging down to the ground is the easiest expedient, but with a deep snow cover this is not practical (you don't want to have to lower pots to the fire with a line). Often the best alternative is to build on the top of a boulder when a suitable one is available, which also puts the fire at a convenient height. When this is not practical you must have a base on the snow to prevent the fire from melting its way out of sight and drowning. Use rotten chunks of logs. These are usually wet and punky enough to hold up a fire for quite a while, but they may also be buried in deep snow where you can't find them.

With a heating fire, a reflector is even more important in winter than in summer. Without a reflector, you'll need a conflagration to keep you warm and half a day to get the wood to feed it. In winter you have a ready material for building the foundation of a reflector wall— banked-up snow works to hold up a wall of logs. The snow also provides an easy method of controlling drafts. With big fire, though, you will find that melting will force frequent revision of fireplace architecture.*

Backpackers using stoves for cooking in winter gen-

---

*If you can't stand the heat, the saying goes, get out of the kitchen. Conversely, if you can't stand the frost, come in from the cold. The Sierra Club feels strongly that heating fires are for emergencies only.—The eds./Sierra Club Books.

erally work from the comfortable interiors of their sleeping bags. Once the strenuous activity of the trail and setting up camp is over, it tends to get cold waiting around for the snow to melt and the food to heat, and the luxurious warmth of a down bag makes it a nice place to wait. Make sure you get all the chores done first. It's hard to get out of that snug bag once you're in.

When the snow cover is light, it is usually easiest to clear a spot for the tent, but with a deeper layer, a platform has to be stamped out. Start with your skis or snowshoes on; sidestep with skis and just walk around with snowshoes. Be sure to cover a large enough area, since you'll need space to walk around the tent, and you'll want a platform in front.

When you reach the point of diminishing returns with walking, start hopping up and down on the boards or webs until you are convinced that you've done all the packing you can with them on (wearing the pack will give you more oomph). Now try stepping off onto your platform to see whether you've really done all you can with the skis or snowshoes. Pack for a while with your boots. Make it smooth—bumps and holes will soon freeze solid.

Set up the tent using whatever anchors are at hand that are appropriate to the snow. Sticks may work as stakes in snow of medium consistency. They can be buried and stamped down in soft snow, with the tent loops tied around them before burial. Skis, poles, ice axes, and snowshoes will all serve as anchors, but think a little beforehand. Don't use your skis to hold the main guys for the tent and then find you need them to go for water.

Cooking and Water

Cooking in snow camps should be kept as simple as possible, since it is usually done inside the tent or snow shelter. Stick to one-pot meals. The danger of spilling the stew in a cramped tent is bad enough without attempting any six-course suppers. In very cold weather you may be able to count on keeping some fresh food like meat without worrying about spoilage, but the main problem in winter cooking is that liquid water is often not available. Find some if at all possible. Melting snow is time-consuming and takes a lot of fuel. It takes almost as much to convert the snow to water as it does to heat that water all the way to boiling. If you must melt snow, try to find crust, ice or granular snow. Incredible quantities of light powder snow are required to get any amount of water. Melt a little snow and then keep adding more. If you start with a full pot of snow, you are liable to scorch the pan, giving a burned taste to the water and the stew. With powder snow, you are sure to scorch the pot unless the snow is added bit by bit, because the powder acts like a blotter and soaks up the water as fast as it is melted. Get plenty of liquid at meals to replace what you lost during the day, and fill your water bottle to take to bed.

A few other tips on winter cooking. Use a lot of fat. You will find that it tastes good. You need the calories, and the extra heat that is produced in digesting fat will help keep you warm. Use a cover during cooking, keep the tent door open if you can, and avoid meals that require long periods of boiling. Water vapor inside the tent in winter will condense as water or frost, and some of it will end up in your insulation.

Other Winter Camping Notes

Use all of your insulation at night. Fluff up sleeping bags carefully and prepare your bed well. You may not wear your extra clothing, but you can put it in waterproof sacks or shells and use it for insulation underneath the legs and feet, as a pillow, or as extra insulation under the upper body.

Do not leave anything lying about loose outside the tent. Even a light snowfall at night will cover it up, providing it isn't blown away. Skis, poles, and snowshoes that aren't used for anchoring the tent should be stuck upright so that you won't have to dig them out.

Snow shelters are warm and protected from the wind. Learn to build them on mild afternoons. It takes practice. Igloos are hard to build except when snow conditions are right. A snow cave is generally best. It is most easily dug into the side of a large drift, preferably with a light shovel carried for the purpose. Wait for consolidated spring or wind-packed snow for your first attempt—powder snow just collapses. Make the cave just large enough to enable you to get in and make necessary movements. Dig the entrance a little lower than your sleeping spot, so that cold air will go down. Punch an air hole above you. Take your digging tools in with you in case of drifting during the night—*this is important!* Don't leave your equipment where it could be buried outside. Take it in or leave it where it could not be snowed into featureless landscapes. Practice with snow shelters before you depend on using them. They are very effective, but they require experience.

The Backcountry Navigator

From *Be Expert with Map and Compass.*
By Bjorn Kjellstrom

There is a tale in the Arabian Nights' entertainment of a magnificent contraption: A magic carpet. The lucky owner could seat himself on his carpet, recite the magic formula—and suddenly the carpet would rise in the air and carry him wherever he wanted to go.

It is likely that your early wanderings will be supervised by someone whose formula is no more magical than the time and effort it took to achieve navigational know-how. Once you get scent of exploring new trails or bushwacking through unknown terrain, you will enjoy becoming your own guide.

With map and compass for your steady companions, the art of *Orienteering*—the skill of finding your way along highways and country roads, through woods and fields, through mountain territory and over lakes —becomes an intriguing hobby and an interesting sport, whether you travel alone or with a buddy or with a group of like-minded friends.

Map

The map is navigation's most important tool. Actually,

you can at times manage without a compass but you cannot get "from here to there" without a map. Look upon a map—a reduced representation of a portion of the earth's surface—as if you were flying directly over the area. Directions are identical and all distances are in the same proportion on the map as they are on the landscape. The grade of reduction from reality to the map is called the map scale.

Topographic Maps

The best maps available to backpackers are topographic maps—derived from the Greek *topos,* place, and *graphein,* to write or draw: a drawing or a picture of a place or an area. They are updated and printed by the U.S. Geological Survey and are available for large areas of the United States. These maps can be acquired by sending a postcard to

Map Information Office
U.S. Geological Survey
Washington, D.C. 20242

Request a Topographic Map Index Circular of the state in which the actual backpacking area is located. Also, ask for the Geological Survey booklet on topographic maps. This material is free.

From the Index Circular you can decide what maps you need. Send your order with the required payment for areas EAST of the Mississippi River to

Distribution Section
Geological Survey
Washington, D.C. 20242

and for areas WEST of the Mississippi River to
              Distribution Section
              Geological Survey
              Denver Federal Center
              Denver, Colorado 80225.

Other Maps

For some areas there are other useful maps available
with additional valuable information for the backpacker. Such maps are the U.S. Forest Service maps
(obtainable from U.S. Forest Service, Washington
D.C. 20250) or National Parks maps (from U.S.
National Park Service, Washington, D.C. 20252).
Your local Chamber of Commerce or surveying office,
or your state's Department of Conservation may also
have information and suggestions, as may the Army,
Air Force or Marine Corps training centers or the
regional Boy Scout offices. Thanks to the spreading
of Orienteering, modern and very detailed maps in
larger scales of certain areas are becoming available,
but so far they are fairly rare in the United States.
Local Orienteering clubs (where they exist) will be able
to advise you.

What the Map Tells You

You will soon find that a map is just as easy to read
as a book. It tells a complete story of an area, and
that story can be fascinating, inspiring explorations
into new territories. When planning your trip it will
tell you what route to choose, how difficult it will be

and where to expect a nice place for rest. It will explain the geographical features of the area in which you intend to travel. It manages all this under the five categories called the "Five D's of Map Reading." To understand what is meant by these headings, unroll the topographic map you ordered, spread it out flat, and take a good look at it.

Description: The description of the map is found in its margin. The "Name of the Map Area" is found at the center top margin. This is the quadrangle name you used in ordering the map. In small type at top and bottom, at each side, and at each corner, are the names of the quadrangles that border on your map. This will be helpful when you find you need maps of the neighboring areas.

The "Location" of your map on the globe is clearly indicated. The degrees of longitude are the numbers just outside the top and bottom lines that frame the map area. The numbers for the degrees of latitude are at the sides. If you connect the tiny line marks for the degrees of longitude at the top with the corresponding marks at the bottom, you are drawing meridians—lines that run true north to true south. If they were drawn far enough, they would hit the North Pole in one direction (up on the map) and the South Pole in the other. The degrees of longitude given are figured westward from the zero degree line running through Greenwich, England.

If in the same way you connect the tiny line marks from the degrees of latitude at one side of the map with the corresponding marks at the other, you are drawing parallels—lines which run parallel to the Equator. The degrees of latitude shown are figured northward from the Equator in the Northern Hemisphere, and southward in the Southern Hemisphere.

Down at the bottom of the map you find important dates: dates of the basic material used for the map including the years of the field check and the date of printing. If the field check was completed in 1950, a number of changes are probable. A town may have grown. The road through that town may have become a highway. Some trails may have grown together and new trails appeared. Consider these possible changes when you plan any excursion.

Details—map symbols: To give you a clear picture of the terrain, the mapmaker has used easily identifiable signs—the map symbols, sometimes called mapping's alphabet. There are four main groups of symbols, each with a distinctive color:

1) *Man-made or cultural features*. Roads and trails, houses and buildings, railroads and power lines, etc. shown on the map in black, except for some important highways which may be overprinted in red.

2) *Water or hydrographic features*. Rivers and canals, lakes and oceans, swamps and marshes and other bodies of water, printed in blue.

3) *Vegetation features*. Wooded areas, orchards, vineyards and scrub are on recent maps in green tint.

4) *Elevation or hypsographic features*. The ups and downs of an area—its mountains and hills, valleys and plains—are indicated on the map by thin brown lines, the so-called contour lines.

You will find that most map symbols are self-evident and will be easily learned. The contour lines will need further explanation and more careful study and practice. You may find them somewhat confusing in the beginning, but perhaps it is some consolation to know that fairly experienced map readers have occasional difficulties interpreting them correctly.

The contour line, by defintion, is an imaginary line on the ground along which every point is at the same height above sea level. The difference in height between each contour line—the contour interval—may vary from map to map and is stated in the information in the map margin.

On a map of a rather level area, the contour interval may be only five feet whereas on maps of mountainous terrain it may be 50 feet or more. Quite often every fifth line is heavier than the others and has a number on it giving the height above sea level in feet (or meters). The pictures shown may help you in understanding and interpreting the contour lines, but the important thing is to take every chance to practice the reading of contour lines in the field, on any and every trip.

A good indoor practice to get a general idea of how map symbols relate to one another is to copy by memory a section of your map. Study a small section of your map, then get out a letterhead-size piece of paper and a pencil. Attempt to sketch, from memory, the map section you have just studied, incorporating in it as many map symbols as possible. Start with such base lines as roads, trails, rivers and creeks. Then compare the result with the real map. Try it again with another section.

Directions: A quick glance at your map will show you the relative direction in which any point lies from any other point. The base line for deciding directions is the north-south line, the meridian line, through the point from which a direction is to be decided. What is north and what is south? When you place a topographic map before you with the reading matter right side up, north is up and south is down on the map, the left margin is west and the right one is east. There is, as a rule, an indication on any map where north is. On topographic maps you find a diagram as pictured, showing true north and magnetic north. The difference will be explained later. Check that the true north leg on the diagram runs parallel to the lines that frame the map—which it usually does.

Now spread the map in front of you. Find a longitude number along the top line of the map frame, and the corresponding number on the bottom line. With a ruler and pencil, draw a line between the two marks at the longitude numbers. This is the true north-south line, the meridian line described above.

In a similar way, draw a parallel line from the left to the right margin of the map by connecting a latitude number on the left line of the map frame with the corresponding number on the right. Where these two lines cross, you have your "base of operations" for some practice in understanding directions on the map.

If you follow the meridian line from your "base of operations" toward the top of the map, any point on the line is directly north of your "base." If you follow the line southwards, toward the bottom of the map, any point on the line is directly south of your "base." Follow the parallel toward the left margin and every point on that line is directly west of your "base." Go along the parallel to the right—any point on the line is east of the spot.

So much for the basic directions, north, south, east and west, called the cardinal points. They may suffice for a general indication of directions. But what about all the other directions from your "base?" The first step toward a more precise way of reading directions from the map is to use the intercardinal points of the compass. To assist you in learning them, take a piece of paper, about three inches square. Fold it in half, then in eights, finally in sixteenths. Round the free edges with scissors. Open the paper, and mark the folds clockwise: North, North-North-East, North-East, East-North-East, East, East-South-East, etc., or simply N, NNE, NE, ENE, E, ESE, SE, SSE, S, SSW, SW, WSW, W, WNW, NW, NNW. Make a small hole in the center of the paper. Place this hole directly over your "base" on the map with the fold marked N(orth) lying over the meridian and pointing toward north of the map. Now you can go from your "base" in 16 specific directions, along the north-east "road" or the south-south-west "road" or in any of the other directions.

The cardinal and intercardinal points of the compass give you only 16 specific directions to work with. You need more than that for precise and exact work from the map to the terrain and vice versa, as need may arise. For this the 360 degrees of a full circle are used. From your "base" you get 360 different highways to choose from, numbered 1 to 360 clockwise from north, which is 0 and 360. As a first step to get a feel of these directions, turn your folded-paper circle into a simple protractor by providing it with the degree numbers for each cardinal and intercardinal point.

Your folded-paper protractor will, of course, not be very accurate. But you learn the principle for determining directions on the map. Whether you actually use a real protractor or a protractor type of compass for taking the bearings (directions) from the map, the principle is the same.

Distances: The scales in the bottom margin of your map give you the means for measuring distances on the map. These scales are usually given in four ways: (1) as a fraction—1:24,000 or 1:62,500; (2) as a ruler divided into miles and fractions of a mile; (3) as a ruler divided into thousands of feet; and (4) as a ruler divided into kilometers and fractions of kilometers.

On a map in the scale of 1:24,000, one inch on the map will represent 24,000 inches or 2,000 feet in the field. On the map in the scale 1:62,500 the number of inches on the map will give the number of miles in the field. Practice the measuring of distances on your maps, converting them to the proper distances in the terrain.

Designations: Places and other map features are designated by name in various lettering styles. Regular Roman (upright) type is used for places, boundary lines and area names, while hydrographic names are in italics (slanting type). Hypsographic (elevation) names are given in block letters and finally, names of public works and special descriptive notes are in leaning block letters. This refers to topographic maps. On other maps different styles may be used.

If you have to indicate to someone else an exact location on the map not designated with a place name, you can do this by using the closest place name and give direction and map distance from it to the point.

Traveling by Map

Now that you know the features of a map, it is time to take a map walk. For a first practice, look at the illustration over-leaf. Lets say that you decide to start from the crossroad south of the Log Chapel, and take a "hike" that will bring you in a counter-clockwise direction— east, south-east, east, north, west, south and west— along the route shown on the illustration back to the cross-roads.

You arrive at the Log Chapel, proceed south to the crossroads and are ready to start out. But, in what direction?

Orienting the map: As a rule, the map should always be oriented when you use it for traveling in the terrain. This is most important. It will make it quite simple to decide from the map what direction to take in the field.

To "orient" the map means to turn it in such a way that what is north on the map fits north in the landscape. Roads, creeks, hillsides or any direction between two points on the map will then be in accord with the same features and directions in the terrain. The map can be oriented "by inspection," by comparing map and landscape and turning the map to fit the landscape and its directions. It also can be done by using the compass and turning the map until the north end of the magnetic needle points to north of the map. This will be explained later.

Now place the illustration on a table. Turn it until

the top of the map illustration faces north, or what you
assume is north, in your room. Theoretically, the map
is now oriented. If you were at the Log Chapel the
picture of the terrain on the map and the terrain itself
would look like the illustration opposite. You would see
that to walk to the crossroads you would walk straight
ahead along the road—south on the map and south on
the terrain. When reading the map you should hold the
map that way in front of you "walking" southward
along the road.

When you have come to the crossroads in your im-

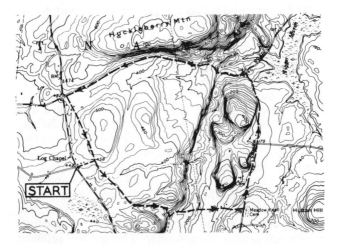

*Follow imaginary map "walk" described on the following
pages. Begin at Start and go counter-clockwise.*

Compare map with landscape: Log Chapel on correct side of road.

aginary hike you should turn left toward point 458 to follow the route indicated on the first illustration. Now you change place and walk over to the side of the table prepared to walk east. The map is left in the same position. In other words, it remains oriented. Arriving at point 458 you prepare to walk south. As you "walk along" you will see that features in the terrain that are on the right will also be on the right side of the map.

Approaching the turn of the route, you walk over to the side of the table or chair preparing to walk east again. At Meadow Knoll Cemetery you move to the next side of the table or chair and so on to complete the imaginary hike. Remember: The map should always be oriented when being read for comparison with the terrain or for travel. The habit of orienting the map at all times will substantially simplify your map reading problems. In areas without clear landmarks to use for orienting the map "by inspection" you have to use the compass.

The Real Map-Walk

Now return to your topographic map. Studying it carefully, plan a trip on it. A walk of four to five miles (in familiar territory, at first) will give you a good grasp of map use. On the next trip you can be a bit more ambitious.

You should try to get along on these first practice trips without reference to the compass. Therefore, your map-reading walks should follow roads, trails and creeks or other similar terrain features clearly identifiable both on the map and in the terrain. And it is not a bad practice at all to follow trails or hike in an area well known to you but perhaps not hiked with a map.

Compass

The heart of the compass is the magnetic needle swinging freely on a pinpoint. When it comes to rest, one end is pointing toward the North Pole and the other one to the South. The magnetized needle is being attracted or directed by the magnetism of the earth. This invisible force of direction which was discovered thousands of years ago is at the wayfinder's or navigator's aid at any time and any place. It is "floating" around you when you read this—yes, right there. All you need to make use of it is to have a small magnetic needle.

Unfortunately, the magnetic North Pole does not coincide with the "true" or geographic North Pole. Maps are drawn to True North and compasses point to magnetic north. The difference in degrees is called "declination." To make things worse, the declination varies—in the United States from 25 degrees west in the eastern part of the country to 25 degrees east in the western part.

There are also local variations in the declination and it does decrease or increase annually depending upon the location. This change, however, is very small and can generally be ignored. Try to get updated information on the declination, and you are all set for years.

Any good quality compass can be used with a map. When purchasing your compass remember that the money saved buying the inferior and cheap alternative won't hire you a taxi when you get lost in the woods.

The modern protractor or orienteering compass is considered far superior to the conventional ones. The combination of a revolving compass housing on a transparent base plate makes for a true precision protractor and direction finder instrument. The best models are liquid filled, where the magnetic needle can be quickly brought to rest.

The housing has one or more compass meridian lines. The base plate has one or more direction of travel lines. The revolving housing can be turned so that the compass meridian lines are in a specific angle to the direction of travel lines of the plate.

When you work with the compass on the map to transfer a bearing from the map to the compass, you forget about the magnetic needle and work with the compass meridian lines and the direction of travel lines of the plate. When transfering a bearing from the compass to the field, the setting should not be changed. Turn the entire compass around until the magnetic needle lines up with the meridian lines of the housing. Personal experience will prove that the advantages of protractor compasses are far superior to those of the conventional types.

Basic Uses of the Compass

The compass is used for these four main purposes:

(1) To follow a degree reading (compass bearing) in the field:
   a) Decide on the direction expressed in compass degrees that you want to follow.
   b) Twist the compass housing until the number on the outside rim of the compass housing for the degrees decided on is at the spot where the direction line touches the housing.
   c) Hold the orienteering compass level before you in your hand, at waist height or a little heigher, with the direction-of-travel arrowhead pointing straight ahead of you.

d) Move your whole body around with small tripping steps, until the compass needle lies over the orienting arrow on the inside bottom of the compass housing, with its north part pointing to the letter N on top of the housing.

e) Raise your head and look straight ahead of you toward some landmark—such as a rock or a large tree.

f) Walk directly toward the landmark without looking further at your compass.

(2) To take a degree reading (compass bearing) from where you are towards a point in the terrain:

a) Face squarely the point toward which you want to take the direction reading expressed in compass degrees.

b) Hold the orienteering compass level before you in your hand, at waist height or a little higher, with the direction-of-travel arrowhead pointing straight ahead of you toward the distant point.

c) Twist the compass housing until the compass needle lies over the orienting arrow on the inside bottom of the compass housing, with its north part pointing to the letter N on top of the housing.

d) Read the number of degrees on the outside rim of the compass housing at the spot where the direction line touches the housing.

(3) To orient a map with the compass:

a) Set the orienteering compass at 360 degrees—i.e. with the 360 degree marking of the compass housing touching the direction line of the base plate.

b) Place the compass so that the wide edge of the base plate lies along the magnetic north arrow on the map, or parallel to it, with the direction arrow of plate pointing towards north of map.

c) Turn the map with the compass lying on it until the north part of the compass needle points to the N of the compass housing. The compass is now oriented—and so is the map.

(4) To set a degree reading (compass bearing) on a compass from a map:

a) Place the orienteering compass on the map with the edge of the base plate touching the starting point (where you are standing) and the place to which you want to go (your destination).

b) Turn the compass housing until the orienting arrow on the inside bottom lies parallel with the nearest meridian (the true north-south line drawn across map from north to south)—the compass is now set.

To proceed toward the destination for which the compass is set, pick up the compass without moving the housing, and then follow points c), d), e), and f) in instructions given above for following a degree reading in the field.

Traveling by Compass

Try a simple test first, of a compass walk over a short distance. Place a marker on the ground between your feet. Set the compass for an arbitrary direction between 0 and 120 degrees, as described under (1) basic uses, above, perhaps for 40 degrees. Then proceed as further described in that specific direction for 40 steps—around 100 feet. Stop!

Now, add 120 degrees to your original 40 degrees—making it 160 degrees. Reset your compass housing and proceed in the new direction for another 40 steps. Stop!

Again, add 120 degrees to your setting of 160 degrees—making it 280 degrees. Set your compass, determine the direction to walk and take 40 steps in the new direction. Stop! Bend down and pick up your marker. It should be right at your feet. How come? You have been walking the three sides of an equilateral triangle, mathematically correct, returning to your starting point.

Adjusting for Declination

It is important to know the declination of your loca-

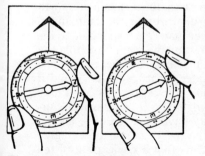

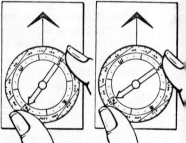

To compensate if declination is WEST: check number of degrees at base of direction line. ADD declination, reset compass to new number.

To compensate if declination is EAST: check number of degrees at base of direction line. SUBTRACT declination, reset compass to new number.

tion. If you depend on a compass direction taken from a map without considering the declination, you may get thrown off your intended course.

You have two choices as to how you will accomplish this: (1) By resetting the compass each time you set it from the map or (2) by making your map speak "compass language." Resetting the compass after you have taken the bearing from the map is done as shown by these illustrations:

There is, however, the much simpler way of compensating for declination, by providing the map with magnetic-north lines. By using these lines instead of the true-north lines of the regular meridian lines, your map speaks the same language as your compass. The settings you take on your compass using these lines do not require resetting as explained above to compensate for declination—the declination is taken care of.

To provide your map with these magnetic-north lines, first draw a line up through the map in an angle to one of the true meridians corresponding to the degrees of declination given on the map. Note that the declination diagram as such may not be exact. The number of degrees indicates what to abide by and if the declination information is several years old it may be wise to find out from the U.S. Geological Survey to what extent it may have changed. The annual change may be nil. It may be one-sixth of a degree easterly and if it is it means that a declination of ten degrees west will decrease by one degree for every sixth year and for all practical purposes you may use the same magnetic-north lines for more than five years anyway. And this may be longer than the lifetime of your map.

The Real Thing

Most of what you have read thus far is theoretical. Nothing, but nothing can replace practice if your goal is navigational expertise. If you've digested the above instruction you should now make a habit of carrying your map and compass on even the shortest excursions.

There is always something new to learn about your map and compass. One important technique is learning to determine the location by taking cross-bearings to two or more definable points. A backpacker should also get acquainted with keeping a map-log for areas not covered by good maps. Carrying along a notebook, one tries to make a habit of taking notes of directions and distances—by time, by counting steps or estimations—as he hikes along. Also, by making note of discrepancies in existing maps or by finding exciting look-out points or campsites, he can then relate them to friends.

In my opinion, it would be wrong to attempt writing more about "the real thing." With this basic knowledge of wilderness navigational tools, the map and the compass, I am confident you will be able to go from here on your own.

Remember: Make it a habit always to carry along your map and compass! And use them—even when you don't need them!

The Weather Eye

From *Finding Your Way in the Outdoors*.
By Robert L. Mooers, Jr.*

Weather is of critical importance to any outdoor activity, but particularly to those pursuits which take people more than a few hours from warmth and shelter. Accurate weather forecasting in the outdoors by an untrained individual is out of the question, but so too is the blind acceptance of whatever comes from the weather gods without even an attempt at second-guessing them. The alternative, somewhere between blind acceptance and sheer guesswork, is to develop a "weather eye" in the tradition of farmers, sailors, and other self-reliant peoples the world over.

Long before the days of global weather reporting and weather satellites, these people depended on their own observations to learn when and how the weather would change. The lore they developed is no less valid today. With a little science added, it is perhaps even more reliable.

Cultivating a weather eye consists of learning some of the fundamentals of meteorology and knowing a few of the weather's typical patterns and signs of change. The more you learn, and the more astute your observations, the more accurate will be your guesses.

With one excerpt from another source as indicated.

Some Old (Semi-) Reliable Weather Signs

Each of the following has some basis in fact, though like most wise old sayings, exceptions occur often enough to keep one guessing.

Bad Weather Indicators

- A ring around the sun or moon means rain or snow.
- Wind-shifts from N to W then S are often accompanied by rain.
- Unusual sky tints—green, yellow, dark red or gloomy blue—bring rain and/or wind.
- Small inky clouds bring rain.
- "Red sky in the morning, sailor take warning. Red sky at night, sailor's delight."
- Clouds hanging on the heights indicate wind and rain unless they lift by midday.
- Scud clouds (small, dark, scurrying cumulus types) sweeping beneath a dark stratus layer mean that wind and rain may be near. If above the stratus layer, which may be difficult to determine, there will be wind only.
- Cloud layers moving in different directions foretell a change in wind direction corresponding to that of the upper layer.

Fair Weather Indicators

- A gray dawn means fine weather.
- Fog in the valleys will burn off and clear.
- Rain rarely falls after dew forms.
- Cumulus clouds, especially those found on bright

sunny days, mean fair weather unless they tower and flatten on top.

• Red sky in the evening means fine, generally hot, next day. Wind shifts from S to W to N are often accompanied by clearing.

What "Makes" Weather

At the heart of the weather-making process are differences in the density of air masses due in turn to differences in their temperatures. The sun heats the earth's blanket of air unevenly, causing the warmer masses to expand, become lighter (less dense) and thus, to rise. Cooler and heavier air masses (more dense) immediately move into the void and a cycle has begun. The moving air is, of course, wind.

Weathermen speak in terms of low and high pressure rather than of heavy and light air masses. Since lighter air pushes downward with less force, it exerts low atmospheric pressure on the earth, and the opposite is true of heavier air. Measuring differences in atmospheric pressure is the function of the barometer, a key instrument in guessing the weather and the only one necessary for the outdoorsman-forecaster.

In its movement over land and sea, air picks up evaporated moisture. The warmer the air, the more moisture it can hold; thus at any given temperature it will reach a saturation point. As it rises into the upper atmosphere, warm air must cool. It does so at the normal rate of about 3½°F for every 1,000 feet. When its temperature drops below the saturation point for the amount of moisture it is carrying, some of it must condense back into liquid water droplets, which as they become larger and larger, will eventually overcome the upward air currents and fall as rain. The several other forms of precipitation are variations of this same condensing process.

Air Masses and Weather Fronts

Air masses affecting the contiguous United States originate northward in the polar regions, southward in tropical zones, and in the two great maritime areas to the east and west, particularly westward over the Pacific Ocean. As they enter the country the polar and tropical contributions are deflected eastward by the great mid-latitude wind belt known as the "Prevailing Westerlies." The colder air of the polar masses actually takes a compromise southeast course while the moist tropical air typically moves to the northeast. Daily weather maps in newspapers often show the two different masses to be on such a southeast-northeast collision course.

Many things can happen to modify the "typical" sequence of events with any type of front. Only the gathering of widespread and numerous, as well as frequent, reports can hope to keep up with the whims of such a vast and dynamic force. One confusing variation in weather patterns is the occluded front. An occlusion occurs when two air masses of similar disposition trap a smaller and different mass between them. The associated weather usually has characteristics of a cold front, that is, gusty and violent, but the sequence of activities will seem haphazard to the weather eye.

A second frontal event which tends to complicate weather guessing is the stationary front. For one reason or another an air mass may camp in an area for days or even weeks. In this case the barometer might serve to notify when a change is finally forthcoming, but will be of little use in the jockeying back and forth from storm to clearing and more of each. Air, like people with nothing to do, often gets into trouble.

This is a highly simplified version of air-mass movement, but the point to be made is that most of our storms arrive from the western quadrants. The actual winds in any weather pattern may blow from any quarter since winds behave in a circular manner independent of the direction of the storm itself. Winds spawned in northern hemispheric high-pressure cells rotate in a clockwise direction while those in a low-pressure cell rotate counterclockwise. The effects south of the equator are reversed.

A weather front is the leading edge of a mass of air with well-defined characteristics of density, temperature and moisture content. More exactly, it is the meeting point between two differing masses. Since nature insists on achieving a balance, the greater these differences the more violent will be the adjustment, which of course, we know as "weather."

Fronts are classed primarily as warm and cold, referring to relative differences between air masses and between ground temperatures and air masses. Each behaves in a characteristic manner, announcing its approach and passage in predictable fashion. The weather is likely to be good when either is in firm control. Here are a few general facts about each type of front:

Cold fronts: Cold air is unstable and, therefore, restless. Weather associated with it is often of an aggressive and violent nature, though ordinarily of shorter duration than that accompanying warm fronts. Cold air is typically clear and dry, with ceilings high and visibility good except during precipitation. A cold front moves at about 20 to 35 mph or from 500 to 700 miles per day. Because the air in a cold front is dry, thus having less extensive cloud layers, it often arrives with only a few hours' warning. The actual front may be preceded by a squall line of thunderstorms as much as 50 to 200 miles in advance. In the interim between squall line and the frontal weather itself, conditions may be unsettled.

Warm fronts: Warm air contrasts with cold air in every respect. It tends to be more stable, more moist, with lower ceilings and poorer visibility even when not precipitating. Weather associated with a warm front is usually limited to rain which may last several days. Clearing is typically followed by several more days of good weather. In contrast to cold fronts, warm fronts move slowly, perhaps 10 to 25 mph, or 250 to 500 miles per day. Their coming is forecast as much as two days ahead by a typical sequence of clouds and a drop in barometric pressure. Clouds and cloud sequences figure very prominently in our forecasting.

Cloud Identification

A cloud is the visible evidence of moisture content in

Top: Cumulus. Bottom: Stratus. Facing page: Cirrus.

the air. The words used to describe the different kinds of clouds may seem clumsy at first, but do not take very long to learn. Learning which name to give to which cloud, however, takes a bit more practice.

Clouds are named in three families which define their shape. *Cirrus* clouds are always high and are thin and wispy, sometimes filmlike in appearance. *Cumulus* clouds are billowy and puffy, like mounds of soapsuds. They are formed by vertical currents carrying moist air upward, and are consequently very active. They roll and surge upward and outward, changing shape in a markedly short time. *Stratus* clouds are layered. After rising moisture has begun to condense, it typically slows its vertical ascent and begins to form in horizontal or stratified layers. Cumulus and stratus clouds may form at any height, while cirrus, as noted, are always very high.

Each of the three families occur separately, but as often as not, are found in combination which make identification a bit more arbitrary. Very high, puffy-looking clouds may be *cirrocumulus,* while very high, filmlike cloud sheets become *cirrostratus.* The same is true, for example, of puffy-looking clouds which are tending toward a flattish layer; these are called *strato-cumulus.* There are a few more combinations, but no cloud name uses more than two of these word elements.

While the family names define cloud shape, the prefix *alto* tells us that a cloud mass is in the middle range of heights, below the cirrus family. It is used with cumulus and stratus to define middle-high *altocumulus* and *altostratus* clouds. One more designation, *nimbus,* means "rain bearing." Like alto, it is used only with the cumulus and stratus family named to give us *cumulonimbus* and *nimbostratus.* You might have noticed that the order in these two is changed around a bit, but this is hardly important. Ham and eggs is the same dish as eggs and ham; the important thing is to get them both on the same plate. A third descriptive term, *fracto*, is used to denote the broken or ragged underside of a rain cloud. *Fractonimbus* is the final pronouncement that if you are not already being dripped upon, the time is near. The accompanying chart shows all of the important cloud name combinations.

Cirrus: Highest of all clouds, like wispy locks of hair or frost patterns on a window. Often form on leading edge of warm front as it rides up over colder mass before it. Composed of ice crystals. Usually indicators of change in the weather within two days.

Cirrus clouds may be the first to appear in a clear blue sky, or may appear over other forms and from a different direction.

Cirrocumulus: High, rolling, wavy groups, the true "mackerel sky." Looks like winnowed hay or gently rolling waves on the ocean. Not a frequent cloud form. Its presence is a good indicator of violent weather with the approaching front. (Distinguish carefully from altocumulus.)

Cirrostratus: High, whitish, filmlike sheets. Like all high clouds, cirrostratus never cast a shadow or completely block sun or moon. Cirrus generally degrade to this form rather than to a mackerel sky. Due to ice-crystal content, may produce a halo of yellowish brightness around sun or moon.

Altocumulus: White to grayish rolling or scrambled patches looking like chunks of various-sized cotton. May be arranged in wavy rows and be confused with cirrocumulus. Puffs are larger than in the cirro form; they are and tend to look lower than cirrocumulus. If cirrus clouds appear in the same sky they will be an obvious overlayer to the altocumulus but will seem more adjacent to or grading into cirrocumulus. Altocumulus masses may produce a sun corona or disk of color around the sun. The corona, formed by sunlight shining through water droplets rather than through ice crystals, is more compact than the halo of cirrostatus, seeming to replace the body rather than ringing it. The corona is more highly colored, ranging from pale yellow in the center to bluish or reddish edges.

Stratocumulus: Masses of spread out and flattening

cumulus clouds in a layered formation. Not usually rain bearing, but may close to form nimbostratus.

Altostratus: Gray, layered mass. Blocks sun and moon but occasionally lets them peak through between thicker areas. Usually drop precipitation beginning as drizzle.

Stratus: The single family name of stratus is given to low continuous gray masses which may hang on for days, producing only drizzle at the most. Uniform appearance indicates lack of internal vertical motion which is necessary for formation of raindrops of any larger size.

Nimbostratus: Precipitating low, thick, layered mass, the true rain cloud. Completely blocks sun and moon. Often presents ragged or fracto underside as rain falls on somebody else.

Cumulus: Puffy, billowy, white clouds with flat, grayish bottoms. These are fair-weather clouds which form on warm afternoons as sun heats the earth, forcing moistened air to rise. Cumulus clouds usually dissipate with cooling of evening, but may develop into towering cumulonimbus. Clouds given the family name of cumulus tend to be large and distinctive. In combination with other forms the cumulus puffiness is retained, but the individuality is lost.

Cumulonimbus: Towering cumulus thunderheads, often with visible anvil-shaped tops and dark, boiling underreaches. Upper fringes develop brilliantly defined outlines as interiors darken. Tremendous internal vertical air currents may reach speeds of 200 mph. Cumulonimbus clouds unleash thunder, lightning, rain, hail, or snow flurries on the earth. These violent ac-

tivities often appear to come from altostratus or nimbostratus cloud cover just in advance of the front, but
are generated by cumulonimbus above.

Approach of a Cold Front

Most storms are closely enough allied with weather
fronts that by watching the front we can pretty much
predict the coming weather. Fronts vary and change
constantly within themselves, but often retain a definite
identification.

Cloud sequences in a cold front: Altostratus two to
four hours in advance, then nimbostratus, possibly
preceded by cumulonimbus.

Conditions: Barometer drops (altimeter rises)
steadily, then rapidly as front arrives. Temperature
falls. Winds from N or NW quadrant, shifting to S or
SW.

Description: Cold air on the leading edge of the
front slides under the warmer mass ahead of it, causing
a rapid rise and cooling of the warm air's moisture
content. Resulting altrostratus clouds appear first on
W or NW horizon. Rain begins, perhaps as a steady
drizzle, then heavier as clouds lower and thicken to
nimbostratus. Particularly fast-moving fronts will be
signaled by cumulus cloud forms along with the stratus
layers. These foretell gusty winds and possibly
thunder and lightning with more severe forms of
precipitation. Cumulonimbus clouds may be hidden
from view above the stratus clouds, or precede the
front by 50 to 200 miles as a squall line. If they appear
in advance, the barometer will show a quick drop, then

steady before dropping again with the approach of the front. Cloud conditions in between will typify unsettled skies.

As the center of the disturbances arrives over the observer, the barometer will hit its lowest point and begin to rise. This low extreme is referred to as the "trough." With its passage, winds shift back around to the W or NW, the temperature falls, and the sky begins to clear. Broken masses of cumulus and cumulonimbus clouds may bring occasional showers as skies remain unsettled for a time. Settling is indicated by formation of stratocumulus bands, then higher alto- cumulus clouds as the cover breaks and lifts. If no further disturbance is near, clearing will follow.

Approach of a Warm Front

Cloud sequences in a warm front:
Cirrus up to 48 hours in advance
Cirrostratus
Altostratus
Nimbostratus

As with the cold front, any cumulus cloud forms appearing in the sequence warn of more violent weather with the coming rains.

Conditions: Barometer drops (altimeter rises) slowly. Temperature rises. Visibility is poor with fog, haze and lowering ceilings. Winds are light to calm.

Description: Warm fronts are signaled as much as 48 hours in advance by high, thin, innocuous-looking cir- rus clouds formed as the leading edge of warm air rides up over the colder mass ahead of it. Cirrus wisps join to form milky cirrostratus sheets, then thicken and lower to become darkening altostratus bands. Rain begins and increases with the formation of nimbostratus layers. The barometer continues its slow decline. With passage of the front, pressure begins a slow rise, while alto and nimbostratus clouds hang on for one, two, or even more days. Clearing typically lasts a corresponding period before arrival of the next front.

Change, rather than the exact form it will take, is what the weather forecaster is concerned with. For route-finding and decision-making, this itself may be enough. Rather than planning activities on the basis of what the weather *will* be, decisions can be based on what the worst *might* bring. The weatherman in a party of mountain climbers might say, "There's a cold front on its way. I don't like the idea of being caught on the exposed west face in lightning. Let's do the east ridge and hope to beat the weather." Or perhaps after three wet days in a cheerless camp a weather prophet might announce to his companions, "Indications are for clearing in 12 to 18 hours. Let's wait one more day before giving up."

Of course we weren't there for the reply, but one of the others might have said, "That's what you told us Tuesday."

Lightning Strikes*

Electrical storms are commonplace in mountainous areas, and occasionally an outdoorsman may become the victim of a lightning strike. By far the best approach to lightning injuries is to avoid being struck in the first

*From *The Outdoorsman's Medical Guide* by Alan E. Nourse, M.D.

place. Get away from summits and peaks when a thunderstorm comes up and seek protection on low, flat ground or in shallow declivities when possible. Open rock faces and high rock outcroppings can draw lightning strikes even when they are not the summit of mountains. As a cardinal rule, if you are in high, exposed country, when you see a thunderstorm coming *get to lower ground quickly.* A *deep* cave or overhang can provide ideal protection, but the openings of shallow caves, narrow rock leges, or stream gullies can all be dangerous because of the movement of ground currents that occurs after a nearby lightning strike. In wooded areas avoid standing under tall, solitary trees and seek shelter instead in thickets of shorter trees. Finally, when you have found reasonable shelter, isolate the metal objects among your equipment—metal pack frame, ice axe, knife, or what-have-you—and keep them at a distance from you until the storm passes over.

Many people erroneously believe that the individual who is struck by lightning is invariably going to be killed. The fact is that many an apparently dead victim of lightning strike has merely suffered from an arrest of breathing and heartbeat, and can be revived by the swift application of mouth-to-mouth artificial respiration and external cardiac compression until his natural respirations and heartbeat resume. Either or both of these procedures should be continued as needed for an hour or more before abandoning them as futile. Once breathing and heartbeat are restored, there is time enough to dress any burns that may have occurred where the lightning bolt entered or left the body.

Dealing with Heat and Cold

From *The Outdoorsman's Medical Guide*
By Alan E. Nourse, M.D.

[*Rather than belabor the usual first aid favorites (massive mosquito bite, grizzly scratch and on-trail treatment for coronary thrombosis), we felt that a comprehensive discussion of the heat and cold—the practical problems—would be more useful. The chances of severing an artery in the backcountry, or being bitten by a rattlesnake, are really not deserving of the aura of panic that surrounds them. One should, however, certainly be informed. The serious backpacker should study a complete first aid text, or enroll in a Red Cross Course, or purchase a copy of the excellent book from which this excerpt was taken. The eds./Sierra Club Books*]

Dealing with the Heat

By far the greatest amount of outdoor recreation is pursued during the spring, summer, and early fall when thousands of hikers and backpackers all over the country are taking to the woods and trails. The reasons for this seasonal increase in outdoor activity are obvious.

With the weather generally temperate, the hiker can travel lightly with a minimum of heavy clothing and equipment. Dry fuel is likely to be abundant, only a light tent or rain fly is needed for sleeping protection, and there is little concern about such cold-weather hazards as frostbite or exposure—except, of course, in the case of high-mountain travel.

Hot-weather hiking does, however, involve certain potential health hazards of its own. While hardly life-threatening, such problems as sunburn, dehydration, or muscle cramps owing to salt depletion can cause great discomfort and seriously diminish one's pleasure on the trail. Such other conditions as heat exhaustion or heat stroke can be far more serious and could well, if not speedily diagnosed and treated, bring an otherwise pleasant summer outing to a catastrophic end. Every outdoorsman should know how to recognize such hot-weather problems, how to prevent them from arising whenever possible, and how to deal with them effectively if they do occur.

Sunburn

Among the problems that can arise from solar radiation, sunburn is by far the most familiar. A mild sunburn may produce only minor discomfort and require no special treatment at all, but a bad sunburn can be severely disabling. What is more, serious sunburns are particularly likely to occur under the special conditions of exposure commonly encountered by hikers, backpackers, or fishermen unless adequate preventive measures are taken.

Sunburn is caused by exposure to the ultraviolet rays present in unfiltered sunlight. The severity of a sunburn will depend upon the amount of natural pigmentation in your skin, the depth of protective tan you have acquired prior to exposure, and the intensity and duration of your exposure to the sun. Fair-skinned people with blond or red hair are more susceptible to severe sunburn than brunet individuals because they have less natural skin pigmentation and do not tan as readily or deeply. Such a person may develop a mild sunburn in as little as a half-hour of exposure to intense sunlight, or a severe, blistering burn in the course of a single hour. Oriental, Amerindian, or Negroid individuals burn much less freely, but even they can be seriously disabled by sunburn, given sufficient unprotected exposure to the sun.

Aside from natural susceptibility, certain hiking and backpacking conditions may expose you to extraordinary amounts of ultraviolet radiation. More of the burning ultraviolet rays reach the earth at high altitudes than at sea level because there is far less atmosphere to filter the sunlight. Exposure to the sun on a lake can double the amount of ultraviolet radiation you receive because of reflection, and the conditions on high-altitude snow fields can compound the sunburn threat even more. Even the reflection of sunlight from light-covered rock faces can lead to sunburn in such unexpected places as under the chin, in the ears, or within the nostrils. Also bear in mind that severe sunburning can easily occur on days when the sun is partly obscured by high thin clouds, and that some degree of sunburn can occur even *through* a light, loosely woven summer shirt.

The signs and symptoms of sunburn occur within a few hours of exposure and vary according to the severity. A mild sunburn produces little more than a reddening or *erythema* of the exposed areas. The skin feels warm immediately after exposure, and the next day it develops a feeling of tightness or scratchiness. With more prolonged exposure the skin becomes a deep, angry red, and blistering may occur on such tender areas as the lips, the nose, or the sides of the neck. The burn is painful to touch, and toxic symptoms such as headache, nausea, chilling, or fever may appear. Still more severe exposure leads to widespread blistering and extreme pain, together with an exaggeration of the toxic symptoms and, in many cases, noticeable swelling of the injured tissues.

The best way to prevent a serious sunburn on the trail is to prepare in advance by gradually exposing yourself to the sun daily for increasing intervals during the first few weeks of warm spring sunshine. This procedure will stimulate the development of protective pigments in your skin so that any later sunburn will be relatively mild. Exposures of fifteen to twenty minutes per day at first, increasing to an hour at a time later, will help develop a protective tan. Don't bother with so-called tanning lotions during this process; you are seeking the skin's natural reaction to sunlight at this time, not the action of a surface chemical. If mild burning and peeling occur at first, don't worry; this will enhance the tanning process rather than hinder it.

On the trail the most obvious way to prevent sunburn is to wear adequate protective clothing—long trousers, a long-sleeved shirt, and a hat with an adequate brim.

To protect such exposed areas as the hands, lips, neck, face, and ears, use liberal applications of one of the suntan lotions containing screening agents which filter out the ultraviolet rays before they can penetrate to the skin's surface. Preparations such as Sea and Ski, containing glyceryl-para-amino-benzoate, are highly successful in protecting against sunburn and help speed tanning. Others containing menthyl salicylate (Coppertone, Aztec) or oxybenzone (Solbar) are also good. In addition to screening protection during the day, these lotions can also provide relief from the tightness and discomfort of a minor sunburn if reapplied copiously before retiring on the evening of the exposure. Unfortunately these preparations tend to wash off with swimming or heavy perspiration and must be reapplied frequently during the day for continuing protection. They must be avoided altogether by anyone who has become allergic to the active ingredients. High climbers on snow fields and glaciers often prefer the complete protection of an oil-based opaque white pigment such as titanium dioxide (A-Fil) or zinc oxide (Zincofax Cream) to coat such sensitive areas as the lips, the nose, the ears, or the eyelids.

What can be done to treat sunburn when it occurs? A mild burn requires no treatment other than the reapplication of a suntan lotion to the reddened areas before retiring to help prevent dryness and peeling of the skin later. If there has been blistering of the skin, avoid the use of lotions or oils, which can contribute to later infection. Such sunburns can be made more comfortable by applying cold moist dressings soaked in water that has been sterilized by boiling and then cooled. The

same applies to severely blistered, swollen sunburns.
Pain can be combated with one or two ordinary 5-grain
aspirin or, when severe, with a Darvon Compound
capsule or a ½-grain codeine tablet. Since any blistered
sunburn is vulnerable to later infection, the victim
should be seen by a physician for further treatment as
soon as he has returned home.

Dehydration, Salt Loss, and Muscle Cramps

Other problems, both minor and major, can arise during
hot-weather hiking as a result of the body's natural
efforts to cool itself down when it becomes overheated.
The human body is a remarkable heat-production machine. Under ordinary circumstances it uses nutri-
ents assimilated from the digestive tract to produce a
steady flow of heat and energy. Additional heat is generated by muscular activity. At the same time, heat is
steadily being lost by the breathing out of warm, moist
air during respiration, and by the evaporation of perspiration that flows to the surface of the body. Normally
such a delicate balance is maintained between heat
produced and heat lost that the body's internal temperature seldom varies more than a degree or so from a
normal level of 99° Fahrenheit.
    When the body's muscular activity is suddenly
greatly increased, however, a huge surplus of internal
heat is produced, and the body's natural cooling
mechanisms must shift into high gear to prevent over-
heating. A backpacker on a mountain trail can easily
generate six to eight times as much internal heat as he
would sitting at a desk in his office, and in summer the

sun's radiation adds even more to his body's heat burden. At the same time the amount of heat lost by increasingly rapid respirations may be doubled or tripled during strenuous hiking, and the amount of perspiration is vastly increased. During vigorous exercise on an extremely warm day the hiker may easily shed quarts or even gallons of perspiration in the course of a few hours.

Obviously such a loss of fluid can cause the body to become badly dehydrated unless the fluid is promptly replaced. In addition, the increased amount of perspiration can carry out of the body a considerable quantity of salt, a substance which is vital to the body's normal, healthy chemical balance. When fluid and salt are being lost much faster than they are being replenished on a long, hot hike, the resulting imbalance may be manifested in such uncomfortable symptoms as marked and increasing thirst, increasing breathlessness, generalized weakness and lethargy, and, finally, cramping of the muscles, especially in the legs, thighs, or back. These cramps can be painfully disabling, but tend to subside, at least temporarily, whenever the victim takes a break to rest and cool off.

The best way to prevent dehydration, salt loss, and muscle cramping on the trail is to take in adequate amounts of water by mouth at regular intervals to make up for the fluid lost in perspiration, and to replenish the salt loss by taking salt tablets (with ample amounts of water) from time to time throughout the day. These tablets, each containing about 500 milligrams of salt, are available inexpensively and without prescription at drugstores under such brand names as Thermotabs or

Thermodex Tablets. For most adults, two tablets taken by mouth with two cups of water three or four times a day will be ample to replenish the salt lost through perspiration on a very hot day's hiking. Children under twelve should take no more than half that dosage. In addition, plan your summer camping meals to contain somewhat more salt than you might normally use for seasoning. Be careful, however, not to take too many salt tablets in too brief a period. The excessive salt in concentrated form can irritate the stomach, causing nausea or vomiting, and too much salt assimilated into the body can cause swelling of the tissues due to retention of excessive fluids. Fortunately, most out-doorsmen find that muscle cramping is an early-season annoyance which occurs less and less frequently as the muscles become conditioned to hiking and the body's cooling mechanisms begin to work more efficiently.

The Major Heat Threats

At the worst the muscle cramping described above is a transitory hot-weather nuisance which can be treated effectively by the simple measures noted, and it rarely poses any dangerous or long-term health hazard. There are two conditions, however, that constitute a more serious threat to the outdoorsman hiking in hot weather. The first, known as *heat exhaustion*, is more alarming than dangerous, but the second, *heat stroke*, can develop into a life-threatening emergency. Every outdoorsman should be able to recognize and distinguish these forms of heat injury, and know what first-aid measures can be taken to combat them.

Heat exhaustion: Typically this benign but alarming disorder strikes quite suddenly in the course of a hot-weather hiking trip, and can afflict individuals who are in excellent physical condition as well as those who are not. The disorder most commonly occurs when the victim has been engaging in strenuous physical activity for a prolonged time in a hot environment. Under such conditions the blood vessels at the surface of the body enlarge or dilate, so that excessive internal heat can be dispelled from the skin surface by radiation and cooling of perspiration. When the heat is extreme, this rush of blood into the surface blood vessels can sharply diminish the amount of blood being circulated to the brain and other vital internal organs.

The result is a sudden and startling physiological reaction. The victim suddenly feels faint and becomes aware of a very rapid, fluttery heartbeat. He becomes nauseated, and may vomit. In most cases he will be perspiring profusely, but his face appears pale and his skin feels cold and clammy. In extreme cases he may even pass out momentarily. Characteristically, however, *his body temperature is not significantly elevated*—in fact, it may be slightly below normal. He simply feels faint, exhausted, and unable to go on.

Treatment of heat exhaustion is simple and conservative. First, bring the victim to rest, lying down with his head slightly lower than his feet. Loosen restrictive clothing and give him sips of cool liquids as long as he is conscious. (*Never* try to give fluids to an unconscious person.) Alarming as it may seem, heat exhaustion is almost completely self-limited—that is, recovery occurs spontaneously as soon as the victim lies down and rests for a while. Keep him resting in the shade, off his feet, for a period of half an hour or so, or until his pulse settles down to 90 beats per minute or less, his perspiration is diminished, and he feels capable of going on. At the same time, take steps to prevent a recurrence. Both salt and water loss should be replenished and trail snacks such as cheese, chocolate, raisins, or salted nuts should be used as a rapid source of energy. If possible, relieve the victim of part of his pack until any likelihood of recurrence is past. Once he has recovered, he can usually carry on at a somewhat slower pace unless he is suffering from heart disease, kidney disease, or some other condition in which heat exhaustion might be adding insult to injury.

Heat stroke, also known as *sun stroke* or *hyperpyrexia,* can occur under much the same circumstances as heat exhaustion, but it is a totally different and far more serious condition. Unlike heat exhaustion, in which the body's natural cooling mechanisms are working perhaps too efficiently, heat stroke occurs when those natural cooling mechanisms break down so completely that the body becomes excessively overheated and *cannot cool itself down by natural means.* The victim, who may previously have been perspiring copiously for a prolonged period, suddenly begins to perspire less and less, and his internal body temperature begins climbing to dangerous levels. Typically he complains of feeling unbearably hot; presently he becomes confused and poorly coordinated, then delirious, and may even suddenly lose consciousness. Quite unlike the picture in heat exhaustion, the victim's face is flushed and his skin hot to touch and *completely dry of perspiration.* If his temperature is taken, it could be found to be in the neighborhood of 105° and still rising. In merely a few minutes the victim is prostrated and shows no signs of spontaneous recovery such as is seen in heat exhaustion when the victim if placed at rest.

No one knows for sure why heat stroke occurs, or why it may affect one person and not another under the same circumstances. Perhaps it results from exhaustion of the sweat glands' capacity to form perspiration. It seldom occurs if there has been some relief from sweating in the course of a 24-hour period—a cool night for sleeping, for example, or merely a prolonged rest in the shade during the heat of the day—and seems more likely to occur when the victim is wearing no hat to protect his head from the blazing noonday sun. Whatever the exact mechanism may be, however, heat stroke is a serious medical emergency when it occurs. Unless swiftly and vigorously treated, the victim may die on the spot, or suffer permanent brain damage, as a result of the dangerously high body temperature.

To treat heat stroke effectively you must *cool the victim's body down as quickly as possible* by whatever means you can find available. Ideal treatment on the trail is to immerse him completely in the cool water of a stream or lake until his body temperature drops to 102° or less and he becomes conscious and rational again. If there is no such water supply at hand, cover the victim with cloths soaked with water from canteens, or even with alcohol if any is available, and then fan him vigorously to promote evaporation. If ice or chemical cold packs are available, these can be used to help cool the victim's body. At the same time, massage his arms and legs to stimulate circulation of blood to and from the extremities, so that it can help cool down the vital internal organs. Finally, as soon as he is cool enough to be out of immediate danger, make arrangements to evacuate him to a physician's care. All too often the victim of heat stroke begins warming up again as soon as measures to cool him off are relaxed, and he may retain some degree of intolerance to heat for a prolonged period after recovery. To try immediately to continue a hike or other outing is to beg for trouble.

Obviously it is far better to prevent heat stroke, if possible, than to have to treat it. Anyone hiking in hot weather should wear a hat with a brim wide enough to protect the head and face from the direct rays of the sun. Stop frequently to cool off in the course of your hiking day, and take a quick dip in a mountain stream or lake once or twice a day if this is possible. Such a practice is not only very pleasant, but it may also provide your body's natural cooling mechanisms just the breather they need to maintain their efficient function throughout the day.

Dealing with the Cold

During the past ten years the popularity of winter wilderness recreation has been increasing on a geometric curve. Backpackers, snowshoe hikers, cross-country skiers, snow campers, bow hunters, and snowmobilers have been penetrating the winter wilderness in ever increasing numbers. Nor is this accelerating interest likely to flag in the near future. As outdoorsmen become bolder and more experienced in winter recreation, increasing multitudes of people will be encountering the singular pleasures—and the singular dangers —of the cold-weather wilderness for the first time.

The still, dry cold, in itself, does not present a hazard to anyone who is adequately dressed for the weather. On the other hand, the deadly combination of coldness, wetness, and wind can confound the most experienced and well-equipped outdoorsman unless he is prepared in advance to recognize and protect himself from certain extraordinary cold-weather threats that can arise—and especially from the hazards of disabling frostbite or life-threatening hypothermia.

The Hazard of Frostbite

In the simplest of terms, frostbite is the actual freezing of the skin and underlying tissues of certain parts of the body owing to exposure to the cold and chilling of these tissues below the freezing point. The parts most commonly affected are the extremities—the fingers or toes—and such exposed parts of the body as the ears, the nose, the cheeks, or the chin. When the injury involves only the skin and the layers of cells immediately beneath it, we speak of *superficial frostbite* or "frost nip." When the injury involves deeper layers of tissues, including muscle, tendon, or bone, it is called *deep frostbite*. The distinction is important, since the approach to treatment of minor frost nip is quite different from the approach to deep frostbite.

Obviously mere exposure to the cold, in itself, does not invariably lead to frostbite; certain *predisposing conditions* are almost always present. Cardinal among these are fatigue or exhaustion, the lack of adequate heat-producing food, and dehydration resulting from inadequate intake of fluids. External factors often play a part: the victim of frostbite may have been trapped by a sudden storm, separated and lost from his party, or injured in some way before the frostbite occurs. Certain internal physical factors can also predispose to frostbite and set the stage for trouble. For example, enormous quantities of body heat can be lost through perspiration, panting, and overexertion in the extreme cold. Excessive activity under such circumstances not only exhausts the body's energy supplies but chills the body to the bone as well. When this occurs, natural physiological mechanisms sharply reduce the flow of blood to the surface areas of the body in a desperate effort to retain all possible heat at the body's core. As a result, the extremities or exposed parts of the body, faced with the chilling effects of cold, dampness, and wind—or all three—become colder and colder until the tissues begin to freeze and frostbite develops.

What exactly happens in the tissues when frostbite occurs? Even today medical authorities do not know the whole story. We do know, however, that two different kinds of change take place as the tissues chill below the freezing point of water. First, ice crystals form between the cells and then water is withdrawn from within the cells as the ice crystals increase in size. Second, biochemical changes take place within the cells which can, unless promptly reversed, result in the death of the cells and permanent tissue damage. Curiously enough, there is a critical temperature, some 5° below the freezing point of water, at which these

biochemical changes become irreversible. If the frostbite is detected and treated before that critical temperature is reached, the tissues can be thawed without any
lasting residual damage; below that temperature, however, some degree of permanent tissue damage will
usually result. It is at this point, too, that blood within
the tiny arteries and veins supplying the area becomes
clotted so that these vessels cannot perform their normal circulatory chores even when the frozen tissue is
thawed.

Signs and symptoms of frostbite: Whether the frostbite is superficial or deep, a sequence of signs and
symptoms occurs to warn that the injury is developing.
The affected area at first feels bitingly cold, and then
becomes numb and loses all feeling. As the chilling
continues it may even begin to feel warm, an alarming
symptom that suggests that the frostbite is progressing
from superficial to deep. The skin over the superficially
frost-nipped area takes on a dead, yellowish white,
waxy appearance, but the underlying tissue is not yet
frozen, so that the area feels doughy or boggy when
touched, stiff on the surface but still soft and resilient
underneath. In the case of deep frostbite, however, the
injured part becomes hard through and through with a
tell-tale solid, woody feeling.

Treatment of frostbite: The approach to treatment of
a case of frostbite depends very largely on the degree of
frostbite present—that is, whether the injury is superficial or deep. Superficial frostbite or frost nip can often
be treated on the spot the moment it is first detected and
the hike continued, provided that the frost-nipped area
can be rapidly rewarmed and then protected from re-

current freezing. The tip-off to superficial frostbite is the blanching of the skin over the affected area and the loss of feeling in the region.

The treatment of choice is *rapid rewarming* of the frost-nipped area by any gentle means available until thawing has taken place, followed by protection of the area to prevent refreezing. A frost-nipped ear or cheek, for example, can be covered with a warm hand and then protected from further exposure until thawing is complete. Frost-nipped fingertips can be thrust into the victim's own armpits for rapid warming. Frost-nipped toes can first be rewarmed on a trail companion's warm abdomen and then be dressed in dry wool socks with the boots laced up loosely to allow good circulation. Thawing of superficial frostbite is first accompanied by a tingling and burning in the affected area followed by the appearance of a purplish or mottled color in the area as blood circulation is restored. Blisters may form over the frost-nipped area once it is thawed, and there may be some swelling of the surrounding tissue. When this occurs, take great care not to break the blisters or tamper with the tissue in any way. *Never rub a frost-nipped area;* any physical manipulation may cause further tissue damage and compound the injury that has already occurred. Aside from the changes noted above, superficial frostbite promptly treated will usually recover with no permanent tissue damage whatever; it is only when the frostbite is deep that lasting injury may occur.

Treatment of deep frostbite is a different matter altogether. Slow or inadequate rewarming of deep frostbite on the trail, with the risk of refreezing later, can do far more damage than leaving the frostbitten extremity alone—frozen—until the victim can be transported to a place where he can be kept warm, comfortable, and at rest while rapid rewarming of the frostbite is accomplished. In a sense the treatment of deep frostbite involves burning your bridges behind you: once you have begun you must continue without any reversal, and it is better not to begin treatment at all until the victim can be assured of continuing treatment without interruption. A person can actually walk on frostbitten feet for hours or even days, if necessary, without injuring himself further; in such a case the victim might well safely walk out to find help. If the frostbite were rewarmed on the trail, he would have to be carried out.

Once the victim has reached a place where rewarming can be effected and maintained—at a well-protected camp, for example, from which further aid can be sought—the frozen area should be *rewarmed rapidly* by immersing it (or bathing it copiously) in water warmed to a temperature between 108° and 112° Fahrenheit. If you have no thermometer to check the temperature, test the water by dipping your elbow in it; if it feels slightly warmer than body temperature but not uncomfortably warm, it will be suitable. Rewarming under these circumstances will take a matter of 20 or 30 minutes and will be accompanied by increasingly severe pain. Experience has shown, however, that such rapid rewarming, painful though it may be, results in saving more tissue than any system of slower rewarming; aspirin, Darvon, or codeine can be given to help ease the discomfort. At the same time that the frostbitten area is being rewarmed the rest of the victim's body should be rewarmed as well, getting him into a prewarmed sleeping bag and providing him with hot drinks and warm food. Alcohol and tobacco should both be avoided until the frostbite is completely healed. Smoking in particular causes a constriction of the small arterioles in the superficial tissues and thus actively interferes with the healing of deep frostbite.

In addition to the treatment measures discussed above, there are certain *vital precautions* to keep in mind when you are dealing with any degree of frostbite, superficial or deep:

1. *Never* rub a frozen part before, during or after rewarming. *Use no massage whatever* in treating frostbite.

2. *Never* rub a frozen part with snow, or try to rewarm it in cool or cold water. Such "slow warming" is an antiquated and discredited approach to frostbite treatment; in the long run it is just as painful as rapid rewarming in water at 108° to 112° and results in more, rather than less, tissue damage.

3. *Never* try to rewarm a frozen part by exercising it. If it is really frozen, attempts at exercise before, during, or immediately after rewarming will almost invariably *increase the extent* of the injury.

4. *Never* attempt to rewarm a frozen part by the dry heat of an open fire, with water hotter than 112°, or with any other form of intense heat. Remember the patient *will not be able to feel excessive heat* and can easily be injured further unless the rewarming is carefully controlled.

After rewarming, the deeply frostibtten part should be kept warm, clean, and protected in precisely the same way you would protect an open wound or a burn. *Never* attempt to use a deeply frostbitten part after rewarming until a doctor has examined the injury. Gently *dab off* any dirt from the area, using sterile gauze or cotton and sterile water; then dress the injury with light bandages to keep it clean. Use no antiseptics other than mild soap and thoroughly cooled boiled water. If blisters form, leave them alone. *Never* cut off any tissue.

Once a deep frostbite has been rewarmed, the victim should remain under a doctor's careful observation until healing is complete. In most cases definitive medical treatment is conservative—a matter of protecting the injured area and waiting for nature to do its work without interfering or causing more damage. Often the most hideous-appearing cases of deep frostbite, properly cared for, recover with remarkably little permanent tissue damage—but the long-term care of deep frostbite most emphatically lies in the province of the doctor, not the amateur.

Prevention of frostbite: Whether it is superficial or deep, frostbite is an ugly and potentially disabling injury, and its occurrence is particularly tragic considering that it can almost always be prevented. It has been said that the well-equipped individual who is alert and using his head is seldom bothered with frostbite; the most frequent victims are the inexperienced, the poorly equipped and the unprepared. The prevention of frostbite involves both *general* measures to maintain body heat and prevent chilling, and *specific* measures to protect the vulnerable parts of the body whenever frostbite conditions prevail.

Most important of the general measures is to do everything possible to protect the heat-producing capacity of your body whenever you venture out in cold weather. In large measure this depends upon:

1. Good general physical conditioning.
2. An ample supply of warm and tasty food, including plenty of carbohydrate to enhance heat production.
3. Adequate intake of fluids to make up for the drying effect of breathing in cold air.
4. Provision for ample rest and avoidance of general fatigue.

Second in importance is the conservation of body heat once it has been produced. Be sure to wear adequate insulative clothing, with extra dry clothes on hand to change to when necessary. Keep moving about and exercising, within moderate limits; wiggle your toes, clench and unclench your fingers, and undertake isometric exercises—the tensing and relaxing of muscles in opposition to each other—to keep warm, while avoiding heavy physical exercise with deep breathing, panting, and perspiration in which more heat is lost by the body than is produced.

As for specific measures, take special care to protect the exposed areas of the body from chilling. Avoid snug-fitting clothes that might impair circulation, particularly to the hands or the feet. Try to avoid perspiring, and change out of perspiration-dampened clothing as soon as possible—wet clothes lose virtually all their insulative value and drain body heat away ten times faster than dry. Protect your hands with woolen mittens or gloves worn inside leather or canvas outer mitts, and carry extra dry mittens and socks in your pack. Avoid *any* bare-skin contact with metal (camera, ice ax, etc.), and use extreme care in handling white gas or other volatile fuel which can cause swift and extreme chilling of tissues when it evaporates. Above all, remember that conditions of cold, wind, and dampness make a dangerous trio. *Be alert that frostbite may occur* under such conditions, pay attention to your own vulnerable areas, and watch your trail companions as well for signs of frostbite. Awareness of the danger, alertness, and common sense are by far your best protection against frostbite injuries.

The Hazard of Hypothermia

One morning in late October several years ago an eight-year-old boy and his dog left home for a hike on nearby Tiger Mountain, one of the densely wooded foothills of the Cascade Mountains near Issaquah, Washington. The weather, dry and overcast at the beginning of the day, deteriorated into cold rain, and a chilling wind came up. The boy's mother became alarmed when he did not return home for lunch; she knew he was wearing only tennis shoes and a light jacket over cotton clothing. At four in the afternoon she mustered help to go search for the boy, and searchers continued through the night, stumbling by flashlight through the sodden rain forest jungle of the mountain's slopes as the wind continued and the temperature dipped down almost to 45°. Just before dawn the boy and dog were found, huddled together in a hollow beneath an ancient cedar stump. Ironically, the stump was less than 50 yards from a clearing from which the lights of a neighboring farm could be seen. The dog was alive, but the boy was dead, one more tragic victim of the most insidious and treacherous of all forms of cold injury.

According to the newspaper, the boy had died of exposure. From a medical viewpoint "exposure" is a vague and inaccurate term describing a combination of factors which can, under certain circumstances, lead to progressive physiological deterioration, collapse, unconsciousness, and ultimately death. Four of these factors—physical exhaustion, inadequate food intake, dehydration of the body, and such psychological elements as fear, panic, or despair—may or may not be present in any given case. The fifth and major factor, invariably present, is the medical condition known as *hypothermia:* the gradual cooling of the body's inner core to the degree that normal metabolism breaks down, with death the end result if the heat loss is not discovered and reversed.

To understand how exposure in general and hypothermia in particular can pose such a threat to life, we must consider how the body produces and conserves heat, and how heat can inadvertently be lost by those who venture out in cold, wet, or windy weather. On a very basic level the human body is a highly effective heat-producing machine. The foods that we eat, after digestion and assimilation, are utilized by cells in the tissues all over the body to produce both heat and energy. In general, carbohydrates (sugars and starches, etc.) produce heat the most quickly; proteins from eggs, cheese, or meat provide a slower but equally dependable source of heat; and fats produce twice as much heat, weight for weight, as carbohydrates or proteins.

Muscular activity is a second major source of heat for the body. The exercise involved in carrying a heavy pack up a trail, for example, can produce six times as much heat in the body as is produced by sitting in the shade on a rock. Short periods of extremely heavy exertion can increase heat production to as much as ten times the resting or "basal" metabolic rate. In addition, outside sources—the sun, a fire, or the warming effect of hot liquids that are drunk—can add heat to the body. Finally, the process of *shivering*, an involuntary contraction of muscles all over the body, is an important heat-producing mechanism that is triggered automatically whenever the body begins to cool down even slightly below the normal internal body temperature of approximately 99° Fahrenheit.

Once heat is produced, the body also has natural mechanisms for *conserving* it. As soon as the body begins to chill, there is constriction of surface blood vessels all over the body which tends to reduce circulation of blood in the skin layers and in the extremities and to keep the warm blood nearer to the central core of the body. Thus, in conditions of cold, dampness, and wind, the temperature of extremities and skin areas may drop very sharply, to as low as 50° or 60°, while the internal core of the body still maintains its warmth at 99°. In addition, the body is covered by a layer of subcutaneous fat, which acts as an excellent insulating material when the outside of the body is chilling, and this helps the interior maintain its inner warmth. The

fact that women have a slightly thicker padding of subcutaneous fat than men is one reason that women seem
to withstand the effects of cold better than men do.
Finally, the process of heat conservation can be greatly
aided by wearing adequate quantities of dry, insulative
clothing.

Just as body heat is continually produced, however,
it is also continually lost. A large amount of heat es-
capes from the body during respiration. In addition, the
evaporation of perspiration from the skin is continually
robbing the body of heat. Contact with cold equipment,
being drenched in rain, or sitting in snow or wet rocks
can result in a steady loss of heat. *Freezing temperatures are by no means necessary for this heat loss to
take place;* in fact, dangerous degrees of heat loss can
occur in the presence of wind and rain at outside temperatures in the 40s and 50s. Heat is also lost by radiation
from uncovered surfaces such as the head, face, or
hands; a major amount of heat can be conserved by
wearing dry woolen mittens and wearing a down-filled
parka hood in place during cold wet weather. Finally,
the body is continually warming a layer of air near the
surface of the skin. If this air is held close to the body by
layers of dry, insulative clothing the body stays warm.
If the clothing becomes wet and allows escape of this
heat, the body will chill very quickly. What is more, the
lightest of breezes can be sufficient to vastly increase
heat loss from wet clothing unless some kind of outside
windbreaker garment is worn.

Hypothermia—"body-core cooling"—will occur at
any time that the heat being lost from the body *exceeds*
the heat being produced. Neither extreme cold nor

altitude is necessary for hypothermia to develop; back-packers on trails along ocean beaches have fallen victim to hypothermia in 50° weather. The three external factors that *do* set the stage for hypothermia are *coldness* (though not necessarily extreme coldness); *wetness*, due to rainfall, fog, snow, immersion of the body, or even excessive perspiration; and *wind*, though not necessarily a high wind, since a two-mile-an-hour breeze can drag down body temperatures as effectively as a twenty-mile gale if the victim's clothes are wet.

Now we can see how the other factors that make up the condition of "exposure" can all contribute, some-times very rapidly, to the development of hypothermia. The hiker who has become physically exhausted in cold damp weather moves more and more slowly, producing less and less heat through muscular activity. If he has not eaten sufficient food, his body may not have enough fuel for adequate heat production. If he has no extra clothing, he may suffer very rapid heat loss with no dry clothes to change to. Finally, psychological factors play an important role in hypothermia. The potential victim who recognizes when hypothermia is possible, understands how to counteract it, and proceeds to do so with vigor and enthusiasm is likely to escape un-scathed; the one who is overcome with fright, panic, or despair is the one who is likely to be striken. Case after case has indicated that an upbeat, optimistic point of view can be a vital factor in survival from hypothermia, while a pessimistic attitude of bleak desperation can contribute mightily to hypothermia death.

The symptoms of hypothermia: Unfortunately, a steady loss of body heat can occur insidiously and

proceed to the danger point before it is even recognized
unless the individual is alert to the threat. In general,
the symptoms of hypothermia occur in an orderly pattern, although the order may vary somewhat from one
person to another. As the internal body temperature
drops from the normal of 99° to 96° or 97° Fahrenheit,
the victim begins uncontrollable shivering, often to
such a degree that he cannot perform such simple tasks
as striking a match, buttoning clothes, or working a zipper. As the core temperature drops further to 91° or 92°,
the shivering becomes even more violent, occuring in
waves. The victim begins to have difficulty speaking;
his coordination deteriorates, his pace slows, and he
begins stumbling, perhaps even falling. At this point he
may also find his thinking slowed down, or seem unable
to carry the thread of a conversation. As his body
continues to cool down to 86° or 87° the shivering ceases
and the muscles become stiff and rigid; muscular coordination at this point is seriously impaired, and the
individual shows clear evidence of irrational thinking
and impaired judgment even though he still seems to be
in contact with his surroundings. Even that tenuous
contact vanishes as his temperature drops to 81° or 82°;
the muscular rigidity continues; his pulse and respiration are slowed, and he may enter into a zombielike
stupor. As his body temperature drops below 80°, unconsciousness prevails; the victim collapses, no longer
responds to the spoken word, and may begin to show
evidence of terminal pulmonary edema—the coughing
up of white foamy fluid from the lungs. Soon after this
point is reached, if the chilling continues, the victim
reaches a point where both heartbeat and respirations

fail and death ensues.

How fast can these progressive symptoms occur? In some cases, very swiftly indeed. The person who falls overboard from a ship into Arctic waters can be suffering from a dangerous degree of hypothermia in as little as ninety seconds and be dead within three minutes. Hikers or climbers have been known to progress to the point of unconsciousness in as little as half an hour. In most cases, however, the body chills down more slowly, with ample opportunity for the victim himself—or his trail companions—to recognize what is happening, as long as one is alert to the threat. Obviously, identifying the danger can be all-important. Once the victim has reached the point that heartbeat and respirations have ceased, there is nothing that can be done to revive him. But at any earlier point, properly directed emergency measures can save a life. The earlier the hypothermia is recognized, the more swiftly counter-measures can be taken and the less risk there is that the condition will have reached a point of no return.

Treatment of hypothermia: The vigorous treatment of hypothermia on the trail involves three key measures: first, preventing any further heat loss; second, using external heat sources to warm the victim's body; and third, supplying the victim with hot fluids and food, both for their immediate warming effect and to help resupply his body with energy-giving fuels. The first and most vital step is to get the victim into some kind of shelter, however improvised, out of the wind and wetness. Since chilling will continue as long as wet clothing is being worn, strip the victim of all wet garments and redress him in dry clothes. He should then be placed in a sleeping bag which has already been prewarmed by a companion. If the chilling is profound, rewarming may better be accomplished by huddling the victim against the bodies of one or more trail companions, all kept warm with an insulating layer of sleeping bag both underneath and above them. If a fire can be kindled, it will help to rewarm the victim—and two fires, one on either side of him, can be even more effective. As long as he is conscious, he should be given hot fluids such as soup or tea, as well as candy, dried fruit, or other sugar-containing foods for the fast energy they can produce. Then, once the crisis is over—that is, once the body temperature is up to normal, shivering has ceased, and the victim is entirely mentally clear—get him to civilization (and to a doctor for a checkout) as quickly as possible. Bear in mind that the rewarming process is slow. It may require six or eight hours to completely rewarm a person after a serious brush with hypothermia, and he must be kept as dry and warm as possible on the way home, with care being taken to prevent rechilling.

Prevention of hypothermia: The major key to preventing hypothermia is to be clearly aware of the insidious nature of the condition and the climatic conditions which can bring it about. Any hike or outing in which you meet the combination of cold, wetness, and wind carries with it the threat of hypothermia; *everyone in the party* should be alert to the early symptoms. The second key to prevention is to travel equipped with adequate clothing to protect against cold, wet, and wind. It is far better to wear more insulative clothing than you need and have to take some off than to go out with inadequate clothing and find yourself trapped. Be sure that at least one set of outer clothing, top and bottom, is made of wool, the only fabric that can help keep you warm even when it is wet. Some type of water-proof outer protection should also be carried.

Adequate food consumption is the next important consideration in preventing hypothermia. Carry ample extra food and eat trail munchies from time to time for quick energy. *Never skimp on any meals* on a cold-weather outing; your body may need three or four times its normal amount of food in order to maintain body heat and energy.

In addition to adequate clothing and food, carry some type of emergency shelter on any cold weather outing. A small mountain tent, a plastic-coated nylon "tube tent" or even a large heavy-gauge plastic tarp can fill the bill. In a pinch, a "space blanket" made of plastic with a reflective coating can be used for a temporary shelter. Then do not hesitate to make camp early—long before dark—if anyone in your party is showing any signs of chilling. A cheering fire, a hearty meal, and a good night's rest in a warm, dry sleeping bag will re-plenish body heat and in many cases may avert a situation which could have deteriorated into deadly danger in a very short while. Finally, when chilling is present, *keep moving*, exercise your muscles, chop firewood, or use isometric exercises to produce additional warmth. With an awareness of the conditions that can result in hypothermia, with active preventive measures to avoid body cooling, and with a clear understanding of what to do when hypothermia occurs, cold weather hiking, backpacking, ski touring, or snowshoeing can be en-joyed with a maximum of pleasure and a minimum of risk.

Out

From *The Backpacker*.
By Albert Saijo

You made it. You went in and you came out. You did your trip. It was both harder and easier than you thought it would be. It was harder physical exertion than you anticipated, but it was easier than you imagined keeping the trip together. The beauty of wilderness was overwhelming, both overall and in detail. It took you far away from your usual frame of mind and gave you a long perspective on your life.

Now there are some things you won't do anymore, and there are those new things you feel but can't see the shape of yet. You understand who you are a little better. You got some work done on your secret puzzles. You pounded out a few conundrums on the trail. You got to know your friends better. Outdoor fellowship is special.

You went in fat and you came out lean. You came out with a greater respect for your body. You are going to treat it better now and stay in shape for the next time.

You saw your head through some changes. You started out nervous and excited—like a virgin. Then the hard work of backpacking got to you, and you went into a more serious mood. That broke as you acclimatized, and the trip became pure delight. Each trip has a high point. A point when you feel absolutely with it. You can't plan it. But when you get there, you know it's what you came out for.

Then as you neared the end of your trip, you found your head less in wilderness, even as you were in it, and more and more into thoughts of home. What's happening back there? What have you missed? You began thinking of extraordinary things you'll do once back. The foods you're going to eat—you're starving! You began to feel awfully deprived so that when you finally got back to the roadhead you felt positively liberated.

How strange, because when you finally saw the cars and people, heard the radios and mean dogs barking, you wanted to go right back into wilderness. You felt the strangeness of our civilization. How foreign it is to the part of your nature that blossomed in wilderness.

But you're out. You went away and you came back. Now as you head back to civilization, you have a wildness in your heart that wasn't there before. You know you're going outback again.

Appendices